# Situational Identities along the Raiding Frontier of Colonial New Mexico

HISTORICAL ARCHAEOLOGY OF THE AMERICAN WEST

*Series Editors*    Annalies Corbin, Rebecca Allen

# Situational Identities along the Raiding Frontier of Colonial New Mexico

JUN U. SUNSERI

University of Nebraska Press
and the Society for Historical Archaeology
LINCOLN AND LONDON

*For Esperanza and Nelson Gonzales*

# Contents

# Figures and Tables

## Figures

### Tables

# Acknowledgments

I cannot express enough gratitude for the mentors, colleagues, and family who made this project possible. First and foremost, this research was made possible by the community of El Rito, New Mexico. The generosity of these families afforded me every support and inspiration to conduct research on their ancestral land. Their patience and candor kept me honest and accountable to them and the memories of ancestors. I am deeply grateful for their support, guidance, and mentorship and honored by what it means to have them behind me in this endeavor. I will always be at their service.

Without the kind hearts and generous spirit of the Gonzales family, I would not have fallen in love with the work. From day one, Esperanza, Nelson, Chris, Danny, and cj took me under their wings and introduced me to everything wonderful in the area of the Rito Colorado and beyond. I don't know what this work or my life would have looked like were it not for the support, protection, and profound experiences afforded by their incredible generosity. From leaping skunks during midnight *acequia* work, to learning how to chase down and perfectly butcher a goat, to eating warm empanadas and listening to stories of the valley, almost every aspect of my experiences in the Rito Colorado valley are framed by the warmth of their kindness. They made us family, and I feel it deeply.

I am also indebted to the Ussery Family for not only all of the support and relationships that they helped me build around El Rito and surrounding communities but also for a warm place to keep my crew in the New Mexican winter. In the county commissioner's office as well as out in the field, Felipe Martinez and Moises Morales kept me focused and accountable to the goals of land grant communities in the Rio Arriba, something for which I am very grateful. Of course, without the mentorship of Robert Lawrence, District Archaeologist for the U.S. Forest Service, it would have taken me decades to accrue the knowledge required to even begin this endeavor. His guidance and patience were absolutely foundational to this work. Father Chavez and the Garcia family also kindly welcomed me and were patient in their assistance with my historical questions. In forums from the Sustained Yield Unit, to the El Rito Public Library, to the classrooms and district offices of the Mesa Vista Consolidated School District, many members of the El Rito community have made this an endeavor more joyful and worthwhile to me than any archaeological project rightfully should be.

My parents were supremely supportive of me when I decided to throw away my engineering career to go back to grad school in a social science. They didn't even disown me! Seriously, their love and support have been my foundation and are what allowed me to follow my heart. I owe a debt of gratitude to my graduate advisors, Judith Habicht-Mauche and Diane Gifford-Gonzalez, who took a gamble on turning that mechanical engineer into an archaeologist. It is through no small effort that their patience and guidance brought me through this process.

Along the way, I found myself inexplicably graced by a kindness and insightful mentorship that only Linda Cordell could have brought to bear on a newcomer to the archaeology of the Southwest. Her belief in her students was a *fierce* belief, a tireless and powerful commitment to not just our career successes but our happiness, finding our joys, and a full life. She was not one to miss a chance to check in on us, to forget to ask about our families, our work, our next projects and dreams. Linda wanted us full of energy, excited about what we were doing and where we were. And she led by example, always ten steps ahead of me in imagination and scope of her plans. She didn't seem to credit her own charisma, as much as the excitement, the promise of the work, and the adventures of discovery together. As always, Linda was right in that we *should* be excited about the work we get to do. She wanted that for us in all our adventures in life. Just how I lucked out with an advisory committee this great, I may never know.

More mentors would carry me, from my earliest trips, driving around New Mexico looking for a project, to repeated visits for guidance and comradery, I am indebted to a very special network of people who have backed me in this endeavor. Among them, Charlie Carrillo, James

Brooks, and David Snow were unflagging proponents of my project and approach. Were it not for those early meetings at the School for Advanced Research in Santa Fe, I'd probably still be driving loops around the Continental Divide. Debbie Carrillo, Kurt Anschuetz, and Felipe Ortega bestowed gifts of friendship, wisdom, clay, and time spent scrambling around the hot summertime landscape that I'll always treasure. That they could invest so much of themselves in this process is a testament to their generosity and selfless support.

Several other New Mexican friends and scholars guided me to this work and to the El Rito community. Among them, Sylvia Rodriguez, Estèvan Rael-Gàlvez, Beverly Armijo, and Francisco "El Comanche" Gonzales were gracious hosts and kindly vouched for me with friends and family among communities in the north. In addition, I thank Martha Dick, Michael Adler, and the Laboratory of Anthropology staff for going above and beyond the call of duty in their assistance in locating artifacts and records for this work.

This project was supported by the Colorado University Museum's Joe Ben Wheat Scholarship, the University of California Institute for Mexico and the United States (UC MEXUS) Dissertation Research Fellowship, an Individual Research Grant from the Wenner-Gren Foundation for Anthropological Research, and the SRI Foundation Research Fellow Scholarship.

I will be paying back a debt for some time to the members of undergraduate lab and field crews who assisted this research. Molly Adams, Cicely Amato, Sam Atkins, Natalie Bagley, Jennifer Bower, Ben Curry, Stella D'Oro, Lahti Dunstan, Brian Eskanazi, Danny Gilmour, Jenna Haywood, Miguel Jeffrey, Kari Lentz, Josh Noyer, and Miya Yamishita are the best group of students I could have hoped to work with. They not only made the work go faster, but their presence in New Mexico and in the labs in California also consistently excited me about what we were learning together. Along with help from Richard Baldwin and Bruce Tanner, the labs at UCSC and acquisition of comparative specimens were always an adventure.

The team at University of Nebraska Press and the SHA have been bastions of patience and optimism for me in this process. Without Matt Bokovoy, Heather Stauffer, Annalies Corbin, and Rebecca Allen, I would have sunk to the bottom. For colleagues who have endured countless drafts and late-night work sessions, I cannot express my thanks enough. Heather Atherton, Christophe Delage, Sarah Ginn, Krista Lewis, and especially Sus Eckert, Idelle Cooper, and Deb Huntley have racked up quite a tab on me for this. We've got years of conferences to whittle away at that, I suppose. Something to look forward to, Comrades.

Finally, two people have been lifelines to me through sleepless nights spent hacking away at tortured prose that would kill an elephant. For years, Charlotte Sunseri kept me alive and shouldered enormous burdens to support this work and see it through. Rebecca Allen just about carried me over her shoulders to the finish line, with a valor that I didn't think possible in academia. I'm kind of impressed that they will still speak to me after this experience, but there is no doubt in my mind that without them I could not have done this, and there's no chance I can ever thank them enough. The Venda say, "Muthu ndi muthu nga vhanwe vhathu," which means "A person is a person because of some people." They have shown me time and again that it couldn't be more true.

# Situational Identities along the Raiding Frontier of Colonial New Mexico

# 1 /    Standing Fast in the Middle Ground

How do families make homes and community in a warzone? Colonial New Mexico was not unique in having its least privileged making the greatest sacrifices for a dominant regime. In the 18th century, families of lower status committed to borderlands service, hoping that returning soldier-citizens and their communities could expect some reciprocation on the home front. Rewards such as grants of land and titles could solidify their place one rung higher in a social and political order that existed far from the battlefield. But what of those who could expect to live their new deal only upon that very field of arms? This story explores the material record of families who not only built homes, established economies, and organized labor in harm's way but also married their erstwhile enemies, raised children on the front lines, and aligned themselves across the lines of skirmish as both fighters and ambassadors. As an archaeological tale, it tracks the tensions of early Spanish colonial suppositions about the racial hierarchy known as the *sistema de castas* to modern-day silences and stereotypes about pluralistic communities who refuse simple categorization. The material record attests to the lived experiences of people who have long occupied the middle ground (R. White 1991) and defied any straightforward approach to pigeonholing identity.

Northwest from Santa Fe, a two-lane road winds its way into striking mesas of red and buff, a landscape to which Georgia O'Keefe famously moved in order to paint. This beautiful inspiration would likely have been the end of the artist if it had not been for the patience and care of those families who knew it best and for generations had worked to

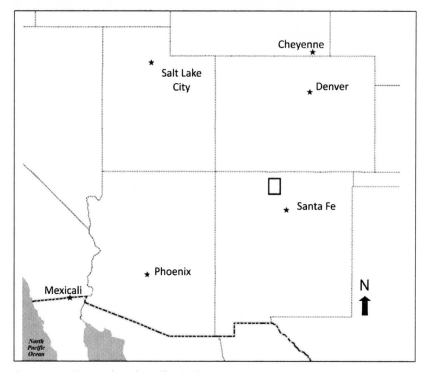

FIGURE 1. Rito Colorado valley in Rio Arriba County, New Mexico.

survive its harsh winters and challenges. Rio Arriba County in northern New Mexico is a land of contrasts. At its heart, the Rito Colorado valley is exemplary in its diversity of environs—rugged hills, open *llanos*, deep arroyos, and vaulted mesas (fig. 1). The southern San Juan Mountains extend from the north, tumbling into maze-like contortions as they meet the Rio Chama valley. Running from the heavily forested embrace of the higher-altitude canyons, the Rito Colorado joins the Chama to the south. Along the way, it has carved out a long, lunate valley from the folds of the Canjilon Hills that signal the end of the San Juans and the beginning of the Colorado Plateau. These mountain mazes are part of the Continental Divide, and although the Rito Colorado valley lies at almost 7,000 feet, the nearby peaks push up from their ponderosa pine and Douglas fir forests to passes higher than 9,000 feet.

Within a single day's walk from the center of the valley, people might find themselves among spiny cholla cactus along the sandy bottom of arroyos, climbing into the punctuated expanse of a piñon juniper forest, scrambling up the talus slopes of steep cliffs, then lunging deep in lush tracts of evergreen forest. At this ecotone, a great diversity of plant, mineral, and animal resources were available to colonial settlers, directly accessible within a few hours' travel. The watershed itself created an environment with agricultural potential. From where the Rito Colorado emerges into the valley from its northern confines, it has deposited a broad expanse of alluvial soils until the water gathers enough critical mass to punch through the constriction at the southern end of the valley.

The result is a broad plain of alluvium in the middle of the valley, with faster-moving water at the north and south extremes that scour their banks clean during spring runoffs. Access to the east side of the valley most often involves fording the Rito Colorado, usually running no more than two to three feet deep. Occasionally, strong rains or heavy snowmelt have been observed to increase traditional fording spots to almost a quarter mile wide by several feet deep. A car left too close to the river during one of these flooding events is a humbling sight, as the Rito Colorado tumbles it end over end, down toward the Rio Chama. Such high flow rates at the valley's entrance and exit make floodplain farming at those locations far less inviting than at midvalley areas.

In the broad middle of the crescent valley, modern fields and the mounded ruins of Sapawe Pueblo, one of the largest adobe pueblos of the 14th century, remain as silent testament to the productive potential of its immediate surrounding area, in the north-center of the valley (fig. 2). The early communities at Sapawe left for greener pastures in the Tewa basin long before the any Spanish colonial-era settlement. So why would the second wave of settlers build a community so far down the valley, three centuries later? Potential answers to that question are many and as complex as the reasons for studying it. Those complexities reflect not only the dynamics of daily life on a dangerous colonial frontier but related and successive waves of identity politics, land tenure, and resource conflict. The most recent of these waves of conflict ripple out through space and time from a tiny, fortified plaza, once occupied in the late 1700s, to the modern courtrooms of Santa Fe. That frontier plaza is known to the descendant community in modern El Rito as Casitas Viejas, and the families who crafted community there are the focus of this story.

A geographic representation of the Spanish colonial administration's system of rights and privileges for its citizens, the Juan Jose Lobato land grant today delimits the Carson National Forest boundary in much of this valley. At the valley's southern constriction, thick adobe walls hide in plain sight on a high bench overlooking the valley. The ruins of Casitas

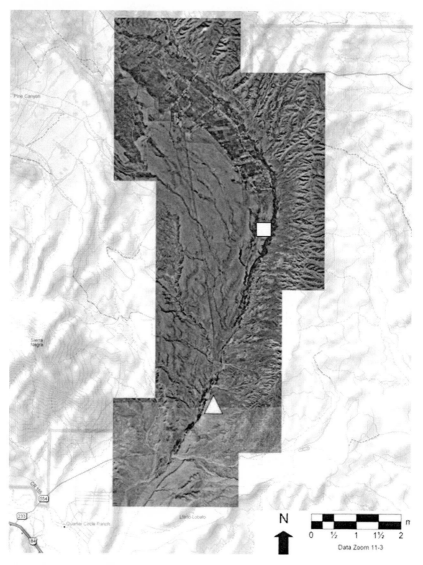

FIGURE 2. Composite aerial photograph of the Rito Colorado valley; triangle marks location of Casitas Viejas (ca. ad 1780); square marks location of Sapawe Pueblo (ca. ad 1400).

Viejas should not be as hard to spot as they are. Although their earthen ramparts still rise up staunchly from the forest and grass cover of the piñon-juniper *llano* after more than three hundred years, the adobes blend into the landscape around them.

Researchers and land managers know this archaeological site as LA 917, a designation itself revealing how prominent the site is in southwestern archaeology. New Mexico is a state where the Laboratory of Anthropology (hence the "LA" designation) of the Museum of Indian Arts and Culture has hundreds of thousands of site numbers to keep track of. Only those sites enumerated in the early era of the Lab's existence could have such a short number. Inside regional archaeology research circles, Casitas Red-on-Buff (or Red-on-Brown) pottery is the ceramic type used to interpret sites across the Southwest as having been occupied during the colonial era. As the "type site," Casitas has had many illustrious (and some not so) visitors through the years since the descendant community moved north to better fields, irrigation, and forest resources at the turn of the 19th century.

Ethnographers, historians, archaeologists, and residents of nearby El Rito and Abiquiú have encountered self-styled "relic hunters" from communities near and far picking at the slowly eroding walls of the chapel and plaza. Some have gone so far as to loot in and around the site, irrevocably damaging the standing walls and roomblock mounds. Deep craters pockmark the back of the nave, evidence that someone had been shooting at the back wall of the chapel. Even modern, high-velocity firearms could not always breach the earthen armor, a testament to the sturdiness and protective efficacy of this ancient architecture. More than one visitor has dropped the potsherds from the adobe in midpluck when warned that such behavior has consequences for those who do not respect the ongoing commitment of community caretakers. Residents of the Rito Colorado valley have long protected their cultural resources and, with on-site patrols and constant invigilation over the long roads up to their community, their watchful eyes have shielded Casitas from the worst of the depredations that have cratered historic sites like it throughout the country.

## Community Research Mandates: A Privilege to Earn
## for Historical Archaeology

Family and friends of community members directed me to El Rito to discuss the potential for a historical archaeological study of frontier community formation. Meetings with various community leaders and the county commissioner of Rio Arriba County, also an El Rito resident and descendant, drove home the privileged position of Casitas in local oral history. Before I stepped foot on the site, these community members made clear that Casitas and other archaeological resources of the valley play a key role in community understandings of place and heritage, as well as contemporary struggles for land, water, and resources use.

A descendant of a long lineage of Rito Colorado valley residents who moved up from Abiquiú to establish Casitas, local historian and community leader Esperanza Gonzales wrote a historical account of the valley as part of a series of evaluations for the installation of a new cemetery north of El Rito (Gonzalez 2001). From our first meetings, she, her children, neighbors, and her husband, Nelson, cemented my commitment to a collaborative research endeavor at Casitas. Their generosity and total support was a seemingly inexhaustible source of narrative material, community introductions, and housing for and protection of project personnel. Their extended family's bottomless patience also provided the deepest examples of historical context and cultural landscape knowledge, as well as opportunities for participant observation in ethnoarchaeological butchery and *acequia* (community irrigation system) maintenance.

Further vetting occurred when sharp-eyed El Rito residents spotted our mapping team on-site at Casitas from the long tar road into the village. Less than three hours later in the Forest Service office, the district ranger took a call from a prominent local resident about possible looters on what descendants call Casitas Viejas. Although the ranger assured him that nothing was being taken from the site, he wanted to speak to the person who happened to be standing in that office. The conversation that followed was terse and serious in getting a clear picture of the intent of proposed research. The next day found me sweating in front of the caller at the county seat of his authority and before several of his most trusted councilors. Their scrutiny and caution turned to encouragement and excitement as we brainstormed the project together. After a thorough, in-depth discussion about research potentials of the site and fielding many questions from the seasoned crew of activists and organizers, we broke into smaller sessions to discuss the utility of such work to community endeavors and struggles for self-determination. Yet, what was most striking was their clear directive to maintain as much archaeological objectivity as possible, regardless of what they, parties in the community, or others said, or what I might perceive as their needs. I hope the work discussed here begins to do some justice to the incredible support and inspiration I have been gifted by my generous hosts and partners.

## A Spanish Colonial Project in a Native American Landscape

The Rito Colorado valley has long been a place that winnowed need from want. Seven miles north of the ruins at Casitas, the contemporary village of El Rito and its outlying hamlets are home to the descendants of those who lived at the site and others like it, clusters of homesteads strung along drainages and dependent upon the community-managed irrigation system. The mother ditch of the El Rito *acequia* irrigation system, which feeds the fields and orchards in El Rito, provides far more water to this top part of the valley than possible where Casitas sits at the other end. The broad, fertile alluvium of this part of the Rito Colorado valley proved better to till and irrigate than the high-relief and hard-scrabble bench at Casitas. But the timing had to be right for the move north from Casitas. Its historic role as a guardian runs deep, situated on a landscape that had long been a frontier between people who chose to live in different ways.

In the rugged mesa lands across the Four Corners region of the American Southwest, groups of people began to leave their canyon homes in the 13th century to start communities elsewhere. As people moved toward the Rio Grande region of northern New Mexico to establish new places and create new traditions (Cordell 2004), the combined push of violence and unpredictable rainfall, as well as the pull of new religious movements based on fertility and world renewal, may have made the northern Rio Grande, as well as places farther west that would come to be known as Zuni and Hopi, more attractive for people in the 14th century (Duff 2002). Large, multiroom architecture was organized in blocks around open plazas and kivas began to reflect people of diverse origins. By the middle decades of the 15th century, some of the largest Puebloan towns ever built grew near the Rio Chama. These aggregated pueblos, too, went through cycles of use, disuse, and reuse (Anschuetz 2007).

In the northwesternmost area of this region, near the Rio Chama, more than a dozen pueblos housed hundreds if not thousands of people. Sapawe was the largest such ruin (fig. 3) identified by Tewa informants (Harrington 1916) as once peopling the Rito Colorado valley. Archaeologists consider it the largest adobe pueblo site in New Mexico (Maxwell 2000:72). The northwestern edge of the Tewa basin, in which the Pueblo communities identify many ancestral sites (Blair and Blair 1986:14) had

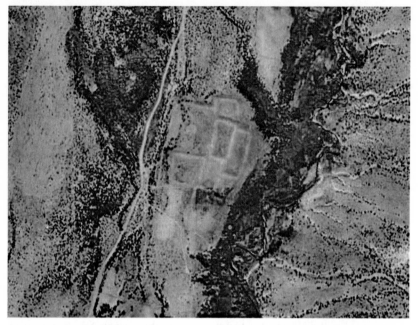

FIGURE 3. Aerial photograph of Sapawe Pueblo, site la 306 (after usgs).

long served as a place of contact and negotiation between indigenous people (Snow 1981). As a middle ground between very mobile groups of people who would later include Utes, Apaches, Navajos, and Comanches, and more sedentary agriculturalist Pueblo people, this landscape framed trading and raiding relationships between indigenous people well before Spanish efforts at colonization (Ebright and Hendricks 2006:16).

By the time Francisco Vásquez de Coronado led his expedition into New Mexico in 1540, Pueblo people lived in as many as 150 distinct villages (Frank 2000:3), though their numbers would later be horribly diminished by death from European-introduced diseases (Ramenofsky 1987). Coronado's expedition included recent Native Mexican allies, including Nahuatl-, Tarascan-, and Caxcán-speaking people of western and central Mexico (Snow 1996; Flint and Flint 2003:59), and perhaps the Tlaxcalteca who warred with them against the Aztec monarchy. These *indios amigos* outnumbered the Spaniards three to one and exercised considerable agency, serving as the expedition vanguard, as principal envoys and negotiators to Pueblos, or, in some cases, leaving the expedition to make their own way (Flint and Flint 2003:59–65). As Coronado returned south, some of them stayed behind with Pueblo hosts and were found living as part of their host community by Espejo in his *entrada* 40 years later (Flint and Flint 2003:65). The colonizing Spanish caravan, which arrived in 1598 with Don Juan de Oñate Salazar, was also anything but demographically homogeneous (Snow 1996).

In this era, Spanish colonial elites had recent ancestral memories of reunifying several kingdoms into an Iberian polity capable of routing a centuries-old Moorish occupation from the peninsula. As a result, the colonizers brought with them people of many Old World heritages as well as New World ethnicities, some of whom, as with the members of the earlier Coronado expedition of African descent, were apparently "of a status too humble to warrant counting" (Flint and Flint 2003:66). Yet these same colonists, of low *casta* status because of their African heritage, impressed Native New Mexicans "to no end" (Kessell 2013:63) and logged remarkable exploratory adventures in advance of elite expedition forces (Weigle 2003:38). Such administrative invisibility extended to the majority of lower-status people in the colony.

The colonists who came to New Mexico also "carried the tensions between Church and State that ran deep in the Spanish World" (John 1975:40), and that, along with other exploitations and violence, would help spell the demise of the first colonial attempt. Disgusted with the pretensions and squabbles between colonial elites over indigenous lives, labor, and resources, Pueblo leaders recognized the internal weaknesses of the domineering Spanish (Kessell 1979). Triggered by extreme coercion, exploitation, and religious oppressions that were at the heart of the Pueblo Revolt of 1680 (Sando 1979; Swadesh 1979:54), a united front of indigenous resistance crushed the fledgling colony and drove the settlers south into Mexico for twelve years.

During this time of Native American reclamation of northern New Mexico, major colonial institutions, not only physical but social, were selectively rejected, appropriated, and/or transformed (Preucel 2002). Missions were destroyed, Catholic marriages among native people were dissolved (Gutiérrez 1991), and alliances between Pueblos and nomadic Native Americans were broken down or realigned. Comanches, Utes, Pawnees, and Plains Caddoan groups went through military fluorescence on the southern Plains (Almaráz 1994:81), and Plains Apaches were dislocated (Eiselt 2006) south and west into New Mexico. Athapaskan populations that moved into what would become the northwestern frontier of the New Mexican colony lived through complex realignments, blendings, and fissions with local Apache groups that intensified until the turn of the 18th century (Eiselt 2006:103). By the time Spanish colonists and their allies returned to New Mexico in 1692, these Athapaskan alliances, as well as the Pueblo confederacy, had weakened. Most significantly, intensified raiding campaigns by a multitude of highly mobile groups were taking their toll, especially the Comanche forces that some describe as empire (Hämäläinen 2008).

At the turn of the 18th century, renegotiations of political, religious, and economic authority set in motion by the Pueblo Revolt of 1680 set the stage for the creation of a new northern frontier of New Mexico. The Recopilación de Leyes de los Reynos de las Indias reimagined the relationship between colonists and indigenous people, ostensibly to create fewer levels of legislated exploitation and more alliances with indigenous people against the growing crisis of raiding by nomadic groups. Near El Paso in 1692, Don Diego de Vargas reentered the colony with a convoy of people, some of whom were returning colonists. Most were an entirely new mix of people seeking their fortunes. Their diversity of origins would lead to New Mexican communities populated by people with heritages from Europe, Africa, indigenous Mexico, Southwest Pueblos, Plains, and other nomadic Native Americans. Ironically, such a plurality of people not only created tension with the elite social classes who administered from Santa Fe but also may have itself been the most enduring asset to the colony's survival.

## (Un)Documented New Mexico

A little more than a century and a half after the Spanish founded the colony of New Mexico, they retook their capital in Santa Fe with the help of their Native American allies. But the northern frontier remained a tenuous front line of violent raids and reprisals. Having renegotiated the relationship between the colonizers and their agriculturalist neighbors, by the mid-1700s many of their settlements shared a common problem. In a 1753 report back to the Viceroyalty of New Spain, one chronicler laid out his take on the situation as one in which "The whole province of New Mexico is surrounded and enclosed on all sides by innumerable and warlike nations of heathen enemies" (A. Thomas 1931:27).

Swift, skilled horsemen ranged between settlements, taking goods, livestock, and captives in lightning raids that ravaged Pueblo and colonial communities alike. These more mobile communities, too, were victims of raids by the Spanish and their allies, leaving few extended families untouched by the experiences of captivity. Because of these

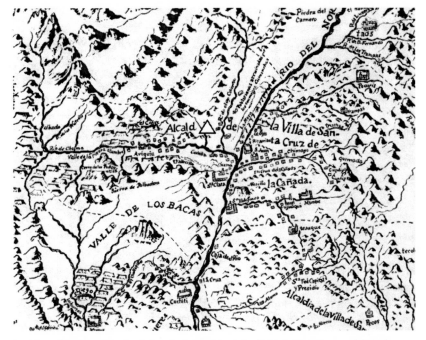

FIGURE 4. Northern New Mexico map (after Miera y Pacheco 1778), with Casitas (triangle) and Santa Fe (star) indicated.

multiple and overlapping histories, cycles of violence were perpetuated from multiple parties (Brooks 2002a, 2002b). The tactical dominance of mounted groups in the north laid bare any conceits about the range and efficacy of the Crown's control. Spanish colonial administrators employed true craftsmen as mapmakers to illustrate these challengers to their imagined domains. The cartographers did far more than locate geographical designations in reference to geological formations. On maps of New Spain's northernmost province, villages, churches, military installations, and routes appear as iconographic loci of familiar and imagined behaviors set among a sea of monsters, enemies, and blank spaces. It was as intentionally misleading to draw Native American villages and place-names in this way as it was to draw colonial settlements and routes. Each is imbued with a specific language, orientation, and set of alliances that would have been unique to the traveler or administrator using the map to understand the colony. Perhaps the most powerful of these devices are the locales that are illustrated between allies and enemies.

In Miera y Pacheco's map of New Mexico (fig. 4), "*los enimigos de cumanches*" frame the intermountain villages of the northern settlers. This juxtaposition is made even more potent by the stark labeling of "*poblaciones arrunidas [sic] por los enemigos cumanches*" (communities in ruins because of enemy Comanches) identified on this frontier, only one valley over from Casitas. Buffer settlements were located in these regions because they were perceived as protecting administrative colonial core places while at the same time isolating people of low status or less-defined social categories far from elites. Not all Comanches were enemies for buffer communities, and many were trade partners, military allies, and close family, "little brother Comanches" in today's celebration memories (Lamadrid 2003). Critically, this entire colonial endeavor was playing out on a canvas already painted with Native American actions, material remains, and meaning. Some of the largest precontact centers of population in New Mexico were located directly underneath the new settlements, huge physical manifestations of their centrality in precolonial landscapes of power and organization.

The map itself is read through the lens of people, in this case, officials such as Friars Francisco Atanasio Domínguez and Silvestre Vélez de Escalante, who visited many places and estimated the populations and locations of many more in their travels (Tjarks 1978). Centuries later these same places, though arranged on colonial papers as frontier peripheries, ended up as crucibles of exchange, alliance, and spiritual amalgams that would create for New Mexican culture its signature resilience. Important historical scholarship has framed these dynamics both from the perspective of the colonizer (Weber 1992; Rivera 1998; Frank 2000; Beebe and Senkewicz 2001; Bustamante 2001; Simmons 2001) and the colonized (Spicer 1962; Swadesh 1974; Chavez 1979; Gutiérrez 1991; Sanchez 1992; Magnaghi 1994; Rodriguez 1996; Wagner 1998; F. Levine 1999). In many historic references, mostly elite perspectives of frontier life are drawn from colonial administration, missionary and military records, anecdotes, litigations, and court settlements. These documents most often reveal the lives of individual actors as they were interpreted by literate scribes and later generations of archival researchers.

Marginalized colonial peoples, whose lives challenged the established social systems that administrators worked so hard to maintain, were less likely to be described fully in the documentary record. Though baptismal records identify and label some of the children and their families who would ultimately live at Casitas Viejas from the Pueblo de Abiquiú and other indigenous origins (T. Martinez 1993), little to nothing else was directly recorded about them and their experiences. On these frontiers, people lived identities in daily contexts that were undoubtedly situational and multifaceted, reflecting their complex origins and ongoing struggles for survival. The reality of systemized racial hierarchy, the *sistema de castas,* discussed in the next chapter, was far more complex than Spanish colonial elites could have envisioned. Their conscious labeling of people and groups was undertaken to define and compartmentalize colonizers and indigenous people alike in a process of racialization engineered to construct and maintain social inequality.

The elaborate *casta* system designed to realize notions of "pure blood" (Bustamante 1989, 2001) was vulnerable to the realities of distance and the logistical impossibilities of stringent enforcement at the farthest reaches of empire. At these critical interfaces, between communities ostensibly organized along colonial principles and legal structures and those who operated outside or in opposition to such frameworks, how people portrayed their identities was a race-focused political strategy in and of itself that might have been organized on a situation-by-situation— *situational*—basis. Such power-laden potential reflects people's awareness of their positions not only within colonial society but also within long-standing and ever-changing indigenous social structures and regional power relations. For many of the settlers at Casitas, these roots ran deep in the community as a direct result of the longevity of such heritages in the communities all around them. Two hundred years later, the material record of that complex social, political, and strategic role-playing stands sentinel at the mouth of the Rito Colorado valley.

## Previous Archaeological Research

Investigation of Government Land Office maps of the preceding century reveals that Casitas Viejas was located at the boundary of the Juan Jose Lobato land grant. Often, colonial land grants boundaries were described by landmarks of the environment (such as the confluence of rivers) and the built properties of neighboring colonial citizens. The Treaty of Guadalupe Hidalgo negotiated ownership of land after the annexation of New Mexico as an American territory in 1850 and included several provisions about the legal standing of land grants. It is well beyond the scope of this work to treat fully the ramifications of unscrupulous land speculation in the shift from Mexican to American territory and then statehood in 1912 (Ebright 1994). Suffice it to say that land grants of many non-Anglo communities, including those living on the Lobato grant, were severely reduced from family holdings (Brown and Robertshaw 1973; Swadesh 1974).

More than a century after Casitas was decommissioned from use as a primary habitation for the community, as they moved north for literally greener pastures to the site of modern El Rito, a temporary city sprang up between the two locations. Housing, offices, and facilities for Civilian Conservation Corps (CCC) workers and their support teams were erected on a high bench overlooking the Rito Colorado in the 1930s. Living this close to the descendant community and their ancestral site, crew chiefs could not have helped but recognize the crumbling landmark as an asset to local culture and history. The CCC's large-scale erosion-control programs can be seen today as check dams, linear cobble grids, and ingenious devices to arrest arroyo head-cutting. Closest to Casitas, they occur in high concentrations not seen elsewhere in the valley. The countless CCC workdays invested to mitigate nature's relentless assault on the site and its associated landscape demonstrate that Casitas has long been identified as worth protecting. It maintained a cultural valence strong enough to mobilize at least a portion of the federal labor investment in the valley. Ironically, this same landscape would serve to shelter local land-reform activists from militarized government pursuit a generation later.

When the first archaeological examination of Casitas began in 1959, the status of land grant properties and federal purview was in a dynamic state of negotiation, contestation, and reimagining by activist groups and their supporting communities. Federal tanks and heavily armed soldiers would course through the valley in 1967, punctuating long-simmering tensions over land and social justice during the dramatic events of the Tierra Amarilla courthouse raid and subsequent manhunt in the mountains and forests near El Rito. The historical injustices and ongoing confrontations surrounding land rights and their social, political, and religious contexts attested then, as it does now, to the need for committed community engagement in pursuing research in the vicinity of Casitas Viejas.

Pioneering efforts to synthesize archaeological research of the Spanish colonial era, in the mid-1950s Dr. Herbert Dick of Colorado State College at Alamosa began work at Casitas. Dr. Dick had long considered several northern New Mexican sites as having high potential for a large-scale project aimed at producing a definitive monograph on Spanish colonial archaeology (Martha Dick 2003, pers. comm.). Casitas clearly fit the bill, and with his graduate students, he excavated there in 1959. Dr. Dick did not have the opportunity to finish his projects at Casitas and later Picuris Pueblo before his death in 1998 (Adler and Dick 1999). The preponderance of evidence indicates that he had extensive plans for the story he found developing in his unfinished studies (Adler 2003, pers. comm.).

In the interim between Dr. Dick's work in the early 1960s and this most recent research at Casitas, generations of archaeologists learned their trade in field schools at nearby Sapawe Pueblo (LA 306). Dr. Florence Hawley Ellis brought many seasons of anthropology students from the University of New Mexico into the Rito Colorado valley to survey cultural resources and learn excavation techniques at the 14th-century adobe pueblo (Ellis 1963). In the process, some of the brightest stars of southwestern archaeology were educated in the Rito Colorado valley and undoubtedly were familiarized with the colonial-era ruins of Casitas in the process. Some of them, including David Snow and John Speth, conducted limited testing near Casitas and at the site itself, most likely in the 1970s (Snow 2004, pers. comm.). Charles Carrillo's surface-collected sample at Casitas was integrated into his dissertation analysis of Hispano pottery craft specialization (Carrillo 1997), which included such colonial-era settlements in New Mexico as the nearby and famous Genízaro pueblo of Abiquiú, as well as El Tajo and Colorado del Sur. Casitas remains classified as it first was, an "Anasazi/Hispanic" site by the New Mexico Cultural Resource Inventory System (NMCRIS, Archaeological Records Management System, Laboratory of Anthropology, Museum of Indian Arts and Culture, Santa Fe). More recent studies complicate this classification.

By the turn of the 21st century, U.S. Forest Service archaeologist Bob Lawrence began a series of evaluations, projects, and excavations at Casitas, nomination of the site to the National Register of Historic Places, and his oversight and collaboration on the work presented here. With the exception of very small assemblages at the USFS Taos office, in descendant community heirloom protection, and at Ghost Ranch, the rest of the known artifacts associated with Casitas are curated at the Museum of New Mexico's Laboratory of Anthropology, along with the databases associated with this research. Importantly, at the site itself, the cooperation and support of the local community for Forest Service efforts allowed for a fence (fig. 5) to protect the site from grazing livestock (Lawrence 1996). In this way and many others, the Forest Service and the descendant community became cochampions of Casita's cause, defending the site from grazers, looters, and vandals—ultimately, a federal complement to El Rito community members' pride and long-standing

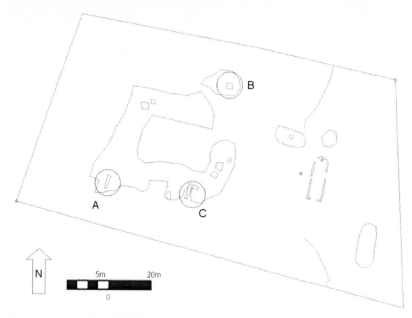

FIGURE 5. Site map of Casitas with protective fenceline and excavated disposal locations (loci A–C).

vigilance. After his careful vetting of the potential of my work with the descendant community in El Rito, Bob brought me in on his final management projects for the community-treasured site before his retirement from the Forest Service. Without him and the support and encouragement of the descendant community, this study would not have happened.

# 2 / Digging out Community

Historical archaeologists studying identity in the material record on a frontier recognize that precontact New Mexico was a dynamic world inhabited by a diverse mix of interconnected indigenous peoples in extensive networks spanning the continent and beyond. Although their arrival had no doubt been presaged by rumors from the east and stories from the south, people aligned with the Spanish colonial endeavor entered this indigenous landscape dramatically in their tiny columns of soldiers, settlers, and allies (Snow 1996; Flint and Flint 2003). Far more powerful than their weapons, infectious diseases, or latitudes of origin (Diamond 1999) were the imaginings they carried with them about their own place in this tapestry of people. To dig deeper into the social structures upon which the colonial enterprise depended requires an examination of the *casta* system and the flexibility with which identities were constituted and materially experienced in the 18th-century Spanish borderlands, the northern extent of which is where Spain's Provincias Internas centered on the frontier of New Mexico. How archaeologists articulate the material evidence of these concepts is in large part what sets historical archaeological work apart from historical studies. Whereas historical research has framed much of the thinking about how people lived together in these places, interpreting the potential meanings of material expressions becomes the archaeology of these communities.

Such perspectives have implications for how lives were historically represented, and in some cases reformulated from colonial pretensions. By teasing apart elite and literate chronicles of indigenous people and the associated dichotomies emphasized by borderlands historians, it is possible to get at a working definition of identity as applied to communities geographically and politically marginal to the colony. The point then is to set up an exploration of how historical colonial ascriptions can be studied archaeologically, particularly as they operated in parallel with or crosscut historically situated definitions.

## Picturing the Cast(a) of the Drama in Northern New Mexico

*La sistema de castas* (Table 1) and all of its preoccupations with skin color, proper dress, occupation, habits, comportment, and capacity for human wickedness had its origins in a recently traumatized Iberia. Having emerged from a long occupation by North African dynasties, the *casta* system was meant to involve control of persons of converted or unconverted Muslim, Jewish, and Christian heritages within the old Indo-European ideological framework of relatedness and blood purity. Such a notion of *limpieza de sangre* (cleanliness of blood) was converted in turn by colonists in the New World context into a classification for a much more diverse set of identities and mixtures (Bustamante 1989; Bustamante 2001; Katzew 2004; Voss 2005). The categories of people represented in the *casta* paintings were popularized by colonial elites who commissioned them for their homes across the Spanish world (Katzew 2004). These depictions served as metonyms for elite colonial perspectives. These paintings portrayed not only socioracial typologies for children of different *casta* parents but also several registers of social rules. Like the ideas that they simultaneously reflected and helped to structure, *casta* paintings incorporated colonial notions about the "appropriateness" of social position, use of material culture, occupation, and the kinds of behavior expected of these imagined subraces (fig. 6).

Several possible arrays of blood admixture were signified, each individually, by one father (e.g., a "pure white" Castilian man) and one mother (perhaps a Native American woman) and their child (labeled a "mestizo" in most of the Spanish colonies). Colonial written and artistic depictions of lower *casta* people were often vicious in their portrayal and, at best, confusing in the complex formulations of blood purity from region to region (Voss 2005). Pictures of pugilistic, domestically violent, or drunk people of lower *casta* designation, such as Genízaros, were carefully formulated in attempts to naturalize low social position, lack of mastery over social skills, and reduced access to materials as a genetically fixed situation resulting from miscegenation (fig. 7).

FIGURE 6. Francisco Clapera, *De Chino, e India, Genizara,*
ca. 1775. (Courtesy of the Denver Art Museum.)

While there was certainly a significant amount of elite paranoia over
a lessening grasp of the resolution of these socioracial categories (Katzew
2004:460), the lower classes in Spain and the colonies were presented
with new opportunities to manipulate this system for their gain. Within
certain strategic contexts, communities and individuals in colonial
New Spain may have expressed belonging to various categories. In New
Mexico, the use of the term *castas* itself went through a transformation
(Bustamante 1989), wherein everyone had a *casta* rank, but the use of
the noun itself referred to people of mixed, indefinable but non-Iberian
ancestry. This process of typological collapse into fewer categories in
New Mexico not only meant a blurring of hierarchical distinction but

Table 1. Select list of *casta* designations in colonial
New Spain

| Father | Mother | Casta child designation |
|--------|--------|-------------------------|
| Español | India | Mestizo* |
| Español | Mestiza | Castizo* |
| Español | Castiza | Torna a Español |
| Español | Negra | Mulato* |
| Español | Mulato | Morisco |
| Morisco | Español | Torna atrás |
| Negro | India | Lobo* |
| Lobo | India | Cambujo |
| Mulato | Mestiza | Cuarteron |
| Cuarteron | Mestiza | Coyote |
| Mestizo | India | Coyote* |
| Español | India | Coyote* |
| Mulato | India | Chino* |
| Cambujo | China | Genízaro |
| Indio | Indio | Genízaro* |

Source: After Bustamante 2001.

* Groups in New Mexico differently defined from other parts of
New Spain.

also created opportunities to reinvent categories. Indeed, Bustamante
(2001:207) relates colonial officials' reports that described *casta* people
passing themselves off for Spaniards as a common occurrence in the
frontier provinces of New Spain.

Multiple and overlapping forms of racial reckoning operated in parallel with the *casta* system. At certain geographical, financial, and expedi-
ent registers, colonial administrators could relate to not only their *vecino*
(neighbor) citizens but also their settled, agricultural, and nominally
Christianized Pueblo neighbors. These they characterized as *la gente de
razón*, or "people of reason." For as much reason as any other, this labeling worked to juxtapose them to the *indios bárbaros*, whom the colonial
elite more or less framed as unredeemable and savage, as their needs
suited them (Weber 2005). In describing how the Spanish colonial technologies, economies, and warfare structured and were restructured by

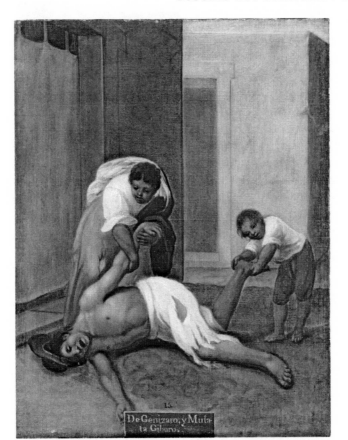

FIGURE 7. Francisco Clapera, *De Genizaro, y Mulata,
Gibaro,* ca. 1775 (Courtesy of the Denver Art Museum.)

the trade in Indian slaves on the northern frontier, Blackhawk (2007:743) suggests that elite chroniclers manipulated notions of rationality and naturalized violence to justify their dehumanizing of noncolonial people:

> When documenting incidents of Indian "savagery," Spanish record-ers, in a sense, bore witness to the violent effects of their own pres-ence while trying to rationalize them. As "*índios bárbaros*" Utes and Comanches, by definition, performed irrational acts of vio-lence. They acted violently due to nature, not in response to eco-nomic or political forces, and Spanish accounts often follow such prescriptions. (Blackhawk 2007:741)

Regardless of the way literate colonists described those who were not part of the colony, the ransoming of captives into New Mexican society introduced large numbers of Native American people into the households of *vecino*, settler-citizen society (Brooks 2002a, 2002b; Rael-Gàlvez 2002). Though worrisome for the elite, the expanding category of *la gente de razón* may have actually served the political and economic machinations of colonial administrators. In new capacities to shift categories of *indio* to *mestizo*, such changes could have satisfied needs to remove rights to traditional land ownership or other responsibilities for taxation or cost (Rothschild 2006:98). In some cases, Spanish colonists may have been more likely to associate certain racial statuses with place of residence and profession rather than strictly race (Jackson 1999:20). Opportunities for families and communities with grants of land were amplified in these ways and were certainly on the radar of those who would otherwise be low status in proximity to elite living in colonial capitals. In such a system of mutable categories, an element of individual and family choice appears built in, which Chance (1978) suggests people sought to exploit to their advantage. The situational aspect of identity in such a context was not as much an indicator of group membership within a static and rigid social system but rather one component of personal identities that could be manipulated and often changed (Chance 1978:131). As the idea of tightly definable identifications among their own *vecinos* broke down, administrators became increasingly creative in how they distanced themselves both figuratively and literally from the lower classes.

## Frontline Families and Opportunities

To colonial elites, the *casta* people placed on the frontier were expendable and obliged to serve as buffers because they were indebted to the colony by virtue of their low position in New Mexican society and commensurate need for land, support, and legal representation. This reinforcement of low status was a structural violence experienced by people in *casta* positions in the colony and a conscious part of elite descriptions of citizens, such as the example in the critical review of colonial holdings (Domínguez [1776] 1956) of "*gente baja*" (lesser people) in the village of Trampas (Bustamante 2001:207). Among occupations available for *casta* people in the colony, proximity to centers of colonial administration had inherent tensions. Near Santa Fe, the barrio of Analco kept *casta* people separated from elite households, even in worship, as they had their own church (Magnaghi 1994:120). From communities such as these, colonial people of higher status extracted labor in the form of household servants, shepherds, and field laborers. In the case of Genízaros, people of Native American descent whose families had at some point experienced captivity, exploitive labor was predicated upon their debt of patronage to household heads. Colonialists "rescued" Native Americans from captivity, often through the payment of "ransoms" at trade fairs, and ostensibly detribalized them by raising them within the precepts of Christian doctrine (Swadesh 1974; Chavez 1979; Magnaghi 1994). Not surprisingly, cases of abuse in such relationships were common and sometimes even filed as complaints with colonial officials (Brooks 2002a:135).

Given these tensions, between the need for Native American labor, military protection, political allegiances and the threat of internal mixing, status mobility, and resistance to oppression, it is stunning how important the Genízaro population became to the colony. Their successes survive as the rural Indo-Hispano (following Lamadrid 2003) villages of today, which have been convincingly argued (Snow 1979:50) to be squarely the products of the last quarter of the 18th century. By that point in New Mexican history, economic, political, and simple corporeal survival depended upon flexibility in dealing with all of the cultural groups that met, were formed, and sometimes clashed, along the borderlands (Twinam 1999; Brooks 2002a, 2002b). But how to populate these dangerous places and by which administrative mechanisms might the administration both offer land and control the communities who took on the challenge?

As in the border wars the Hapsburgs had faced in maintaining their Iberian domains (Good 1984), the later Bourbon administration set ordinances, the Ordenanazas de Descrubriemiento, Nueva Poblacion de las Indias dadas por Felipe ii, by which medieval practices related to land and water were to be enacted in the New World (Simmons 2001:127). It was expected that not only would these practices sustain the livelihood of the settlement but also that they would allow circumscription of the communities into organized, self-invigilating "proper villages" (Nuttall 1921). One principal format was for a village plan around a central plaza for defense. The irrigation committee, comprised of alcaldes, mayors, and other administrative units, was another important form of organization that was established early in the sequence of any colonial site occupation. These local leaders organized labor around the creation and maintenance of the *acequias* that fed intricate agricultural systems for the entire community but were also responsible for adjudicating disputes, negotiating water practices with nearby communities, and defending the interests of the village (Rodríguez 2006). Military service was another primary requirement of these frontier communities. The colonial administration desperately needed militia groups to serve in the campaigns of various governors trying to reign in the deleterious effects of captive and livestock raiding by neighboring nomadic groups. The cycles of violence were renewed and magnified by colonial counterraids against communities during particularly intense episodes of frontier violence.

Despite these dangers, frontier land grants provided lower *casta* colonists with rare opportunities to develop and hold title to land. Once settled, the fear of losing a land grant could be used to pressure these types of communities to maintain or reinforce occupancy regardless of the volatile conditions around them (Poling-Kempes 1997). A primary means by which a settler community could meet the challenges of the required terms of occupancy was to construct the well-fortified plaza required by the Spanish colonial administration. This was a challenge itself as the majority of settlements in the region were residences (*ranchos*) dispersed across the landscape so that families could be close to their fields and flocks. Since this was a common characteristic of settlement patterns of that time period in northern New Mexico (Snow 1979), it meant more difficult defense during raids, a situation lamented by authorities (Simmons 1969:17). Navigating the reality of these conflicting interests in the face of difficult frontier defense was something only the communities themselves could manage on a daily basis.

Intentionally or not, in making land grants to pluralistic communities the Spanish colonial administration rewarded the cultural fluency of those who blurred identities. Ostensibly they were placed far from centers of administrative life, protection, and prestige. But social mobility and economic fortunes were thusly uniquely situated to blossom far from elite invigilation. An example of this tension is the acknowledgment of the need for the fighting prowess of the Genízaros, who became frontline defenders of New Mexico, yet who retained a low *casta* status (Chavez 1979). Their possible European namesakes had origins in Turkish military history: *yeni cerci* for "new troops," these seized Christian captives were renowned for their fighting prowess, discipline, and loyalty to the society they had been adopted into (Magnaghi 1994:125). Governors such as Vélez Cachupín attempted to legislate a frontier strategy of containment of nomadic raiders through community land grants on the frontier to Genízaros, such as those at Abiquiú (Poling-Kempes 1997).

In doing so, they opened a space for renegotiation of Genízaro status in the colony.

Their liminal position between recent captivity and newly minted citizen made Genízaros perfect candidates for settlement of hostile territories away from central towns. Genízaro people epitomized new, mutable categories of frontier *casta* designation. The potential for advancement in the social order through grants of land on the frontier and development of economic and military prowess offered a strong motivation for people to live in harm's way who would otherwise have been denied such opportunities (Chavez 1979). While developing the northwestern frontier, they were reimmersed in indigenous systems of matrilineal resource ownership and labor practiced by their Indian neighbors. Less sedentary groups such as the Navajo divided labor by having women and children tend fields, crops, and flocks, while men hunted, raided, and defended their family from raiders (Brooks 2002a:91). Within the model of the patriarchal colonial household, divisions of labor along age and sex meant women controlled domestic domains and crops only after planting, while men and maturing boys managed herds, hunting, and militia duties (Van Ness 1991:125). In this context, there was potential for frontier *vecinos* to translocate the *casta* categories of their colonial overlords, simultaneously shifting status for themselves upward (Swadesh 1974) while retaining some degree of differentiation in their new communities to control their own captives and servile classes.

## A Turning Point on a Critical Frontier

Increasingly volatile conditions on the northwestern frontier of the colony culminated in the devastating joint Ute and Comanche attacks of 1747, which almost emptied the Upper Rio Chama basin villages as settlers retreated to the town of Santa Cruz and to settlements of various Pueblo allies to the south (Poling-Kempes 1997:36). Prior to this time, considerable administrative consternation was directed at the characteristic organization of northern settlements into loose clusters of dwellings and associated farm buildings scattered across the countryside (Simmons 1969:16). Community dwellings surrounded their *placitas,* small central areas, in a highly irregular fashion, seemingly without order. Yet the nature of the topography, a desire to be near close kinsmen, and convenience have been identified as the principal criteria in organizing these spaces (Van Ness 1991:172). In response to the increased raiding, Vélez

Cachupín's prescriptions for security measures reiterated concentration of populations with fortified plazas and heavy gates.

Calling the closed plaza of Casitas a "modest sample of *plazuela* construction," Swadesh speculated that the layout of this main structure represents a unified set of roomblocks with a massive front gate (Swadesh 1974:179). Sixteen miles away, near the mother village of Abiquiú, the plaza of Santa Rosa de Lima at 370 feet square or 135 *varas* (Carrillo 1997:121) was much larger than that observed at *Casitas*. But this settlement had been abandoned after a raid and was replaced by the current set of *plazuelas* up on the bench above the river where Abiquiú remains to this day.

The author's high-resolution archaeological mapping and limited testing reveals a fortified *plazuela*, and the erosional exposure of massive foundation stones at the gateway suggests support for heavy doors. Ongoing work by the author at a smaller *plazuela* on the main quadrangle at Abiquiú suggests that these fortified households might manifest at multiple scales, particularly if there are defense strategies that include multiple *plazuelas* added through time to a settlement. If one *plazuela* was breached, retreat to another nearby might preclude full flight to another population center. Modern El Rito retains some vestiges of this kind of layout, but a smaller and more defensible example may be observed at Chimayo, downriver and closer to Española. The plaza of San Buenaventura, now called the Plaza del Cerro, was built around 1740 and consists of a square of contiguous adobe buildings with only two entrances, a *torreón* (small fortified defensive tower) on the south side, and a small chapel bounding the western side (Usner 1995). Within similar residential units at Casitas, it is likely that extended families and close kin occupied the "restricted plaza" of the main quadrangle (Simmons 1969:14). In times of attack, multiple aligned kin groups and neighbors likely joined the main *plazuela* families, such as those who may have constructed the nearby unattached blocks at Casitas, as well as the only slightly more distant and unprotected *ranchos* up and down the valley (e.g., LA 112951). But who constituted family or kin among the dispersed *poblaciones*, or loosely grouped *ranchos* of such tributary valleys?

In 1750, at San Juan Pueblo, the alcalde mayor of Abiquiú, Juan José Lobato (for whom the land grant on which Casitas is located is named) read Vélez Cachupín's decree to fortify to the other Abiquiú settlers (Carrillo 1997:120) and forbade the building of isolated houses. Lobato was in charge of the resettlement of the Abiquiú area. There is much debate regarding whether or not Lobato himself actually was the progenitor of settlement in the Rito Colorado valley (Swadesh 1974; Quintana and Snow 1980:45), but census data from Abiquiú indicate that the settler population was growing rapidly, creating new villages as groups of families settled in previously unsecured secondary drainage basins such as the Rito Colorado valley (Carrillo 1997:36). From a tactical standpoint, it makes sense to have settled the alternate routes to Chama villages in order to avoid having Abiquiú flanked by raiding parties coming through the southern San Juan Mountains via passes from Canjilon, Vallecitos, and Ojo Caliente. As the labor of whole families was necessary to make any new settlement viable, extended kin groups would likely have been deployed to settle the Rito Colorado valley.

Recent historical work (Brooks 2002a, 2002b; Rael-Gàlvez 2002) complicates what such family compositions could have looked like. Even as late as 1860, census takers in the Chama precinct that included the Rito Colorado valley found that family units living under one roof "contained such an admixture of names and ages that it was virtually impossible to ascertain each individual's relation to the rest of the family and precinct" (Brown and Robertshaw 1973:44). Carrillo (1997:112) states plainly that the inhabitants of Casitas Viejas came from Abiquiú, and this idea that the settlement at Casitas budded off from the founding village of Genízaros is supported by a concomitant increase in Rito Colorado valley population following petitions from Abiquiú for more land (Quintana and Snow 1980:46).

Kin relations with an established outpost hub like Abiquiú are implicit in the settlement of a place like Casitas. As the basis of membership in plaza-based frontier networks, kinship coupled with residence would have been enacted daily in the localized activities of people living there (Van Ness 1991:130). Anthropologists and historians have long distinguished Spanish colonial frontier villages from other colonial communities by describing their traditions as hybridized (Swadesh 1974; Chavez 1979; Kessell 1979; Gutiérrez 1991; F. Levine 1992; Magnaghi 1994), that is, taking on aspects of both colonial and native cultures. This only complicated matters for administrators attempting to reify socioracial statuses.

Attaining legal title to land from the government created an implicit tension in colonial communities, because certain requirements of ethnicity and religion, a Spanish or Hispanicized identity, had to be met by grantees (Jimenez 1972; Jones 1979), as well as the legislated layouts for settlement and defense (Simmons 1969). These buffer villages continued to be distinguished from many colonial communities by continuing some measure of unregimented settlement structure and the agricultural production and maintenance of syncretic culinary traditions (Simmons 2001). Such traits are only now beginning to be fully explored as hallmarks of the formation of new corporate identities on the frontier. At the very heart of the matter, understanding how a community or a family could mobilize different aspects of their heritages in making a home and a network of allies has daunting potential illegibility for historical and archaeological studies.

## Viewing Borderlands Research from a Distance

The development of the concept of the Spanish borderlands represents a particular moment in American historical research and nationalist dialogues. Historian Herbert Eugene Bolton is largely responsible for the nucleus of what became the field of Spanish borderlands research. His seminal work, *The Spanish Borderlands: A Chronicle of Old Florida and the Southwest* (Bolton 1921), examined a part of North America that was truly distinct from the historical projects of other nationalist authors (Turner 1894). Rather than timeless and static backwaters whose contribution to America was to be assimilated by the eastern colonial tide of Manifest Destiny, Bolton's borderlands were a romanticized narrative of cultured European adventures in a rugged landscape. Perhaps most importantly, Native Americans were present in this portrayal of how the historical landscape was peopled, although the portrayal of political economies was oversimplified. Leading up to this, Hubert Howe Bancroft's work (Bancroft 1889) influenced a new, idealized representation of the Spanish New World, though his large body of historical works revealed an ambivalence toward Hispanic culture (Weber 1991). Scholars such as Snow (1992) and (Lamadrid 1992) would identify the legacy of such ambivalence for archaeologists and historians a century later when they pointedly critiqued the dual assault of stereotyping Indianism and Hispanophobia and glossing over the contributions of this era to American history. Overall, the body of research that came to be known as Spanish borderlands studies was broad in scope and sweeping in concept. Words like "pageant" and "epic" titled these scholars' studies of Spanish accomplishments in the New World, which left little room for the complexities of individual or local experiences in their grand narratives.

The scale of these studies makes understanding the nature of everyday life for the many kinds of people who inhabited the Spanish borderlands extremely difficult. Military and diplomatic themes, while very important in framing the initial exploration and settlement of the borderlands (Weber 1991:13), do not permit the fine-grained examination required to question who colonial people really were and what their daily lives were like. In this early body of Spanish borderlands research, the region was written as a play with characters that played to stereotypes of Anglo-American xenophobia: the cruel, greedy Spanish colonizer of the infamous "black legend" oppressing the Native American "noble savages." The most immediate dichotomy that becomes apparent in early borderlands studies is that of "Spanish" and "Indian." Yet contemporary records systems and reports on archaeological sites often make simplified use of these monikers. In the life of such documents and historical narratives, the actions of these communities are implicitly uniform. By extension, their operative principles were shared and enacted by a homogeneous colonizing population and reacted to by stable and consistently organized populations of indigenous people. Again, this idea is part of Bolton's concept of a "Spanish imprint" upon the indigenous landscape of the New World (Weber 1991).

In the situation of the northern frontier of New Mexico, the "Spanish" themselves might not have pictured such a clear-cut dichotomous position with respect to indigenous people. It has been pointed out that, unlike in other European New World colonies, people in Spanish provinces created and maintained a smaller social distance from indigenous communities (Rothschild 2003:163) even with the elaborate *casta* system ever-present at many levels. It could be read that in the very act of marking relations that crossed *casta* designations, the Spanish colonials were signaling a certain level of acceptance of the fact there was indeed substantial mixing of indigenous, European, and African blood. Moreover, those men who came to the North America did so in the context of huge disparities in gender ratios in the settler populations yet were ultimately enumerated as heads of household (F. Levine 1992). The Spanish Crown considered the practice of Spanish immigrant men incorporating indigenous women into their households to be advantageous in the conversion process in the New World (Brooks 2002a, 2002b). By acknowledging these processes, ethnohistorians began a discipline-wide rejection of dichotomous stereotypes and the concept of a static borderlands where Spain's imprint lived on "deep and clear" (Bolton 1921) into the present day. By an explicit rejection of the direct historic model of analysis, analytic frameworks for studying long-term culture contact between colonizers and indigenous people could be formulated.

Edward Spicer did just this in a critical piece of ethnohistoric scholarship (Spicer 1962), where his dynamic perspective allowed for different groups in the borderlands to have different colonial experiences. Spicer organized his analyses by defining two contact situations: directed and nondirected. Situations in which power was not a factor were considered to be nondirected. In directed situations, Spanish colonial society used force against indigenous people and those within the colony who did not conform to social and political mandates. Spicer's main focus was identity maintenance throughout the ages, despite unequal power relations during acculturation. Acculturation theory in this vein modeled these processes along a continuum with varying amounts of retention of indigenous cultural traditions. The trajectory was in only one direction, with Spicer identifying a general pattern that inevitably led to "acceptance of domination" (Spicer 1962:16). Not all Indian people experienced contact with the Spanish in the same way. Differences between Franciscan and Jesuit missionary tactics and cultural differences between the Opata Indians of central Sonora and the Pueblo Indians of New Mexico led to different responses in indigenous responses to missionization attempts (Spicer 1962). Long-term persistence of cultural identity is attributed to contact being mostly a transfer of "things" rather than of core cultural ideas or beliefs. Such an acculturation perspective seems to weaken the agency of the acculturated group, while simultaneously denying them a history of complex and dynamic relationships that crosscut categories of colonist and *casta*. Cusick (1998) points out that some of this thinking is probably the result of the political atmosphere within which it was formulated, in that Spicer was a real-world participant in what he might have theorized as a "directed contact" situation of administration for Japanese American relocation camps.

Unfortunately, these ideas still did not offer escape from the basic tenets of static tradition. The recurrent themes of dichotomy in "continuity and change" that were mobilized by early Spanish borderlands historians conceptualized colonial people as incapable of acting across and between *casta* categories. Rather, they were forever locked into distinctive roles. So even though people may have had extremely varied daily experiences, dependent on who they interacted with, arguments of continuity projected static traditions onto them while simultaneously constraining them to only externally caused change. A classic example of an enduring "static" theme is Bancroft's interpretation of the New Mexican economy as a backwater. This was based on a single 1770 report from Consular Morfi that portrayed a stagnant Hispanic enclave waiting for outside economic stimulation rather than a network of sophisticated daily negotiations which would have been a necessity in a regional economy with little hard currency (Frank 2000:143). Such assumptions of stability in ethnic cultures are cautioned against (Wolf 1982; Sahlins 1985) because static models basically posit that memory is defining and experience corrupting (Upton 1996).

Stereotypes persist in academia as in other realms of thinking and marking otherness. Scholarship that frames stereotypical ways of life (type lists) denies the potential for situational identity performances, drawing upon a repertoire of tools, cultural knowledge, and strategies. Shifting identities could be used by individuals and communities in self-fashioning their place in a society—sometimes a distillation of particular, chosen traits and ideas; sometimes a synthesis of introduced and adopted characteristics. In fact, debate exists whether certain versions of stereotypical institutions, such as the *hacienda*, ever truly existed in pre-Pueblo Revolt New Mexico (Snow 1983). Historical archaeologists argue with historians about which processes actually structured the nature and scale of socioeconomic relations, organization, and landscapes (Simmons 1969; Snow 1992). The life of such a debate centers on whether the dichotomy of continuity and change represents realistic parameters to describe what was going on in, across, and between *casta* positions on these "frontline" contexts of culture contact.

## Borderlands Identities as Strategy

Recent generations of southwestern scholars have reenvisioned historical processes, centering less on dichotomies and unidirectional processes while becoming more invested in exploring webs of interaction. In these narratives, frontier people strategized not only their position in colonial society but also their kin and alliance relationships within and across indigenous groups by drawing from complex repertoires of identity.

Historians point out that when Spanish colonists wrote about the indigenous people upon whose land they were establishing a new economy and way of life, it was always in the context of an underlying recognition that the survival of the colony depended upon them (Gutiérrez 1991). If the diverse cast of newly arrived people were going to create a situation for themselves that enhanced or maintained their prestige and honor in New Mexican, continental, and global societies, they needed to reinforce and reinvent distances between themselves and other members of their colonial society. For this to work in ever-changing circumstances, the maintenance and performance of social distance must have also been situational and changing over time (Frank 1998; Rothschild 2003). Part and parcel of an identity label such as *español* that colonial people were creating was the understanding that others had to fill lower social ranks in order to buoy newly emerging categories (Frank 1998:178).

On paper, people manipulated these rankings administratively using the *padron*, or official colonial census. This record was an instrument of social control for people both inside and outside colonial society (Radding 1997). By the use of labels and counting, census takers enumerated details about geographic communities that led to the enforcement of matrimony and delineated the kinds of alliances most strategic to military and ecclesiastical authorities in their separate projects. Furthermore, tenure and genealogy recorded in the census data led to relations of power tied intricately to limited resource bases of land and water within colonial control. Again, a hierarchy of ethnic and other identities was promulgated within and between groups, including indigenous peoples, as illustrated by an example from Sonora where access to an economic base led to one indigenous group treating another as inferiors within a repositioned social system (Radding 1997:149). Ongoing negotiations of status among indigenous people and their choice to articulate new affiliations played out in parallel to increasing use of recontextualized, but nonetheless mostly foreign, categories of status. Petitions by individual Native Americans to gain the status of *vecino*, or colonial citizen, and thus fully integrate with the market system of the new colony represented a substantial gamble. For some indigenous people, to seek this new social identity and try to find advantageous positions within the colonial labor market meant abandoning traditional entitlements to the products of communal labor as well as protected access to Indian lands and legal standing under Spanish law (Radding 1997).

James Brooks's (2002a, 2002b) examination of Spanish colonial and Native American traditions of capture, servitude, and kinship identifies frontier people as preeminent negotiators between cultural groups. Indigenous groups and colonists alike, as a part of their systems of capture and servitude, seem to have separately cognized the people they captured or bought by race, age, and gender, which in turn conditioned the captives' experience of enslavement. Far from the dichotomies of earlier historical research, this key work explores the mutual understandings among all of the societies ensconced in the frontier setting and allows for the potential of direct translations across cultural gaps. Within the value of gendered and extracted labor, Brooks makes space in his work for historical peoples themselves to manipulate and assign their own meanings and values to expressions of different kinds of identity.

On a frontier where raiding and counterraiding was part of everyday life, the particular value that a perceived membership carried for a captive was central to their social and economic status in both colonial and indigenous societies. If a party of raiders from a Plains community captured a girl from a New Mexican colonial settlement, her worth in the complex negotiations of trade to others or incorporation into the community would vary, depending on her perceived "Spanish-ness." This in turn would be only part of the complex of values associated with her enslavement—"a member of the conquering people held in bondage by her erstwhile subjects" (Brooks 2002a:187). Depending on their *casta* status, female captives might have passed to their children particular types of rights and privileges accorded their perceived identity. Among other identity aspects, Brooks describes a captive's value in a colonial or indigenous household as having amounted to not only what labor they could contribute but also the claims to their membership that a captor and a family could pursue once children were born (Brooks 2002a).

A similar framework of captivity and cultural capital, flexible and powerful in performance as well as latent potential for alliances, is detailed in Estèvan Rael-Gàlvez's work on Indian slavery in Colorado and New Mexico (2002). By addressing the centrality of the lived experiences of enslaved as well as reintegrated Native American peoples, the described mixture of heritages that occurred in southern Colorado and northern New Mexico frames the development of frontier society (Rael-Gàlvez 2002). In these constructions of community, the negotiation of identity was a product of the encounters that produced a sense of historical consciousness, a process that is continuously negotiated. In that process, identities are "grounded in the particular relationships formed through histories of race, gender, class, and place" (Haas 1995). Historical work like this, which positions gender-centered regional community (Deutsch 1987) as one of many important frameworks to illuminate the intersection of class, culture, and racialized relationships are powerful lenses through which to examine the frontier.

## Historical Archaeology of Identity as a Complex of Possibilities

The New Western Historians and their intellectual heirs demonstrated that stories of frontier intergroup relations were more complicated than

the unidirectional transfer of things and traits envisioned by earlier borderlands historians and acculturation theorists. Archaeologists following this shift are challenged to find conceptual tools that allow us to more
satisfactorily explore historically silenced aspects of these processes. The
*casta* system established a hierarchy in Spanish colonial society, placing
Iberian peninsula–born at the top and indigenous slaves at the bottom.
But to start from this perspective on identity in examinations of multi-
cultural but hierarchical societies risks overrepresenting the view from
above (Clifford 1997). How affiliations were negotiated across various
levels and contexts remains unclear. Similarly, alliances between communities were multifaceted in their possible range. It is important to recognize that just as administratively confusing and liminal "becoming"
any given status could be, such as the processes lived by Indo-Hispano
communities (Lamadrid 2003) in New Mexico, so was it a result of where
one was.

Cultural revolutions were in the making in northern New Mexico.
Rather than some periphery off of the core of Spanish colonialism, cultural crossroads such as the Rito Colorado valley were sites for refor-
mulating the process of "becoming" citizens. These challenges to a
supposedly set system of race-dependent values could resonate well
beyond the adobe walls of homes at Casitas. Developing a more flexible
view of identity in the borderlands requires another set of tools to see
how people performed these pluralistic social roles from the bottom up,
or in daily life. Archaeology is particularly well suited to gaining this
perspective, and Casitas serves as the perfect test-bed for the kinds of
theoretical approaches that illuminate the situational nature of identity.

For a historical archaeology of frontier living, identities might be
framed as historically contextualized, situational, and multiscalar means
of synthesizing imposed and adopted practices in ways that demonstrate
part of a person's or group's membership in a community. It follows,
then, that people and the groups to which they belong exist within social
constraints along a spectrum of what they may or may not be aware of,
but that they reproduce and modify through their daily practices (Bourdieu 1977). Different situations affect the ways people relate to the material and social constraints that they perceive, and prompt changes in
how they position themselves with respect to others (Barth 1969).

Because the archaeological record does not often have the resolution
to deal with the rapidity with which some situations could change, we
must look elsewhere to find the reproduction and modifications of practices signaling identity. Fortunately, identity practices occur on varying

scales, including the intimate, local, and regional. At one end of the spectrum, what constitutes behavior that signals membership within a private family household context may be quite different than what happens on the other side of the same wall where a plaza (public) performance could be staged. At the other end of the scale, when identity is situated in contexts of conflict and confrontation (Schortman and Urban 1998), identity aspects can be seen as the critical conjuncture (Sahlins 1985) for a regionally based conceptualization of opposing sides in contestations of power. Historical archaeological theories of competition and intergroup power differentials can be expanded to a scale that connects large social groupings and geographically linked aspects of society (McGuire 1982).

Perhaps most easily approached by an archaeologist working within the constraints of a site-focused project, the smaller scope of macro- versus microscale expressions of community membership might be explored via landscape processes of settlement, agricultural elaboration, and defensive posture, versus household uses of space, foodway choices, and plaza use. If the *habitus* of a particular group were embedded in family and cultural memory and reproduced in the daily routines of kitchen and hearth, foodway practices should be manifest in the material record as traces of labor and production in which smaller-scale expressions of identity affect uses of space, culinary materials, and tools. At a larger scale, if community members differentially participated in the transformation and maintenance of what was once a largely indigenous landscape into one that incorporated new Spanish colonial structures and functions, they would have imprinted the signature of a new kind of corporate community.

Although presentations of ethnicity can be a powerful way to not only reinforce but also create bonds of kinship between people, that is only one part of an array of variable strategies, processes, and practices that make up identity. The concept of ethnicity itself may not have had the same meanings or been experienced similarly for everyone in New Spain or even in Iberian Spain. Yet, socioracial identity aspects had many legal, economic, and sexual repercussions for people living in colonial contexts. And because these aspects were recorded in some colonial documents, the material expressions of these traits are rich resources for exploring the reality of daily life for people who may or may not have lived the roles ascribed by their ethnic labels. Processes, not trait lists, reflected in the archaeological record permit some exploration of these ideas. Notions of shared identity and the maintenance of social boundaries related

to ethnic and other designations sometimes crosscut geographic, economic, or social categories.      Expressions of identity as reflected in
material behavior can be more easily understood in the context of imag-
ining colonial identities in terms of nested networks rather than boundaries (Cordell 2004). So rather than conceptualize groupings of people
as mutually exclusive, thinking how their experiences may have been
crosscut by different kinds of relationships allows for an archaeology of
pluralism. Even if people were not constantly or consciously focused on
which groupings they were a part of, Bourdieu's analogy for not seeing,
but *being* and *becoming* (emphasis mine) a part of a community of behavior via practice, is compelling about the unconscious nature of learning
rules (Bourdieu 1977). In her particularly insightful interpretation, Stone
highlighted the analogy of young children who learn vocabulary and
the underlying rules of grammar and syntax without ever having been
taught the difference between a noun and an adverb (Stone 2003). In
archaeological materials, this concept can be applied to having a meal
by working with the "vocabulary" of ingredients, portioning, presentation, and consumption without necessarily obsessing over just how the
marrow got from the bone into the soup. Conceptually similar, the act of
laying out a field uses an implicit "vocabulary" of tilling, irrigation, seed,
and weeding that is almost universal to agriculturalists, but not every
society lays out *suertes* based on household demographics. The approach
advocated in this book bridges these scales of practice by nesting them
within multiple layers of intra- and intercommunity cultural dynamics.

In this realm of differential and recursive ideological forms, where
even the colonially labeled "Spanish" actors were a mix of Iberian, African, and Indian heritages, what people did could have been more important than their pasts, which were in turn grounded in ethnicity or even
race. Such marking activities or performances of belonging are exactly
the situational processes of becoming that I seek to identify through patterns of material practice. Those concepts are aligned with the ideas of
structure and practice in Bourdieu's (1977) framing of *habitus* as "regu-
lated improvisations." Successful improvisations take maximum advantage of small modifications and on-the-fly adaptations, so their place
in performing identity is powerful. Improvising one's membership in a
community of practice allows for fewer digressions in new situations as
well as an outlet for the agency for people trying to manipulate identity
in their favor. It is improbable that absolutely all aspects of those processes could be archaeologically visible, and especially whether or not
the participants recognized them. Yet the potters' practices left material

traces that, when nested within other scales and independent lines of evidence (i.e., other material categories), may in their combination reveal the situational nature of different aspects of the potters' experiences.

On the other hand, it seems improbable that all people are conscious and active agents in the negotiation of their identity all of the time. Pottery production and *acequia* construction by communities living in New Mexican villages like Casitas certainly exhibited certain aspects that were both formal and informal in their execution, such as vessel shapes or the construction of headgates. But these practices were not daily activities for just anyone in the community and therefore can be used as examples of identity production at different temporal and spatial scales, on both conscious and unconscious levels. It is for this reason that I combine both within frameworks of foodway and landscape behaviors that also consider more quotidian practices. Synthesizing these two lines of investigation further exposes how various modes of identity and expressions of community membership correlate or crosscut each other, situates different aspects of historic identities in tension with each other, and builds upon recent, successful studies of culture contact in places such as Florida and California (K. Lightfoot et al. 1993; Lightfoot, Martinez, and Schiff 1998; Voss 2002; K. Lightfoot 2005; Voss 2005; Voss 2008). In New Mexico, archaeological narratives that examine small slices of time on several sides of a historical conjuncture—the lives of Spanish, *mestizos*, Native Americans, and others along the colonial frontier—can include flexible models of group membership and identity. In such cases, people, families, and perhaps whole communities may have used strategies associated with multiple cultural practices to secure their interests. These kinds of situational identities are not neatly bounded entities and cannot be explored meaningfully outside of their social and historical contexts, in the present or the past. The concept of mutable identity is a critical pivot for studies of multiple and changing forms of social belonging, allowing for a focus on the ways people could move between and among interstices between identity labels (Casella and Fowler 2005:6). The investigation of frontier community formation can be pursued most fruitfully by the application of practice theory to the material record of mutable micro- and macroscale behavior, as understood within historical structures of the Spanish colonial *casta* system. Building upon these crucial areas of research, my study of Casitas emphasizes the important roles that diet and foodways play in the construction and protection of affinities to or exclusion from communities of practice. To link this approach with archaeological investigation at multiple scales, the organization and maintenance of foodways in relation to community-constructed landscapes must be linked as microscale practices of identity and representation with the macroscale practices of place.

At Casitas, two-sided understandings of low *casta* status were a necessity for Genízaro service. These processes can be framed in terms of how they are enacted by individuals out of experience. These performances at their core actually *entail* change and lend themselves to iterative improvisations. Investigation of the material signature of both modes of practice, organic and intentional, lends itself to archaeological description of what has been called the emergence of a people via Genízaro consciousness (Lamadrid 2000), which in turn can be considered a uniquely New Mexican Indo-Hispano community formation on the frontier.

With this in mind, this archaeological study of identity on the northern frontier of New Mexico is predicated upon two assertions: (1) that the multifaceted array of practices and daily activities that create community can be studied through careful examination of diversities reflected in patterns of the material record; and (2) that the places where historic colonial endeavors met in relative parity of strength with those of indigenous groups are particularly rich for exploring the kinds of self-fashioning and identity performances of people and groups. By extension, the examination of the material residues of the behaviors of frontier communities can expose ties of common practice and expose unique connections underlying common ideas about belonging. At different temporal and spatial scales, such commonalities may have been subsumed under multiple, overlapping strands of identity in ways that reveal their relationships to each other and to the greater constraining structures around them.

If the multiscalar approach outlined above is going to work for investigating the dynamic, pluralistic colonial situation of northern New Mexico, appropriate contextualization of the communities and locations of practice must precede its application. In this respect, focusing on both micro- and macroscale practices—cultural landscape creation and foodways—has the greatest potential to reveal diversity and connections among identity expressions. In addition, this endeavor must be situated within the appropriate historical framework of northern New Mexican buffer communities. At Casitas, an interpretive methodology akin to that used by lithic analysts, called *chaîne opératoire* (operational chain), is central to the investigation of household-level foodways. These practices in turn are evaluated in relation to larger processes of identity marking in the landscape of the Rito Colorado valley. The intent is to identify material evidence for Indo-Hispano community formations within categories of daily actions to avoid categorization of situational practice on any one scale, or material category alone. I cache these nested categories within the two frameworks that I call "homescape" and "hearthscape."

## Concepts of Homescape and Hearthscape

Homescapes, a particular form of cultural landscape, are multidimensional and composed of overlapping and reinforcing elements including, but not limited to, natural environment, agricultural systems, ritual place, processional routes, military jurisdictions, and seasonal hunting territories. In short, these are different dimensions of archaeological landscape which in their interaction created a sense of home place for a community. Homescape describes how people navigate, manage, and reinvent the immediate geographic, physical communities in which they live. This macroscale of practice is more readily visible and part of the ongoing process of landscape creation and maintenance. Homescape processes can operate at village to regional scales, with linked levels of involvement. For this study, the Rito Colorado valley constrains a macroscale of behavior that represents a homescape for the communities with which Casitas settlers engaged. Multiscalar investigation of this homescape is not constrained by actions within the immediate vicinity of Casitas. For example, sources of ceramic raw materials can be local to the larger valley, from the Greater Southern San Juan area (such as the residual micaceous clays of La Madera) or from the Tewa basin. Similarly, animal resources may be from local herds or nearby wild deer and elk, regional sources of antelope or mountain lions, or distant bison from the Plains, and all may be taken at different seasons, pastured in rounds, or exchanged at annual trade fairs. At the same time, the concept of homescape describes a more bounded scale of cultural action for a particular community.

Within the community scale of organization, the household is the basic unit of social production and reproduction, centered around the hearth (Wilk and Netting 1984). Temporally, the creation, maintenance, and re-creation of household structure and function operates at a level archaeologically discernible via processes that constitute what anthropologists call foodways. Household members spatially organize behavior along social relationships, reflecting different communities of practice. In this way, responses to changing social scenarios, adaptation to resource availability, and manipulation of daily practices happen at the hearth, a microscale of practice less visible to Spanish colonial administration. In the intimate setting of the household, people had some measure of refuge from the initiatives imposed upon them by colonial administrators, powerful neighbors, or other circumstances. Examining the material expression of food production, preparation, distribution, consumption, and disposal, using two aspects of the food system (Gumerman 1997), fauna and ceramics, permits an archaeological exploration of social relations. It is possible to specifically investigate Casitas's community foodways by examining the faunal and ceramic assemblages from three disposal loci, each of which represents the aggregates of various households across the site (see fig. 5).

The idea that foodways create and are created by different groups of people, with varying material outcomes, parallels the notion that landscape creates and is created by different communities. The relationship between the two scales links the situational nature of identity on interpersonal levels to the larger scale of community. A person can be simultaneously *india, hispana,* and *riteña* and express certain elements, combinations, or versions thereof depending on the kind of interaction she is having in a particular context. Such is the case, too, of community expressions of relationship to colonial ideals for *la gente de razón.* These depend upon their success as a social performance, considering the experience and context of the people traveling through and living in relation to the community. In this way, homescape is both a producer and a product of social forces that can be approached via a practice theory approach to the material record. In dialogue, they create a narrative that nuances existing stories about communities in ways only the material record can do.

In the main quadrangle, or *plazuela* at Casitas, three disposal loci (A, B, and C) represent distinct modes of deposition and are interpreted as the adobe melt-sealed aggregate of different households at the site. The spatial and material differentiations of these disposal loci are important analytical frameworks for investigating the nature of foodways as they occurred at hearthscape levels of organization. Household practices in selecting and using ceramic and faunal materials are interpreted within and between each locus. Similarities and differences among the loci suggest differential access to and use of those materials, as they reflect relationships built and maintained within the community as well as communities outside Casitas.

Because hearthscape practices relate the day-to-day practices of making and consuming meals as well as the far less frequent practices of selecting, acquiring, and making pottery, and choosing portions of meat and other products from animal carcasses, there are multiple temporal scales addressed by analysis of these activities. The different disposal loci represent not only daily behaviors associated with communities but more private practices of cuisine. They also represent larger connections to wider communities that may have been part of a network of economic and kin relationships, tying Casitas to the wider frontier at longer time scales. Although a family might have sat down to a dinner of *posole*, eaten from individual flange plate bowls with pieces of tortillas resting on the enlarged rim, they may have at other times been engaged in creating foods and associated paraphernalia for use during participation at a seasonal Pueblo dance. Evidence for both activities would make its way into the disposal locus of the one household, so only analysis of the separate stages of production, consumption, and discard of both ceramic and faunal lines of evidence—something akin to the *chaîne opératoire* approach of investigating the sequence of operations for making stone tools—can tease apart the different layers of hearthscape behavior as they are reflected by scalar choices. Analysis of attributes within and between the material categories of ceramics, fauna, and homescape allows comparisons to be made at different temporal and spatial contexts.

Using both the homescape and hearthscape scales of analysis, and putting them in dialogue with each other, is also an attempt to evaluate and complicate long-standing interpretive dichotomies regarding indigenous versus Spanish colonial practices. Chapter 3 addresses the tactical and engineering homescape of the Rito Colorado valley. Chapters 4 and 5 consider foodways at Casitas via the hearthscape, particularly by examining the ceramic tools and faunal ingredients. The core of this work is in its exploration of how the material practices of dynamic, situational forms of identity may be illuminated by study of the static material and documentary record.

# 3 /   Homescape

The weapon shone dull black and lethal as I looked down at it in my hand. I raised my head just enough to peer beneath the brim of my hat, squinting in the bright light to take in the scope of all that was downrange. The position we occupied commanded a field of fire that encompassed every possible route of advance up the small slope. From his crouch next to me, my comrade spoke in low tones, "Man, it's like Tora Bora up here." Our conversation was about a place deeply entangled in the tensions of illicit commerce, memories of sometimes desperate fighting, and the frustrations of faraway administrators sending troops chasing what seemed like ghosts through mazelike mountain passes, just as the enemy hit another village in the other direction. He uncurled and focused on the distance. Watching him, I registered how his time in dangerous borderlands had changed how he moved. Out of necessity, he had rarely been in uniform during his service there, and his loose clothing flowed over his easy steps as he bounded up the broken hillside. Other muscle memories were there too, darker lessons taken home. Instinctively, he moved from cover to concealment and back to cover, never stopping out in the open and eyes up, ever scanning. Back at the house, I could sense him checking corners down every hallway and at every door, a measured hesitation. At ease now, he crouched back down in the shade of a low earthen wall. He picked up something to inspect it and started to say something. Expectantly, I put the projectile point we had found back down on the ground and made a mental note to include it in the site maps later. But really, it was hopeless, overwhelming. I could never incorporate all that was being communicated here.

Shared with me years ago on our walk together, I glimpsed not only this veteran's memories of war but also his connections to his ancestral land by tradition, family lore, regional trauma, heritage, and pride. Stories of the community who made home here among new friends and foes flowed from both past and present, perspectives gathered from oral history, legal disputes, family, and personal narratives about homescape. Four centuries distant yet as dangerous as the mountains of contemporary Afghanistan, the New Mexican frontier this little arrowhead hinted at was as frightening and complex as it was beautiful in our minds' eyes.

## Landscape and Identity

The everyday practices of identity on the 18th-century frontier of New Mexico were at play in all of the places, in and around the Rito Colorado community location, where people lived out the majority of their lives. Homescape is where coordinated labor, rituals, and warfare took place. Such efforts would have left different combinations of evidence on the landscape, in which household-level divergences in ancestry, wealth, habits, etc. would be subsumed both in daily behaviors and in the outcomes of coordinated community action. The homescape is not merely a different spatial scale of analysis; it also encompasses intertwined temporal and social scales.

Inhabiting a land grant community in colonial northern New Mexico came with many attached legal arrangements and social strings that would have long-lasting repercussions (Clark 2005). Notions about the social position of land grantees and expectations for them to fulfill their strategic duties went hand in hand. Genízaros' demonstrations of loyalty to the Spanish colonial society that adopted them from captivity, over and above self-preservation, were implicit in their defense of the frontier. But the Casitas community may or may not have aligned with the top-down colonial identity classifications devised by Spanish officials. When colonial frontier settlers acted within their daily life, the fluidity of a given situation dictated the means and methods by which any given aspect of identity would manifest in the material record. Maintenance of the categories by which the colonial administration pigeonholed people on the frontier required ascribing specific behavior to each *casta* designation. The scale at which these practices were created and at which they constrained further action created different contexts of preservation in the archaeological record. While some activities could be more privately enacted within systemic household foodway contexts (the hearthscape), some scales of behavior must have made it harder to project or conceal practices that may have been differentially received as appropriate or transgressive by invigilating administrators. Building and maintaining architecture and features on the homescape undoubtedly made manipulation of elements through varying choices a more challenging scale of practice.

A distant administration promulgated a discrete set of rules by which settlers were to establish and maintain a new settlement if they were to retain title to a land grant (Nuttall 1921). In the context of lower *casta* people obtaining land grants from the administration, these rules were particularly important to follow, at least in ways that addressed some minimum requirements. A landscape scale of social identity performance likely served as an overt declaration of subscription to colonial practice. But perhaps not always. By combining archaeological and geographic information system (GIS) analyses of homescape creation and maintenance, I explore how the material vestiges of community practices expressed hidden dimensions of multiculturalism in the most public of scales. At a landscape scale, this approach tracks the ways in which people's lived experiences accorded or were in tension with their ascribed social identities on this frontier. This scale of analysis specifically seeks to investigate the strategies employed by frontier settlers to meet the doctrine of settlement in situations that challenged the social, economic, and military practicality of such requirements. I particularly address two dimensions of the homescape engaged with, built, and maintained by the colonial settlers of the Rito Colorado valley: the tactical homescape and the engineered homescape. Casitas is central to both analyses, but study of each employs different methodologies to explore dimensions of behavior suited to specific research questions. Also central to the study of the Casitas homescape is this question: What strategies were employed by frontier settlers to meet the colonial doctrine of settlement in situations that challenged the practicality of such requirements?

For the tactical homescape, my spatial analysis considers the parameters for maintaining a defensive posture on the front lines of a long-lived and episodically intense conflict. In this context, many military decisions and compromises could be systematized in the layout of the settlement with respect to tactical-range decision-making time frames. While the colonial administration had a set of strategic goals for placing communities as buffers on the frontier, the settlements themselves had to deal with surviving the actual tactical engagements. This includes not only monitoring of raiding conduits into and out of the Rito Colorado valley but also maintaining a clear view of what is happening in nearby fields and orchards to command a clear field of fire for ranged weapons like firearms and bows.

I evaluate the record of tactical behavior that created and was created by homescape in the Rito Colorado valley against four historically linked actions: (1) fortifying locations that allow for limited siege protection; (2) creating and maintaining routes of trade and raiding; (3) managing viewsheds of valley routes and agricultural areas; and (4) maintaining agriculture close to fortified defense, allowing subsistence during periods of intensified conflict. How these practices fit or circumvented administrative prescriptions for land grant status is related not only to Spanish notions of military dominance but also to precolonial kin networks among northern settlements.

For the engineered homescape, my spatial analyses consider the parameters for maintaining sustainably integrated agricultural systems in a local environment that afforded only marginal returns. Although pastoral and forestry practices are also engineered systems that alter the homescape, I prominently feature *acequia*-based colonial irrigation systems in my approach. Settlers at Casitas began their occupation in the Rito Colorado valley under the threat of military forces pushing from outside the frontier, and at the same time, internal administrative, economic, and social forces pressed the settlers into buffer locations. Colonial pressures and opportunities included stringent standards for the establishment of new, agriculturally productive land grant communities and regulations for the occupation and maintenance of grant titles.

If homescape practices are representative of a community that overtly subscribed to one identity or another, then a pattern of tactical and engineered homescape aspects should be observable that closely mirrors one of them. Such adherence to the set of colonial and precontact institutions that were in operation in other places and times in New Mexico would be distinct indeed, which is why they were chosen. Unlike the hearthscape scale of analysis featured in the following chapters, the homescape aspects of behavior studied in the landscape of the Rito Colorado valley do not allow for as fine-grained an investigation. A creolized pattern of tactical and engineered homescape-scale practices, if evaluated at this scale alone, may not be discerned differently than landscape creation and management patterns of a community that is manipulating identity performances. This is a result of the much longer (and larger) temporal scale of actions that affected the homescape, wherein irrigation structuring and settlement layout happen perhaps once during the term of occupation.

Creation, re-creation, and management of the engineered systems at Casitas certainly did not occur in a conceptual vacuum, nor on a blank landscape, free from anthropogenic features. A hypothesis that recognizes that separate technological traditions could have variably played out in one place can consider that the late-colonial-era ruins at Casitas were established in an actively indigenous landscape. Approaching these landscape-scale practices as a syncretic amalgam of behaviors can show how the irrigation ideology upon which homescape behavior was organized was created and re-created by people who implemented not only colonial ideas of agriculture but an intimate knowledge of indigenous techniques. Such knowledge must have included understandings of the movement and cycles of occupation that characterized Tewa use, abandonment, and reuse of sites in the Rio Arriba (Lightfoot 1993a; Anschuetz 2001; Rodriguez 2002). With a homescape analysis, I try to explore how the settlement sequence of the Rito Colorado valley, considered with respect to tactical positioning and agricultural potential, might suggest that the site of LA 306 (Sapawe Pueblo, introduced in chapter 1) was still "in play" for some cross-section of people who frequented the valley, if not within the ranks of the settlers themselves. An analysis of the engineered agricultural homescape may reveal to what extent indigenous motivations played out in the Rito Colorado valley.

## Maps and Mappings

I derived the majority of data sets used to construct the geographic information system (GIS) for this project by using modern instrumentation and methods, collated in digital data sets, and integrating them in their multiple formats to qualitatively and quantitatively compare and analyze elements of the Casitas homescape. Digitization of features from field data and aerial interpretation constitute important vector data sets for the project GIS. Features from 21st-century aerial and satellite photos, 20th-century United States Geological Survey (USGS) topographic maps, and 19th-century Government Land Office (GLO) maps—including water-related features, roads, and boundaries of site roomblocks and plazas—were displayed at small scales in order to closely follow their geographic representations.

Digitizing involves creating feature classes (a shapefile that can be edited) within a geodatabase (a data structure that can store all types of vector files) and then creating the desired vector in the GIS with a drawing tool. Hydrological features (*acequias*, Rito Colorado River, tributaries, and springs) digitized from the USGS topo maps and ground-truthed by handheld Global Positioning System (GPS) and Geodetic Total Station (GTS) surveys provided a representation of where modern *acequias* (irrigation ditches) are located. GLO maps, orthorectified to match existing maps and known landscape features, were similarly used to track and digitize *acequias* to compare what hydrological features were recognized by 19th-century surveyors and modern archaeologists. Like the USGS surveyors, these cartographers made some distinction between *acequias* and ditches, as opposed to intermittent streams and tributaries. It is interesting to note the change in perceived function in the intervening century or so between the creation of these maps, as will be discussed later in this chapter.

I digitized homescape features such as roads from GLO maps, USGS topos, and aerial photos to track where historic routes of access in and out of the valley developed and changed. Similarly, agricultural field locations from the GLO maps and other archaeological studies of field systems (Boyer 2002), including field-mapped GPS points, were digitized to incorporate some aspects of historic fields such as location and slope angles. I digitized modern El Rito and Sapawe from aerial photo interpretation because their structural features are easily visible, whereas for Casitas and other archaeological sites, I used the GTS maps as a primary data set. Boundaries digitized around the plazas and/or central roomblocks of Casitas, El Rito, and Sapawe were drawn in discrete sets of points, rather than lines or polygons, for the sake of viewshed calculation. After comparing these disparate map elements to each other, as discrete data layers in the same data frame, I superimposed and orthorectified these vectors on the aerial photos of the area to determine, via aerial photo interpretation, if there were any *acequias* or other features missed by the USGS and GLO that were visible on the aerial photos and/or matched up with the GPS or GTS points generated from ground-truthing and field survey. Although these maps are not nearly as accurate as modern USGS topos, they provide a unique opportunity to examine a representation of the landscape in a time period much closer to that considered in this project. Certain features, such as irrigation works contemporaneous with the GLO surveys, had eroded into a state identified as arroyos or intermittent streams by the time USGS topographic maps were created 100 years after the occupation of Casitas. One example of this palimpsest process will be more closely reviewed later in this chapter.

GLO maps were created in the 1860s by U.S. government employees walking ground transects and measuring distances via survey chains.

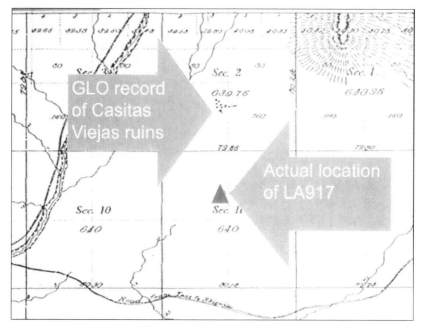

FIGURE 8. 1860 U.S. Government Land Office (GLO) map of Casitas showing location of ruins on wrong side of chain transect.

Where features on the map cross mapping transects, I have observed a fair level of accuracy; these features were encountered and recorded in consistent intervals from known locations. Features that do not intersect these transect lines have to be scrutinized to a much greater degree, with increasing error from transect lines, because these were based on survey crew estimations of distance and bearing relative to the surveyor's current transect line. For example, the cartographic symbol and label for "ruins" representing Casitas were placed on the wrong side of a transect line (fig. 8).

Casitas is in fact located exactly the same distance opposite of the transect line where the GLO cartographers placed it on their map. This may have happened through a common transcription error of writing "north" instead of "south" in the surveyors' note (Bob Lawrence 2003, pers. comm.), but it is hard not to notice the placement of the ruins at the southeastern boundary point of what was the Juan Jose Lobato land grant. This is now the Carson National Forest, so the mapped location of Casitas would have centuries of ramifications for how many hundreds of acres would be effectively placed within new jurisdictions in later transitions to American authority (Church 2001; Church 2002), and what has been described as the land grabs of powerful cabals of speculators in Santa Fe (Ebright 1994). The national and legal processes embedded in mappings of the Casitas homescape ultimately made those representations powerful mediators for descendant communities. But for those who inhabited the little fortified plaza, barely registered in an iteration of Bernardo Miera y Pacheco's 1760 map of the north, such cartographies were not nearly as powerful as the lived experiences of those inhabiting and traveling through it.

Historic documents from New Mexico are rife with anecdotes regarding the crippling state of constant warfare between the colonists and nomadic Indian groups. Cycles of raiding and counterraiding led to countless enumerations of death and abduction among the frontier villages (Rael-Gàlvez 2002). As the number of incidents abated into the 19th century, the dispersed way of living increased, eventually leading to the establishment of the modern plaza of El Rito (Parish records, Church of San Juan Nepomuceno). The majority of testimonies from El Rito descendant community members concerning Casitas and El Rito highlight that there were fewer families living in Casitas than El Rito and that Casitas was eventually abandoned completely in the mid-19th century. Oral history narratives of its abandonment are accompanied by varying reasons for why and how it occurred. This testimony includes that of Dorothy Parker, a resident of El Rito (Speth 1963). Mrs. Parker's perspective was that environmental conditions worsened over time with less and less snow falling each year until there was not enough water to survive, forcing the settlers to relocate the main village center to El Rito (Speth 1963:12).

If the northern half of the Rito Colorado valley, in which the plaza and field systems of both precontact Sapawe Pueblo and modern El Rito are located, had increased agricultural potential over the site of Casitas, as they do today, why was this not the primary factor in those locations becoming the dominant village plaza of the valley? One explanation may be that the establishment of Casitas farther down the valley represents a decision by the settlers to forego optimal agricultural land based on the historical circumstances of maintaining occupancy in a land characterized by raids from outside nomadic groups. The cornerstone of this hypothesis assumes Casitas was in a better tactical position to maintain this occupancy. As raiding activity declined in the late 18th century and eventually stopped in the mid-19th century, it may have become viable for the settlers to move their village center farther up the valley to where better agricultural land and irrigation resources were located. With this approach, historical circumstance and human agency are considered the dominant factors responsible for how people occupied the landscape. Earlier, settlers would have been caught between requirements of colonial government strategies and raiding nomadic groups to settle in particular locations, but when these constraints lessened they pursued options to seek out the best agricultural land. This hypothesis assumes some measure of tactical superiority to the position of Casitas, such as viewshed of raiding approaches to the valley, would decrease with settlement movement up valley. This must be tempered with some inverse correlation of agricultural potential for these sites to explain tactical choice as a primary motivation.

If the shift in settlement was linked to a decrease in precipitation, this should leave a different signature of spatial relationships as the settlement moved up valley. Some have speculated that the Rito Colorado River could have changed course and washed out floodplain agricultural fields of Casitas, causing the settlers to move north up the valley (Bob Lawrence 2005, pers. comm.). Such a scenario supposes that settlers did not have the foresight to see that Casitas was in a poor agricultural position for the long run and that farther north in the valley, agriculture would have been better. A corollary of this hypothesis posits that the settlers pushed north when the environmental conditions required relocation. In such a scenario, agricultural strategies and style of settlement would be expected to be the same between the two sites because environmental change would have been the only demonstrable thing to have changed. The consistency of *acequia* (irrigation ditch) placement and the degree of plaza fortification can be evaluated to determine whether a significant change between the two sites could attest to other factors besides environmental change. The creation and use of *acequias* is more fully examined later in this chapter. These two hypotheses are evaluated against the observable patterns of homescape behavior below.

## The Tactical Homescape

A tactical homescape is an amalgam of features based upon a larger collection of physical spaces that play stage to armed conflict. For the purposes of this study, the tactical homescape of the Rito Colorado valley includes features used as strongholds (e.g., Casitas), observation points, defensible areas, and lines of advance and retreat. The material

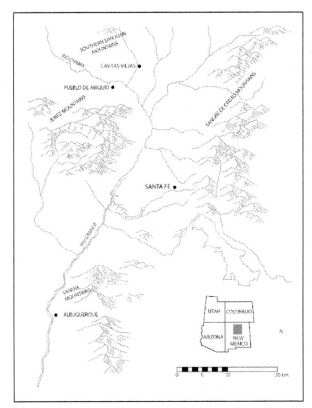

FIGURE 9. Map showing location of Casitas with
respect to major drainages, nearest large settlements
and the capital at Santa Fe (after Habicht-Mauche 1993).

record of tactical behavior is understood by investigating patterns: (1)
locations of fortified defense; (2) historic routes of trade and raiding; (3)
areas within a viewshed of fortified defense that allow observation of
routes of trade and raiding; and (4) areas of agricultural potential within
close proximity to fortified defense, allowing maintenance of subsistence
economy during periods of intensified conflict.

By design, frontier land grants were strategically located as buffers
between the centers of colonial administration and raiding bands of
nomadic peoples not always allied with the colony. The Rito Colorado
valley settlement was a day's travel from the closest administrative settlement of Santa Cruz de la Canada. Santa Cruz was just south of the confluence of the Rio Grande and the Rio Chama (fig. 9). Failing a clear route

via the southwest to Abiquiú, heading southeast to San Juan Pueblo or Santa Cruz was a logical retreat. Settlers had relatives and other connections there (Poling-Kempes 1997).

Land grantees had to be self-sufficient in growing all their own crops and making their own clothes and household goods, as travel down valley to other settlements for such necessities was hazardous. A dispersed community having a fortified plaza nearby, such as the one at Casitas, would have been afforded a temporary fallback position without a full retreat to Abiquiú or Santa Cruz. Additionally, this would have ameliorated the subsequent complications of colonial authorities alleging that the land grants had been vacated. For *ranchos* in close proximity to the fortified plaza, localized agricultural maintenance could still have been possible during some periods of prolonged raiding potential. The presence of fortified *plazuelas* in village centers would not only have helped settlers in the basic survival of a raid but also as a means of preventing the colonial administration from redistributing property to other groups.

How might have the families living at Casitas seen aspects of their tactical homescape, literally scanning the horizon from the tops of the fortified little *plazuela*? I use viewshed analysis to make tactical considerations of the Rito Colorado valley sites, evaluating the potential of site locations to spot an incoming raid along routes of valley entrance (although understanding that raiding groups could have deviated from these routes or come by the cover of darkness). The use of viewshed serves only as a rough guide to the potential that different site locations would have had in spotting a raid. One particularly apt example exposes how settlers at Casitas would have had visibility of the northeastern route of entrance (fig. 10), which is the route that passes into the site of LA 70668.

Local ethnohistory identifies the site of LA 70668 as a camp used by Comanches and other nomadic communities on the banks opposite El Rito, placing the river between them. It was also considered to have been the main route of entrance into the valley (NMCRIS, Vigil family map; Bob Lawrence 2005, pers. comm. 2005). This route goes through the mountains toward Ojo Caliente with a minimal amount of elevation fluctuation (total gain of 387 feet). The other two northern routes into the valley climb farther into the mountains, toward Vallecitos and Canjilon, with much more elevation difference (1,550 and 1,206 feet respectively) (figs. 11–13). This suggests that the northeastern route would have been more accessible and easier to travel because of its connection to the Rio Grande Valley and its elevation consistency, but not necessarily any more desirable as a raiding route than the others.

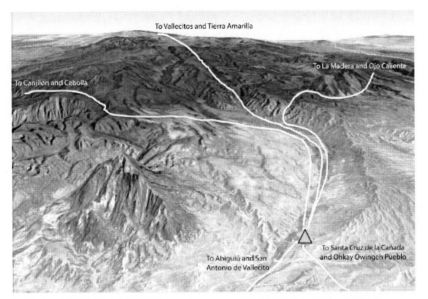

FIGURE 10. Principal raiding and trading routes into the Rito Colorado valley.

I generated viewshed maps of three sites (Casitas, Sapawe, and modern El Rito) from a mosaic of digital elevation models (DEMs) to investigate the potentials of visibility for defense. Testing various sightlines from specific sites allows for quantitative means of exploring which locations had better means of spotting a raid, especially in regard to the known routes of entrance into the valley. Viewsheds can be generated from the GIS via a function that calculates a 360-degree perspective of what can be seen from a given point based on surrounding elevation data from a DEM. I used multiple-point vectors for this because it allowed me to add together viewshed calculations for each point specified. In other words, I tried to calculate through GIS a model of what people in the past might have been able to see by cumulatively adding viewsheds from multiple points along the perimeter of exterior walls of each site. I also adjusted the height of observation, so as to adjust for a sentry at the top of a *torreón* (defensive tower integrated into a defensive wall). The resulting composites simulate what eagle-eyed sentries could have seen from the roof of the outer edge of the roomblocks enclosing the *plazuela* at Casitas (fig. 14). I then overlaid vectors of possible routes of entrance that raiding groups could have taken into the valley with the viewsheds of the three

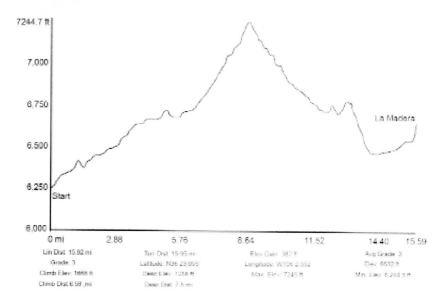

FIGURE 11. Elevation profile for La Madera–Ojo Caliente route.

sites. These routes were derived by digitization of trails from GLO maps and cross-referenced to curated community maps in which raids were sometimes listed by year and location.

I digitized these routes with end points inside the valley because at that point I assumed that a raiding group, no longer constrained by steeper valley walls, could easily travel in any direction across the valley. Along these digitized routes of entry to the valley, I added points at intercepts with the viewsheds. These represent the farthest extents of entrance routes that could have been observable from each of the sites. These points effectively represent when someone from each site location would have first been able to spot a raiding group (or, more likely the dust from their animals) coming into the valley.

From these points, I used a cost-distance calculation—an operation calculating a "Cost-Weighted" function to create a colored isopleth portraying increasing values from a point using distance and slope—to quantify the difficulty of traveling over terrain from each of these locations. Slope surfaces generated by this means are effectively isotropic cost surfaces. I could then visualize a proxy difficulty by this process, based upon the degree of slope angle for each cell around the location considered in 360 degrees of direction, with low values given to flat terrain and

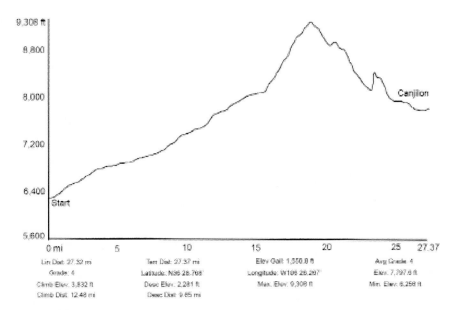

FIGURE 12. Elevation profile for Canjilon route.

high values given to steep terrain. A preponderance of flat terrain results in a portion of cost-distance isopleth represented with high values because there is more linear distance that can be traveled in a given time period than over steep terrain (fig. 15). In this way cost-distance gives a more accurate representation in gauging the relative effort of reaching various locations than would otherwise be apparent through just linear distance measurements.

A major drawback of this model is its lack of energetically realistic representation of effort. Values in the isopleths are unitless and do not reflect any caloric or time factor in and of themselves. This is a common error in using cost surfaces in contemporary landscape archaeology GIS analyses, though it has been pointed out for some time (Gaffney and Stančič 1991:50). A more meaningful model, especially for defining catchment areas within specified human travel time from a given site, must integrate highly developed energetics equations. I used an experimental approach, tracking strings of equid packers through the rugged backcountry trails of the Sierra Nevadas to demonstrate that historical archaeologists must consider horse travel as paramount for reconstructions of travel (J. Sunseri 2015). Work is now in progress to generate energetic equations relating mounted horse travel over composite surfaces

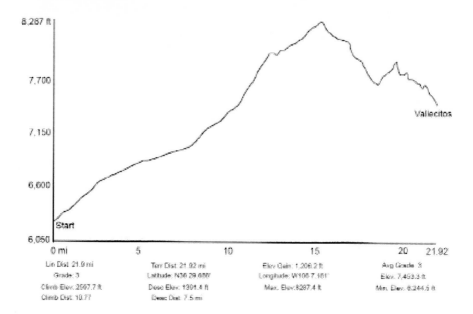

FIGURE 13. Elevation profile for Vallecitos route.

for GIS integration. But in this case, I use cost surface to visualize a proxy for time to engagement for people living at the various sites in the Rito Colorado valley and as a relative measure of their ability to respond.

Further work, using friction surfaces based on horse biomechanics, would result in a finer-grained analysis of this potential but would need to be refined for horseback scenarios (since most raids were by mounted attackers) and interpreted against those generated for foot travel (unmounted shepherds and field hands). In the future, the model could account for flow levels in the Rito Colorado to compare seasonal access to Casitas from upstream raiding parties, something brought to my attention in reference to the "Comanche camp" located on the bank opposite the modern plaza of El Rito. In addition to viewshed and cost-distance, which evaluates the proximity of the three main sites to the routes of entrance from the north, a consideration of proximity to routes of retreat to the south, for fallback to Chama sites, is critical to any analysis of the homescape from a tactical perspective. Although GIS is not needed to calculate these three things, it can provide the statistical means to compare between sites in a similar manner. For now, this limited use of cost surface was useful in projecting a relative comparison

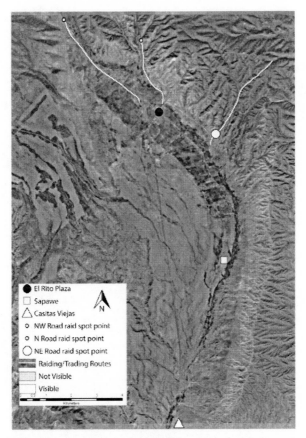

FIGURE 14. Viewshed from Casitas with first points of
visibility along northern raiding and trading routes.

of what sites were most likely farther out from harm's way once a raiding
group entered the valley from the north.

The apparent trend suggests that settlers at Casitas would have had
the advantage in being warned and prepared before a raiding group
travelling along the northeastern route reached the valley. Although El
Rito would have been able to spot a raiding group on the northern and
northwestern route before they reached the valley, this would not confer
a large advantage over the vantage point at Casitas because of its distance from valley entry by these two routes. Finally, it should be noted
that Sapawe's location in the valley conferred some tactical advantage
relative to the location of modern El Rito's plaza. But as it was located

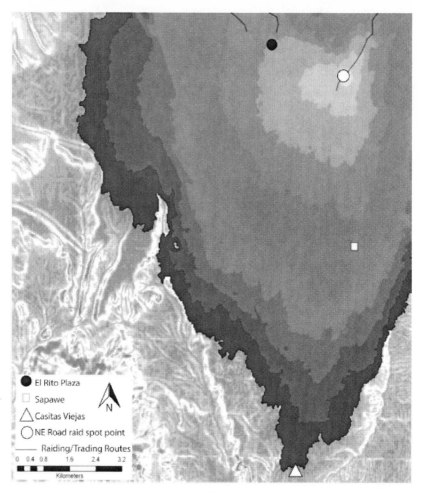

FIGURE 15. Cost-distance proxy raster for time from a viewshed/trail inter-cept to arrival at Casitas.

central to the valley, a large mounted raiding party would have been able to flank a retreat to the Chama valley sites at the natural topographical constriction that begins near Casitas. Precontact Pueblo people living at the zenith of Sapawe occupation were less likely to attempt such a retreat, but colonial settlers were not as numerous and armed in their fortified plazas.

Cost-distance isopleths generated strictly from topography further express the results of the linear distance measurements from the three sites to the locations where raiding groups could have been spotted. Roads should have a lower value (less cost) than other terrain features such as arroyos and the Rito Colorado main channel. Although this would better represent the effort required for the raiding group in traveling over the terrain, the visualization isopleths used here still show the general difficulty and effort required to reach each of the sites. For the plaza of post-19th-century to modern-day El Rito, the raiders at locations on the northeastern and northern routes could reach the plaza while accumulating the least cost-distance units. At least twice as many cost-distance units would be accumulated by using northwestern route. Raiders trying to reach Casitas and Sapawe from the valley raiding entrances within their viewshed could not reach either site within 12,000 cost-distance units. This suggests that it would have taken substantially more time or effort, when compared to the plaza of modern El Rito, for a raiding group to have reached either Casitas or Sapawe from the locations of initial observation by defenders. I calculated another cost-distance analysis from the location that an observer in the El Rito plaza would have first been able to spot a raid on the northeastern route (almost in the valley) for Sapawe and Casitas. The results of this calculation show that Sapawe could be reached in 12,000 cost-distance units and Casitas could be reached in 18,000. Again, this suggests that observers in the modern plaza location of El Rito could spot a raid from the northeastern route and that it would have taken more time or effort to reach Sapawe and another order of magnitude more time or effort to reach the settlers at Casitas. In more highly resolved comparisons than linear measurements alone, this exploratory spatial analysis suggests that the community at Casitas had a tactical advantage in regard to the level of preparedness it would have had for raids originating from the northern entrances to the valley.

When this tactical hypothesis is evaluated in tandem with environmentally based hypotheses for settlement migration in the Rito Colorado valley, the support for the latter set of motivations seems weaker. Based on limited oral tradition, these hypotheses posit that a decrease in precipitation levels or a change in the Rito Colorado River course caused people to move from Casitas to the modern location of El Rito. The agricultural strategies and style of fortification were not consistent between the two sites, which does not support precipitation or river-change scenarios as a sole motivation for the move. For example, the El Rito plaza is much more open and contains three entrances, whereas the much smaller plaza at Casitas is built closer together with only one entrance, implying that defense was probably a greater factor in the earlier construction at Casitas. Also, *acequias* and associated field systems are more numerous and centralized in the vicinity of El Rito than anywhere else. This aspect of agricultural potential is considered in much more depth in the next section of this chapter. Thus, if a change in the environment is posited as the driving force for the movement of people from Casitas to El Rito, it does not explain why people would also change the way they built their plazas or why they only used elaborated *acequia* technology in the northern sections of the valley. Given the spatial relationship of these sites to arable land, irrigation potential, and defensible position, this seems an untenable hypothesis. Tactical issues seem be more the driver of change than environmental issues. A visitor to the modern plaza of El Rito can see that the enclosure was never truly sealed as at Casitas because once defense was reduced in priority, the community could move to the location where agriculture was easier and more productive.

One other, intersecting line of evidence speaks to the large role raiding and trading routes played in shaping lifeways in the Rito Colorado homescape and how different scales of archaeological evidence might be put in dialogue when studying the lives of families at Casitas. The archaeofaunal caprine assemblage from Casitas (further addressed in chapter 5) consistently exhibits morphological elaborations suggesting increased musculature. This intimates that these northern routes were likely traversed frequently by some of the goat and sheep herds (Bower 2006). The deep ponderosa pine forest contexts for these passes suggest drive herding rather than pasturage for these animals. If animals were raided or traded over these higher passes with any frequency, they must have been cardiovascularly and musculoskeletally fit indeed.

Although the viewshed and cost-distance calculations demonstrate that the community at Casitas had a defensive advantage in regard to the northeastern route, its fortified plaza and closer proximity to zones of safety farther south further lend support to the hypothesis that the settlers who first inhabited the Rito Colorado valley chose to forego agriculturally optimal land in favor of a location that was easier to defend against raiding nomadic groups, until such raids began to decline in the 19th century. As compared to the plaza later established at El Rito, which has much flatter terrain for large-scale agriculture, Casitas is much farther from the routes of entrance that raiding groups would have taken into the valley. Modern El Rito's agricultural prominence is also attested to by the many *acequias* that have been built in this section of the valley. Explored more below, Sapawe has slightly less land optimal for Spanish colonial agriculture in its vicinity than El Rito and more so than Casitas, not a significantly different viewshed than either of the two sites, a worse cost-distance than Casitas, and farther from Chama valley sites. This places Sapawe as a prime location for colonial communities to have settled. Their apparent decision not to use this site, unlike the common practice in New Mexico colonial settlements, may have been motivated by more nuanced understandings of tactical and engineered homescapes in the valley. Such motivation is more strongly suggested when the later establishment of El Rito, well upstream from the Sapawe agricultural area, is considered.

## The Engineered Homescape

Holding a frontier has little meaning for a community that cannot feed itself. Time and again, northern villages have proved that hard work and attention to detail can turn hardscrabble pinyon and juniper scrubland into verdant oases of food. Their incredible productivity no doubt was a draw for raiding parties and trading partners. As the heart has its major arteries, *acequia* irrigation systems are conduits of life for these agricultural systems. *Acequia* irrigation, as practiced in New Mexico, was a suite of practices that not only included Roman engineering principles long practiced on the Iberian peninsula (Simmons 2001:125) but was also supplemented significantly by Arabic hydraulic engineering and land-use traditions brought to Spain via the Moorish occupation before the Spanish were able to retake their homeland from the occupiers (Beekman et al. 1999).

The word *acequia* itself is Arabic and along with other words (such as *qanat*) reflects the degree to which engineers and planners had integrated once quite disparate communities of the Iberian Peninsula into more organized North African–style agrarian labor and land management systems. Such community-based practices and ways of cooperating translated well into the New Mexican colonial situation. These practices were institutionalized in the royal *ordenanzas* by which colonial administrators could define prerequisites for land grant occupation. Among the most important were ordinances 35 and 39, requirements that new settlements should be located in areas with "good and plentiful water supply for drinking and irrigation" (Nuttall 1921). These general principles for developing and regulating irrigation were based upon traditional legal codes and practices in Spain (Simmons 2001:130). The very nature of space, ownership, and identity was legislated around the *acequia* system by processes of initial parceling of land into *suertes*, individual sections of land that required layouts conducive to irrigation waterworks (Rivera 1998:6). How subsequent divisions of land were made among family members are overlain on these initial plots and over generations have led to the quilt pattern evident in most arable valleys in northern New Mexico.

As discussed in chapter 2, core frontier communities, such as nearby Abiquiú, often had outlier settlements staffed by extended family and other household members. Casitas was likely established in this same manner, and the surrounding homescape, and the irrigation ideology upon which it was organized, was created and re-created by people who brought not only Spanish ideas of agriculture but also an intimate knowledge of indigenous agricultural histories and practices.

Indigenous knowledge systems, enacted materially upon landscapes of the Greater Tewa basin along the northern Rio Grande, had legal protection in colonial New Mexico. The Leyes de las Indies stipulated that colonists were not to encroach upon Indian lands under cultivation. This was especially true for areas "in which (Indians) have made ditches for irrigation or any other benefit, with which by their personal industry they have fertilized" (Rivera 1998:3). Sapawe's peak occupation had occurred hundreds of years before the settlement at Casitas, and nearby Spanish colonial towns, such as Santa Cruz and Abiquiú, were established on top of or in close proximity to such ruins. The tactical positioning of Casitas was more optimal for observation of raiding routes and escaping to allies than for maximizing agricultural potential. Yet, a different balance might have been struck by locating the fledgling outpost on top of the ruins of Sapawe. Why did this not happen in the Rito Colorado as it had elsewhere in the colony? Historians generally agree that self-sufficiency was a hallmark of colonial communities of this era, especially concerning food production (Simmons 1969; Swadesh 1974; Brooks 2002a). If the settlers of Casitas did not build upon the ruins of Sapawe and did not take advantage of the arable lands in its vicinity, then there must have been a mode of hydrological engineering nearer to the *plazuela* that allowed them to maintain an agricultural base. The style, technology, and execution of this engineered homescape appear to be more complex than a cursory examination of a colonial settlement might suggest. Creation, re-creation, and management of the engineered system certainly did not occur in a conceptual vacuum, or on a blank landscape, free from anthropogenic features.

Historians have documented that at Casitas's mother community of Abiquiú, people of Hopi and Tewa cultural extractions lived with and merged with the Genízaros (Horvath 1977; Poling-Kempes 1997; Ebright and Hendricks 2006). To this day, a delegation regularly makes a journey from the Hopi reservation in Arizona to visit their Tewa roots at the Plaza de Moqui in Abiquiú. If a contingent of this community was tasked with establishing and maintaining a presence at the fortified plaza at Casitas by land grantees connected to that community, then people with Tewa heritage and/or worldviews may have had considerable stake in deciding the location and layout of the site.

Movement and cycles of occupation characterize the Tewa use, abandonment, and reuse of sites in New Mexico (Lightfoot and Eddy 1995; Anschuetz 2001; Rodriguez 2002). The text below explores how the settlement sequence of the Rito Colorado valley, considered with respect to tactical positioning and agricultural potential, might suggest that the ruins of Sapawe were still ideologically "in play" for some cross-section of people still frequenting the valley, if not within the ranks of the settlers themselves. An analysis of the engineered agricultural homescape may clarify to what extent such motivations played out in the Rito Colorado valley.

## Evaluating Topographic Space for Potential as Agricultural Place

To develop some measure of agricultural potential in the valley, I generated slope maps based upon a suite of characteristics of known arable land assumed well-suited for agriculture using Spanish colonial imported technologies of irrigation and crop species. These data sets integrated slopes that surrounded the sites and were of angle ranges similar to known agricultural locations (i.e., low slope angle seemed to be preferred for Spanish colonial agriculture). I generated aspect maps to see what direction the slopes faced for better sunlight reception. The aspect maps proved ultimately less useful because the direction of slope is far less relevant in low slope terrain during the summer months of direct overhead sunlight. In many cases, farmers would likely pay more attention to aspect in terms of drainage directions.

The purpose of this visualization is to clarify areas of low slope angle that would have been best suited for agriculture using Spanish colonial imported technologies of *acequia* irrigation and crop species. I overlaid digitized polygons of historic fields and the data points from Archaeological Records Management System, of the New Mexico Cultural Resource

Inventory System (ARMS) about agricultural features related to Sapawe on the slope map to see what average slope angles they were positioned in, calculated through a zonal statistics function. This was in order to get a sense for what kinds of slope angles were situated on which known historic fields. This helped to determine the potential for similar kinds of agriculture in the rest of the landscape. The average slope angle of the historic field systems was 2.7 degrees and 5.4 degrees for the prehistoric agricultural features related to Sapawe. I characterized the first division of slope to between 0 and 3 degrees, representing the most viable land, and the next category was between 3 and 6 degrees, representing land that had agriculture potential (as demonstrated by Sapawe's agriculture features) but was less able to be as densely planted as the first designation. The main purpose of these categories is to visually represent what areas had much larger areas of low slope terrain. Characterization of the hydrological features associated with Sapawe on higher-sloped terrain is covered more extensively in the next section of this chapter.

These visualizations (fig. 16) exhibit a much larger area around El Rito of low slope angle terrain than at Sapawe or Casitas. The average slope angle within 1,000 meters of proximity around each site was calculated as 2.9 degrees for modern El Rito, 3.5 degrees for Sapawe, and 4.3 degrees for Casitas. Digitized modern *acequias* are also centralized around modern El Rito—and to a lesser extent Sapawe—in the large area that is of low slope angle terrain. Their presence demonstrates the potential of this region of the valley for productive agriculture using colonial methods and species. I interpreted the only linear features near Casitas from aerial photos and ground-truthed them with handheld GPS units. In the future, these may require test excavation to establish duration of use as *acequias* or other hydraulic features. From measurable slope angles and *acequia* placements the data strongly suggest that modern El Rito has better agricultural potential than Casitas and has additional access to arable land in ways that more closely approximates floodplain farming locales in the proximity of Sapawe.

## Modeling Hydrodynamics of *Acequia* Irrigation

*Acequia* irrigation technology assumes a reliable surface water source to supply the system with enough head pressure to reach the farthest channels, or laterals along a serviced field border. To accomplish this without so much flow as to cut through the system banks, erode the channels themselves, or overflow other landscape features such as roads

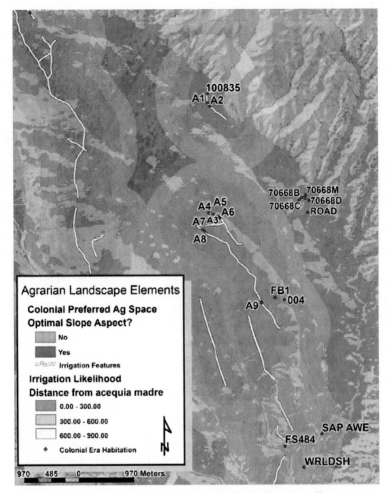

FIGURE 16. Agricultural potential in the Rito Colorado valley.

or plazas, careful design must allow for low-angle approach and departure angles for *acequia* ditch segments. Time and again, colonial communities throughout the New Mexican colony mastered this technique
and were able to engineer water delivery to extensive field systems in the
alluvial plain of river valleys.

Importantly, the style and extent of these hydrological systems were
not similar to the means by which Ancestral Pueblo people brought water
to their crops. In northern New Mexico, several precontact systems of

irrigation have been identified and studied (Lightfoot and Eddy 1995; Anschuetz 1998), most of which have been described by regional archaeologists under the misleading category of "dry farming" technologies. Rarely was flowing water in linear systems of any substantial length a feature of this technology, though some hypothesize that arroyos between terraces may have had some carrying capacity for water between levels of planted beds (Kurt Anschuetz 2003, pers. comm.).

Even a cursory examination of heritage ditch systems that have breached walls suggests that such use of arroyos could not have had any substantial carrying capacity or longevity in comparison to extensive *acequia* systems. The engineering parameters for successful implementation of such long irrigation systems remain quite tight for unlined ditches such as those seen all over northern New Mexico. Ultimately, to explore to what extent colonial irrigation practices were pursued by the community living at Casitas, some measure of hydrological characteristic for *acequias* had to be quantified in the GIS environment.

My first step in the analysis was to intersect the digitized *acequias* of the Rito Colorado valley with digital elevation models. This gives each point along the vector representing an *acequia* an elevation value that can be evaluated against the cells next to it for slope degree and aspect. I prioritized digitizing historic *acequias* of enough antiquity to have names (such as the Acequia Jaral or Acequia Medio) because they were more likely representative of *acequia* creation and management techniques of early settlement. I digitized mid-19th-century maps, orthorectified them, and then overlaid them with mid-20th-century maps, aerial photos, and archaeological site maps to crosscheck for correlates. I made several observations at this stage, including noticing that what had been recorded by mid-19th-century surveyors as "ditches" were later interpreted and drawn as intermittent tributaries to the Rito Colorado by cartographers 100 years later. Aerial photo interpretation in these crucial overlaps show that some surveyors may have inadvertently put roads in contraposed orientation from their transect lines. Like the placement of *Casitas* ruins in the GLO map mentioned above (fig. 8), such a transcription error required only an entry of "west" when "east" is what was meant. Another factor in the series of deductions correlated with aerial interpretation of roads relates to how, in communities practicing *acequia* irrigation, paths often parallel the irrigation works for much of their lengths. In some cases this is for ease of maintenance and observation and, as will be discussed later, can also occur in ways that supplement ritual procession.

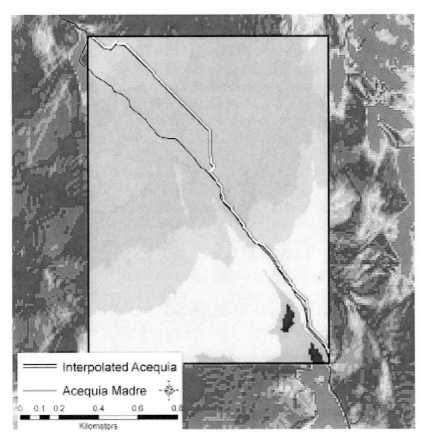

Interpolated Acequia

Acequia Madre

0    0.1   0.2        0.4          0.6          0.8
Kilometers

FIGURE 17. Evaluation of model against known *acequia* segment.

These strategies came together in the investigation of additional suspected irrigation systems surveyed near the site known as DS2, for "David Snow's Casitas 2" (Quintana and Snow 1980). Speth and Snow surveyed and tested this colonial site in the 1960s (David Snow 2004, pers. comm.). I combined examination of the GLO features, aerial interpretation of roads, USGS tributary features, and knowledge of common transcription errors to locate probable irrigation channels that could link to the *acequia* system observed, and then mapped these channels with a total station during intensive site survey (fig. 17). Before I could test these survey results, I needed to develop a working *acequia* hydrology model and evaluate that model against known historic *acequias*.

I sampled and averaged several *acequias* into a range of values that characterized slope per length via GIS modules used widely by ecologists and hydrologists. I chose this suite of computational methods specifically for "length weighted mean" functions. That way, I could make comparisons between potential irrigation features that allowed for characterization of *acequias* that were longer than others, or that had sections that traversed through more extreme changes in topography than the resolution of the digital elevation models they intersected. This characterization consisted of slope values for which water flowing over the preponderance of the channel would have crossed to generate enough pressure to keep moving, but not headcut through the unlined channels. I then reclassified the slope raster generated from the digital elevation model into groupings of cell value that matched the ranges of slope that different *acequias* exhibited. In this way, when modeling the slope characteristic of a known *acequia*, I could tailor the reclassified raster to match those values in adjacent terrain.

I intended the development of this technique for use in scenarios where a segment of *acequia* can be recorded (historically, archaeologically, or by aerial interpretation), but the next section is not visible and/or its path is unknown. Using software to evaluate the most likely, least-cost path of the *acequia* between two points on the landscape, I could further evaluate my projections by aerial interpretation, archaeological foot survey, or test excavation. I chose El Rito's Acequia Madre as the principal development comparative for the hydrological model after I evaluated most of the historic (named) *acequias*, because the Acequia Madre had the longest runs through the valley. As the "mother ditch," it has the longest-known tenure as part of an integrated irrigation system. When I applied the method outlined above to the Acequia Madre, the results were quite satisfactory and could be ground-truthed in all but the most specific of instances. Where the *acequia* has been recently rerouted into culverts under the modern road (the contemporary equivalent of a colonial *canoa*, discussed below), the model does not closely follow the actual observed *acequia* path (fig. 17). But the majority of the model does closely follow the Acequia Madre.

*Canoas* were hollowed-out logs or other planked flumes that could carry water across an arroyo or other depression, although they were most often used in response to extreme headcutting processes that would otherwise cause massive reroute of an *acequia* (fig. 18) . Therefore modeled *acequia* flow compares well to known *acequias* but cannot predict *canoas*. These wooden features were deployed only where

FIGURE 18. Example of *canoas* carrying *acequia* water across an arroyo.

absolutely necessary, as upkeep required significant time, materials, and effort including frequent replacement. It is a minor, though problematic, aspect of this model that it is as of yet unable to faithfully render the constrictions in natural topography with respect to the potential placements of the often-used colonial technology of *canoa* construction. Similarly, this model does not well evaluate locations where a shallow ridgeline or other small elevation change could be breached by deep trenching, to save extensive routing around the topographic feature. Although not very common, because such features would commonly silt up the fastest due to sheetwash or landslide, future models should be designed to predict these locations, hereafter what I will call "topographic risers," after the engineering concept of stress risers in an isotropic vector plane.

A more challenging set of parameters against which to evaluate this model involved applying it to an investigation of a short, unknown *acequia* segment between the "tributaries" of the 1950s USGS topo maps—also observed as "ditches" in the GLO maps of the mid-1800s—and the archaeologically observed *acequia* sections adjacent to site DS2. Again, I used hydrological characteristics of the known sections to develop

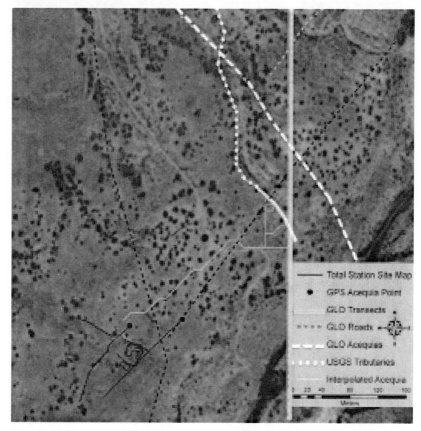

FIGURE 19. Composite map of glo features, usgs features, aerial interpretation, gts site maps, and hydrological model development elements.

length-weighted means and then reclassify a slope raster from the digital elevation model. When I generated the least-cost path between the ends of the historically mapped sections and the archaeologically surveyed sections, the model *acequia* closely followed a historic road (mirrored in the GLO maps but visible in the 1960s aerial photos), a characteristic that matched known preferences of New Mexican communities using *acequias* (fig. 19). This test again verified the utility of this model for interpolating *acequia* direction and length.

Finally, the same tools could be used to characterize the linear features near Casitas. For this, I used a length-weighted mean of slope values to reclassify a slope raster for the entire Rito Colorado valley. By comparison, the characteristic slope of the linear features near Casitas was similar to those of other known *acequias*, suggesting that these features may have been used in a similar capacity for irrigation practices. Additionally, a buffered analysis of the areas that might have been serviced by these features suggests that they could have sustained field systems of similar surface area to historically known agricultural fields. Water from the Rito Colorado itself would be necessary to feed the linear features near Casitas, if they were indeed used in a similar manner as *acequias* elsewhere in the valley. So, I used the reclassified slope raster for the valley to establish where a river intercept for headgates would have to have been located on the Rito in order to get enough water into the system to the known ditches.

I highlighted a particular, narrow band of elevation, interpolated upstream from the characteristic range of slope of the linear features themselves, to demonstrate the intercept point with the Rito Colorado required for water to flow into the linear features near Casitas (fig. 20). To build a dam and headgates at this location would have also required a substantial main ditch to carry water far enough to feed the linear features at Casitas.

This analysis suggests that the linear features near Casitas would have required headgates more than twice as far up the valley as any known *acequia* system in New Mexico. Furthermore, a least-cost path analysis of the topography of the valley between this critical elevation and the linear features at Casitas cuts across so many arroyos and other topographic risers that it would have required more than ten times the number of *canoas* and deep ditches observed in any other known *acequia* system to make such an irrigation system near Casitas workable. No such features have ever been observed on GLO maps, archaeological survey, or aerial interpretation. Evidence thus far strongly suggests that, if the linear features were in fact irrigation works, they did not use the same hydrodynamic characteristics of *acequia* irrigation as were used elsewhere in the Rito Colorado valley.

If these linear features near Casitas were water-bearing, and water was not delivered to them by headgates like those that fed *acequias* elsewhere in the valley, where would water come from? Springs in the Rito Colorado valley area are historically well known, and their Spanish names often tie them to specific events or groups of people. No springs have been known to occur in the immediate vicinity of Casitas. Simple water-lifting technologies such as an Archimedes screw could have been used to lift water from the Rito Colorado up to a ditch system that integrated

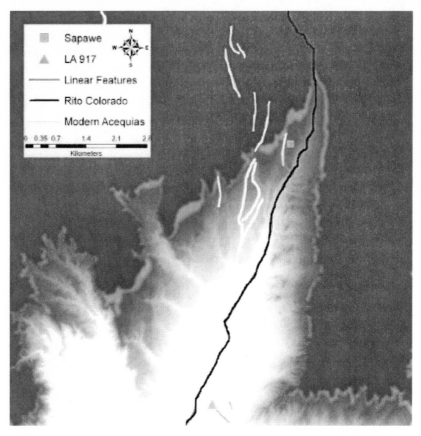

FIGURE 20. Elevation (where band of purple contours intersects blue Rito Colorado river channel) at which headgates would have needed to be located to deliver water to Casitas linear features from the Rito Colorado.

the linear features in question, although this would have required full-time staff and most likely draft animal labor. The use of such technologies in New Mexico are unknown to this author and are proposed as unlikely because it would diminish both human and animal labor needed elsewhere in subsistence agriculture, as well as require a vertical lift in excess of 8 meters, which is longer than similar screws used in North Africa for centuries (Oleson 1984:290). Additionally, it would put those human and animal resources at risk from raiders because of their predictability at the facility and an increased ease of approach without detection because of line-of-sight complications within the Rito gulch.

The only other agricultural water management technology in common use in northern New Mexico at the time of main occupation at *Casitas* was the "dry irrigation" practiced by Tewa communities for centuries (Anschuetz 2001). Such irrigation technologies were in evidence at places like Sapawe, the large precontact Pueblo that was centrally located in the Rito Colorado valley.

## Palimpsests of Place along the Rito Colorado

As discussed in chapter 2, the Rito Colorado valley was anything but a blank slate when the first Spanish colonial land grants were settled. Colonial communities had an intimate knowledge of Pueblo ideas and practices concerning use of the landscape and adapted those techniques as needed. Early Spanish explorers noted Pueblo ruins, and these places retained names in use by contemporary indigenous groups (Harrington 1916; Poling-Kempes 1997). After the Pueblo Revolt of 1680, colonial settlers made significant adjustments to their policies regarding landscape tenure, even beyond those legislated by authorities in the Recopilacion de Leyes de las Indies. As friars accommodated some indigenous practice within the scope of Catholic theology, there was also explicit understanding of an ancient Tewa landscape (Ebright and Hendricks 2006:13). In the Rito Colorado valley, ancestral Pueblo peoples had established one of the largest aggregated settlements in the Southwest and supposedly abandoned it by the time colonial-affiliate settlers arrived in the valley (NMCRIS 2006). This is the 15th-century site of Sapawe (LA 306), which to this day can be found from satellite imagery with ease because of the large footprint its hundreds of adobe rooms and multiple plazas occupy in the valley.

What is unusual about the later, 18th-century settlement pattern is the way colonists divided and exploited space throughout the valley while not incorporating the area of the large ruins at Sapawe. The earliest colonial settlers do not appear to have co-opted Sapawe as space for economic infrastructure nor to have turned Sapawe into a major locale for their settlement architecture in the valley. This was uncharacteristic of the settlement behavior in other areas under Spanish settlement. For example, the pueblo of Abiquiú was established almost on top of ruins to the south. One possible exception to this could be further explored, with future permission from private landowners. On the south edge of the Sapawe ruin there is one historic site consisting of a couple of small adobe room foundations, considered to have been abandoned prior to

1846, from the sparse amount of American trade wares that typically appear in sites after this date (Bob Lawrence 2005, pers. comm.). It remains untested and unknown as to whether or not it was built by a land grant colonizer (Quintana and Snow 1980:47). This may be a dead end, though, as some archaeologists familiar with unpublished work from Florence Hawley Ellis's research consider this site to be a late colonial reoccupation (Maxwell 2000:77). It would make particular sense that this site is characteristic of an individual family residence (*rancho*) such as those dispersed elsewhere throughout the valley, whereas Casitas and modern El Rito are characteristic of fortified plazas (large contiguous roomblocks). Alternatively, if there had been a short-term Tewa reoccupation of Sapawe at this site, it would be a powerful argument for an active cycle of reengagement with this landscape feature.

With this in mind, I turned my analysis to the agricultural systems that had been developed in the Rito Colorado valley before the arrival of the Spanish in New Mexico. Sapawe has more than 50 features associated with it that have been identified as agricultural or hydrological in nature (NMCRIS 2006). Features in the valley bottom, on the west side of the Rito Colorado, and near the pueblo itself are all listed as agricultural, such as the regularly spaced and rock-outlined fields known as waffle gardens. On the east side of the Rito Colorado, agricultural features are located in conjunction with hydrological features, such as check dams, *trincheras* (water-spreading and velocity-arresting devices), cobble mulches, and other elements of water-control technology associated with inaptly named "dry irrigation" systems. These features are in areas of high topographic relief and on sections of the ridge system bordering the entire eastern margin of the Rito Colorado valley. I approached the characterization of this network of features within three parameters: (1) using a regular grid of sample points on which to perform mathematical analyses of neighboring cell values within the digital elevation model; (2) sampling the slope and aspect of the topographic region containing the entirety of recorded hydrological features; and (3) orienting the sample grid in a way that followed the geological ridgeline feature on which the anthropogenic systems were constructed.

To create a rectangular grid sampling array it was necessary to establish a new feature class in the sampling geodatabase. I could then digitize a rectangular area around the hydrological features imported from the ARMS map server and filtered for relevance by their attribute tables (fig. 21). Frequency distributions of slope values for this set of sampling points shows that the modal values of the topography around the hydrological

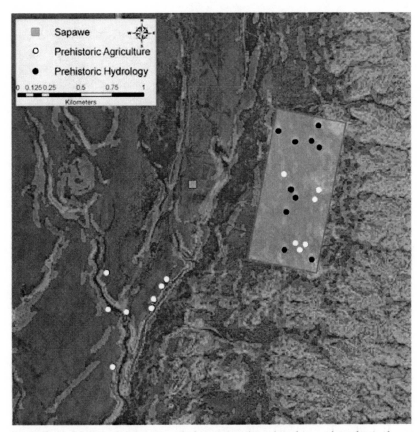

FIGURE 21. Extent of point-sampled topography related to archaeological hydrology features associated with Sapawe Pueblo.

features were at a slope of approximately seven degrees (fig. 23). While there is undoubtedly "noise" introduced by areas that were not selected for water management features, or areas that actually contained agricultural features (and hence were of lower slope value), the preponderance of slope values for this region is considered characteristic of the type of topography in which these kinds of hydrological control technologies were used for agricultural purposes.

Identical techniques were applied to the area of ridgeline nearest Casitas and overlapping with previously identified linear features. I overlaid the sampling grid in this location because it mirrored the orientation along the ridgeline on which the features up the valley had been

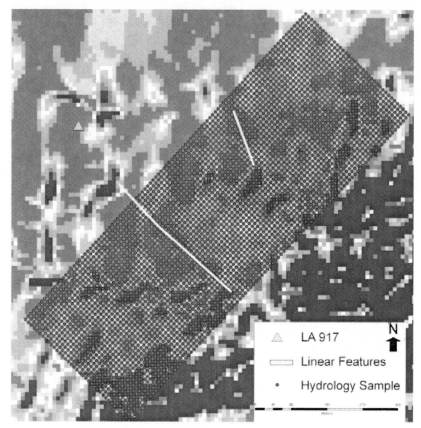

FIGURE 22. Extent of point-sampled topography to characterize hydrological topography near Casitas.

sampled. In essence, this is because the people who built features took advantage of the high-relief and rain-catching aspects of slopes along a ridgeline. They would more likely have used those slope faces that could be incorporated into a cohesive catchment rather than willy-nilly along a single compass orientation. By orienting the sampling grid in a way that was commensurate with the technique used near Sapawe, it intersected the linear features near Casitas (fig. 22). Settlers would have noticed the major drainages and microwatersheds of the ridgeline near Casitas, yet this sampling technique did not preferentially include such geologic particulars. Rather, for consistency's sake, I sampled and characterized by grid values the entire ridgeline topographic area near Casitas, to

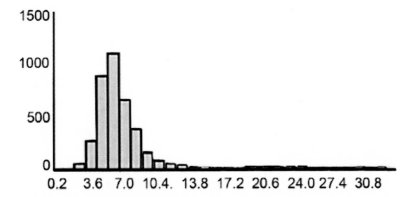

FIGURE 23. Characteristic topography of Sapawe hydrological features (in averaged slope per sample point, N = 1000).

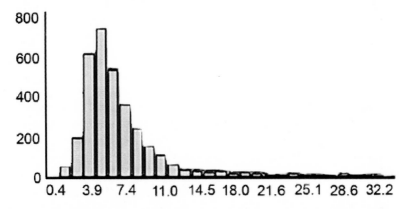

FIGURE 24. Characteristic topography of Casitas hydrological features (in averaged slope per sample point, N = 1000).

resemble the sampling parameters employed at Sapawe. The frequency distribution of slope values of this area shows that the characteristic topography had a modal slope of approximately seven degrees, the same as at Sapawe (figs. 23, 24).

I evaluated hydrological modeling of known and historical *acequias* first by testing on unsampled *acequias*, then at historical and archaeological sites of partial *acequia* observation. The *acequias* were then interpolated for the linear features associated with the agricultural complex at Casitas. This suggested that such a system of irrigation would be impossible at the site. With floodplain agriculture precluded by near-surface geography in the proximity of Casitas, it was unclear how the obvious agricultural features were irrigated. In other words, if settlers had established irrigation agriculture as mandated by the colonial administration but could not actually get water into those required ditches from the river itself, what irrigation strategy did they use? This line of inquiry led to the development of a way to quantify the characteristic topography around the only other example of successful farming to precede the buffer settlement, Sapawe Pueblo. Ancestral Tewa peoples used indigenous techniques (as described above) to manage water flow to agricultural fields, and my comparison of characteristic topographies suggests similar hydrodynamic parameters for integrating "dry" farming techniques with ditch irrigation at Casitas. If this was true, then such integrated practices were a most visible, intentional hybridization of technologies and a way of "hiding in plain sight" what may be deeply rooted understandings of sustainable agricultural processes in the Tewa basin.

## Homescape Dimensions in Dialogue

At my largest scale of analysis, I consider homescape elements to be the material result of processes that incorporate variable ideological constructs of communities over time. In this I followed the tact of many previous researchers (Briggs and Van Ness 1987; Ingold 1993; D. Lightfoot 1993b; Basso 1996; Comer 1996; Beekman et al. 1999; Benes and Zvelebil 1999; F. Levine 2001). When viewed together as coherent landscapes (Anschuetz et al. 2001; Clark 2011), researchers can use homescape elements to describe the economic or social infrastructure on which settler communities experienced frontier life. While individual features or portions of cultural landscapes survive (or sometimes even where they are lost), their connections to historical and material lines of evidence complete the stories of the people that inhabited them.

I use a homescape approach to focus on specific aspects of spatial pattern creation and re-creation to be able to consider multiple material categories. My thinking is that the multidimensional nature of those categories can be put in different kinds of interpretive dialogue with each other, as well as being considered differing scales of practice in the archaeological record. In this case, the broader homescape framework includes what I call the tactical homescape and the engineered homescape. While these landscape aspects centralize the residues of homescape behavior left behind by the families who populated Casitas, each GIS analysis uses a different suite of methodologies to explore material expressions of daily life, suited to specific research questions.

For the tactical homescape, the spatial analysis focused on the parameters for maintaining a defensive posture on the front lines of a long-lived and episodically intense conflict. In this context, colonial settlers systematized many military decisions and compromises in the layout of the settlement. They did so with respect to decision-making time frames that reflected the close-in fighting and retreat options that a community facing a raid might consider. This included not only monitoring of raiding conduits into and out of the Rito Colorado valley but also maintenance of a clear view of what was happening in nearby fields and orchards. The intent of the tactical homescape was to command a clear field of fire as well as to provide access to viable escape routes to allied communities.

For me, the result of my analysis is a more cohesive understanding of the sequence of settlement for Casitas and descendant settlements in the Rito Colorado valley. This is particularly true of the location of contemporary El Rito in the spatial sense it makes after the Comanche truce brokered by Governor Cachupín at the end of the 18th century. What these perspectives on the homescape most poignantly clarify is the delicate and dangerous balance struck by the Casitas community in managing their tactical response to any possible raid while trying to situate themselves on the landscape within required colonial parameters.

Quantitative aspects of those parameters were most clearly demonstrated in the analysis of the engineered homescape. Those spatial analyses considered the requirements for maintaining sustainably integrated agricultural water systems in a marginally productive local environment. Although the *acequia*-based colonial irrigation systems were foregrounded here, pastoral and forestry practices were also engineered systems that altered the landscape. Hydrological modeling of *acequias* helps to define and evaluate linear features associated with Casitas as unlikely candidates for archetypical forms of *acequia* agriculture. The resulting comparison with the characteristic topographic signature of precontact Tewa agricultural practices lends itself to evidence of syncretic practices of landscape creation and management in the most public scale of community practice.

Future homescape analyses of the historic sites in the Rito Colorado valley should further develop cost-distance defining energetics of horse-mounted and unmounted agents (J. Sunseri 2015). In an historical era

where horses were the principal engines of trade, war, and communication, such work is necessary to refine understandings of the tactical costs
and benefits of settlement location. These further cost-distance calculations can be used quantify the amount of effort and thus time required
to retreat to one of the defensive plazas once a raid was spotted from
the surrounding agricultural fields. The assumption is it would have
been possible to work in a field and still make it to a defensive settlement
before the probability of being overtaken in a raid became too high. A
quantitative measure of time to safety would clarify how much of the
agriculturally viable land surrounding the three sites would have been
improbable to use because of unsafe positioning (a nonsufficient length
of time required to travel to safety). By extension, the algorithmic read-
ing of travel times could also be applied to cost-distance studies in which
an interpretation could be made of the amount of time different sites
would have had before a raiding group reached them.

Cost-distance calculations could also be used as an aid in determin-
ing the difficulty in diverting flow from *acequias* by making increases in
elevation an extremely high or infinite value so as to give an idea of the
potential water flow from the *acequias* into the agricultural fields. This
would give an even more convincing estimation of the optimal locations
where agricultural fields could have been placed once *acequias* were in
use. Knowing potential field locations around *acequias* seems to be a
principal element in investigating the social relations between portions
of the settlement with regard to their proximity to *acequia* headgates.
Would households closest to the headgates have first access to water for
their fields? Is this a reflection of differentiated social status within the
community (Ray and Williams 2002)? Alternatively, such a location put
the household in more immediate danger from up-valley raiding parties.

In the end, the balances struck by the Casitas families—between
defense and productivity, community inclusiveness and non-normative
innovation—were the all part of the lived experiences of making a homescape that was itself a double-edged sword. The tactical and engineering aspects of lived experience at Casitas represent new ways of creating
homes in the Spanish colony's evolving concept of place. Those concepts
were materially recorded in the settlement valleys as important counter-
points to New Mexico's cartographic heritage. The latter was crafted by
only a handful of literate elites who knew about and sometimes incorporated the location and names of previous settlements along the Rito Colorado and upper Rio Chama drainages. Archaeological modeling pursues
an importance line of historical evidence. Ground-truthing of expected

features shows sophisticated tactical and agricultural knowledge of people that is not reflected in the documentary record. These families had much to gain in seeking grants of land and then creatively applying their knowledge instead of being blindly obedient to royal decrees of military and agricultural requirements. Putting these interpretive dimensions in context with each other leads to surprising understandings about hidden as well as public realms of identity. The long-term effects of crafting homescapes under these conditions continue to be a part of the experiences of northern New Mexican communities to this day (see discussion in epilogue).

Finding and creating models to interpret hidden as well as public realms of identity is also critical for assessing material remains found in the hearthscapes of these colonial settlers. The next chapters consider these topics.

# 4 /    Hearthscape Tools

*Scraping a bit of beans from the edge of her wooden spoon, Eufemia had just checked the simmering midday meal when she heard the shout from outside. Careful to not again nick the edge of her hardworking and soot-blackened micaceous pot as she drew the spoon out, she put the handful of dried steam corn kernels back in the polychrome jar at her side and stood up. "Those will have to wait, or perhaps go into posole later," she thought to herself as she stooped through the purposefully small doorway into the plaza outside. One glance at the stream of sheep and worried children pouring through the heavy wooden gates and she knew something was terribly wrong.*

*"Utas? Nabajos?" She caught and held the terrified eyes of Ximena as the girl whipped stock into the increasingly tight courtyard of the fortified plazuela. The answer chilled Eufemia through: "Comanches, and coming fast." As this particular child had lived with a band of them for ten years of her life, Eufemia knew not to question the analysis. There was not enough time for the livestock to be herded through the gates, and the majority of the community's warriors were gone on their current campaign for at least another week. Time was running out, and if the small community was going to survive this raid, Eufemia had to make some hard decisions quickly.*

*Of all the people running from their outlying households to this main quadrangle, not a single family remained untouched by the experiences of captivity, violent raids, and counterraids in which the northern communities had been locked for a generation. In the next valley over, a combined force of Utes and Comanches had attacked Ojo Caliente only last year. Men defending the equally remote settlement were killed and every woman and child carried off to be sold at distant trade fairs. Was it time to run, maybe try for shelter at Abiquiú or San Juan? Even with the strategic placement of their fortified plazuela at the constriction of the Rito Colorado valley, not everyone would make it. The raiding party might easily run them down on their swifter mounts. No, they could neither fight nor flee; but there had to be another way.*

*"Estefanita, go get Tonita and Eufilia. We need them to start that dish of panza de cabrito that they do so well." She looked over at a small child who seemed transfixed by the scene, standing wide-eyed in the corner of the plaza. "Mija, you remember your language, no? Help me with the beans and lay on some tortillas . . . quickly, go now." "Nocario, get these animals out of here and get the big Pueblo painted bowls from Santa Clara and San Juan down for me." Setting everyone on hand into motion calmed them only slightly. With a few sharp obsidian edges sitting on the sill of the*

FIGURE 25. Depiction of a New Mexican woman cooking at hearth (after E. Irving Couse).

horno, Eufemia quickly and methodically removed a few portions from the carcass of a goat she had begun butchering that morning. As she stooped back through the doorway into her kitchen command center, she knew that she was asking everyone for near impossible courage.

Outside, a few riders reined their mounts up short as they approached the heavy outer gates of the plaza. They had taken their time getting there, checking through the now empty houses of the outlying ranchos as coordinated units. What they saw here now was confusing, suspicious. The gates were wide open and a little girl, trembling, holding up a tray of something delicious-smelling and welcoming them in their own language. They remained mounted and waited for the raiding party leader to come around from his flanking run. When he did, they followed his lead and entered the plaza together. The feast awaiting them took them completely off guard. They had not seen a spread this good since the last annual trade fair at Pecos. Welcomed as kin, the team warily sat down with their nervous hosts and tucked into the meal.

In different versions of this folktale, common in the Genízaro frontier communities of New Mexico, Eufemia saves the day in slightly different ways. In one version, the fortified plaza remains buttoned up and raiders thrusting lances through the tiny external windows or chimneys are surprised to find tortillas stuck on the points. They eat enough tortillas to be satiated and ride away. In another version, the raiders are lured by feast into the middle of the plaza and are shot down by womenfolk on the surrounding rooftops, lying in wait with their bows and arrows. Sometimes the story ends with the feasted raiding party working out a trade arrangement with the people who have proven their kinship relations with the cultural performance of an appropriate meal and reception. One imagines trading a few choice sheep, a supply of corn and beans, and one of their famous wool weavings in exchange for a questionable bit of buffalo pemmican and a barely serviceable French trade knife. Under such duress, regardless of a potentially uneven exchange, the negotiation would have been a success if no one was taken captive and homes remained standing.

At the center of each version of Eufemia's story is how in these frontier communities—low-status land grantees put in harm's way by a colonial administration to protect central towns like Santa Fe—a matriarch saves them from certain devastation through the quick mobilization of foods that signify kinship and belonging. For archaeologists studying the material context of folk stories like these, the persistence and resilience of memory in our host communities connects violence and negotiations of the distant past with issues of today.

At its core, Eufemia's story is about making a performance out of shared meals and eating in ways that bind people together across a dangerous homescape. No performance occurs without some form of stage or staging. In this case, there is a foodway performance at the hearthscape. Foodways as a concept comes from a description of not only a whole suite of ingredients but also social constraints that a community shares in their eating practices (J. Anderson 1971). In the case of an archaeology of Genízaro foodways, what is most important is how eating and meals might have created bonds between community members who themselves were representatives of many nations both within and from without the Southwest. The kitchens, tables, and tools, all sets and props on their hearthscape stage, were intimately linked to places outside of their homes in which those nations came together in unique ways.

In this chapter and the next, I introduce two of the most durable and robust data sets used for reconstruction of cuisine, class, and status of

Casitas Viejas: pottery and animal bones. Together, ceramic and fauna suites of evidence are robust, precisely because of how mundane much of their use was in the lives of families at Casitas. As food and the tools to create and serve it, these data are a record of daily life, accumulating from the wear and tear on pots and the discarded bones of meals for as long as people lived at the little plaza.

The assemblages that make up the hearthscape evidence at Casitas are predominantly those that Dr. Herb Dick of Trinidad College excavated during the 1950s, from three trash disposal loci (fig. 5) in their entirety. Never written up, Dick's work at Casitas was to be part of a suite of historical archaeological sites that he tested across northern New Mexico to develop a more clear picture of late colonial life (Adler and Dick 1999). Portions of the material assemblages and disparate associated records found at various southwestern institutions and the Dick residence were recovered and curated together by the end of this project, along with the smaller, more recent assemblages. Those smaller assemblages were recovered via volunteer excavations with the U.S. Forest Service during multiple seasons at the Carson Forest under supervision of forest archaeologist Bob Lawrence. Now a coherent material record of Casitas, the collections reside together at the Laboratory of Anthropology curation facility in Santa Fe with tabulated data sets, labels, and digital databases included on various print and media forms that I included in the boxes with the artifacts.

In this chapter, rather than solely expanding on existing typologies of historic New Mexican ceramics, I prefer to examine the living contexts of pottery production, use, and disposal. Pottery has many hearthscape roles in foodway performance: for cooking, storage, preparation, and as serving tools.

## Pottery as Foodway Toolkits

Several times a day, the families who lived at Casitas put valuable equipment to the test. They required reliability from their pottery under some challenging work cycles. In storing supplies, making and serving meals, and carrying away or processing leftovers, ceramic foodway tools had to be well engineered to endure much abuse. Working loads included compressive forces from stacking and filling, hoop stresses from high-mass contents, tension and torsion from carrying, differential contraction and expansion from heating, and shear stress from cutting and asymmetrical loading. Like any good tool, these ceramics bear the scars of their daily jobs. Their numeric dominance over other artifact categories in all three disposal loci at Casitas speaks to how many pottery vessels were pushed beyond their limits. Because of their prominence in shaping and being shaped, the role of ceramics in the social dynamics of community-making gives them interpretive value far deeper than either their durability or their appearance alone. Potters who supplied the Casitas households understood that their products were expected not only to withstand the rigors of daily cooking use but also to perform in other social realms related to food. As they were used to produce meals, so too did ceramics serve food to families, guests, and maybe even enemies, as in the Eufemia tradition. Their shape, decoration, and perhaps even finish meant that how they were used in the routines and rituals of eating made them powerful within recursive repertoires of culinary performance. That is to say, the pottery shaped and was shaped by its foodway roles.

More than one community of potters supplied vessels to different households at Casitas. This complicates the picture, and interpretations of the disposed broken pottery must acknowledge that more than one kind of consumer group structured the demand and usage of those pots. The approach I advocate investigates how these pots functioned as foodway tools. First, technological traits that are manifested in ceramic assemblages point to unique properties that can be used to characterize pottery production (Rice 1987). The second point is to acknowledge the role of ceramic products within household consumption and disposal practices (J. Hill 2002). This parallels what lithic specialists call a *chaîne opératoire* (Leroi-Gourhan [1943] 1973)—the operating chain, that is, the entirety of human activities from raw material acquisition to deposition of the artifact. This approach emphasizes how the processes of use as well as manufacture of material culture may have created environments that crafted and mediated social relations (Stark 1998:7).

Lithic analysts and cultural technologists have long paid close attention to the different stages of tool production and use, from the acquisition of raw material to the final abandonment of the used objects (Leroi-Gourhan 1943; Tixier 1974; Inizan et al. 1999). By reconstructing the *chaîne opératoire*, archaeologists "reveal the choices made by humans" and situate them within structures of access and performance appropriate to anthropological questions about the nature of their production and use. This approach contrasts with typological models, which concentrate on naming and categorizing the final result of production alone, as opposed to whole processes of creation, use, and discard (Grace 1990).

Extending beyond production-centered analyses and Leroi-Gourhan's concept of "people = tools" (Leroi-Gourhan 1981), consideration of the ceramics at Casitas includes material use and discard to view more holistic pictures of the choices made throughout an artifact's use life (Schiffer 1972; Lemonnier 1993). After all, regardless of what particular kinds of production or exchange dominated the flow of pots in New Mexico during colonial times, ceramic producers were certainly aware of what kinds of forms were in demand and driving consumption (Comaroff 1996:20). Pot makers and users were also engaged in how such artifacts would be used within the context of various meals (Blair and Blair 1986:100). Someone who made a ring-based flange plate invested enough in the overall design of that piece to ensure that it would perform well in a particular schema of presentation and use.

Looking for evidence of these kinds of relationships is in line with theorists who emphasize the interrelatedness of pottery's social dimensions and recognize a distinction between different aspects of practice, such as between technological style and use (Lemonnier 1993; Dietler 1998; Stahl 2001). In a similar way, the cultural and material options available on the frontier for production structured the *habitus* of potting communities, as well as the context in which their final products were used. In this way, pots built communities of practice in households via reflexive processes of supply and consumption.

My investigation of pots at Casitas attempts to track potential mental templates evidenced in the stages of production of various recognizable types and forms (Leroi-Gourhan [1943] 1973), as well as the ways that ceramic vessels became part of foodway performance and other forms of identity practice (Pikirayi 2007) within different household contexts and between groups of people. I consider the three archaeologically recovered and distinctly spatially segregated disposal loci (fig. 5) at Casitas to be household-scale contexts, or at least the aggregate of several proximate households over time, as per discussions of extended families in roomblocks of *plazuela* configuration (Swadesh 1974:179). This basic difference in material patterning across the site serves as a comparative framework for relating the various choices made in ceramic production to the families who ultimately made, traded for, used, and then discarded household pottery.

Consideration of the initial stages in ceramic production includes analysis of the material signatures of raw clay acquisition, processing, and addition of temper. Like other stages in ceramic production, use, and disposal, these behaviors drew variably from a range of behavioral repertoires. Clay acquisition operated along a continuum of choices as disparate as transporting usable material over a long distance, in cases as extreme as the Oñate caravan's small supply of clay (Hammond and Rey 1953:225), to establishing settlement locations on top of clay sources to keep acquisition expenditures minimized (Curtis 1962:491). Even within a single potting community, it may have been possible that multiple clay sources were used, such as both sedimentary and residual clays at Picuris Pueblo (Shepard 1956:51; Adler and Dick 1999). Likewise, choices about construction and finishing drew from traditions as distinct as the coil and scrape methods of the Pueblos (Blair and Blair 1986; Kramer 1996) to paddle and anvil techniques of northern Mexico and the Plains (Charlton 1976; Balkansky et al. 1997; Druc 2000). Besides choosing a kiln or pit, firing was the product of preferences in fuel and atmosphere alternatives (Nicklin 1979:446–447). Even within a single fuel choice such as dung (itself a hybrid process incorporating the by-product of a European introduced domesticate), multiple modes of use could occur.

To relate the communities of potters to the communities of customers they were supplying, the next stage of analysis focuses on the material signatures of ceramic use practices (Henrickson and McDonald 1983). Evidence for cooking, serving, and nonfood utility through analysis of vessel forms, sizes, and use wear should be considered. Such traces suggest how ceramics were involved in multiple stages of food storage, preparation, and consumption. It is important to consider these functions within the ceramic assemblage, as it would seem that most material manifestations of foodways in colonial sites were intimately related to the use of ceramics in these steps (Harrington 1916; Cushing 1920; Gilbert 1970; Hughes 1977; Gilbert 1982).This emphasizes the interrelatedness of their contexts and how each built and rebuilt multiscalar communities of practice through their use of pots.

## Who Made These Pots?

Among archaeologists in New Mexico, it has long been assumed that most, if not all, colonial-era low-fired ceramics were of Pueblo Indian manufacture and that making pottery was a marker of Indian practice (Snow 1984:57). In these models of identity, access to clays, understanding of pottery techniques, and ideas about proper use of ceramic material culture are rigidly associated with one another and with ethnic identity. Typologies used to describe most common plain wares reflect this rigidity. Kapo Black is a classic example, fixing both the type and the producer to one, immutable relationship between polished black pottery and its presumed source, Santa Clara Pueblo (Kidder and Shepard 1936).

Conversely, Carrillo (1997) has argued persuasively for a late-18th-century Hispano economy in which not only textile but especially ceramic manufacture fluoresced and was greatly augmented and influenced by Genízaro craftspeople. While his critique challenges assumptions about who made the pottery found on rural colonial sites in northern New Mexico, it continues to reify the time-honored cultural historical association of a type with "a people" (Snow 1984; F. Levine 1992; Carrillo 1997; Eiselt 2004). So, mirroring the example of Kapo Black, using the type name Manzano Blackware might be interpreted to bind the production and use of a partial subset of polished black pottery to colonists of Hispanic or Hispanicized identity.

More than one researcher has tried to tease these two viewpoints apart by identification of fine to coarse sand or fiber temper and friable paste body in proposed Hispanic types, as opposed to vitric ash or tuff-tempered Puebloan types (Hurt and Dick 1946; Dick [1964] 1968; Warren 1979; D. Levine 1990). Slip and polish extent and quality are also used as gauges of the likelihood of such pots having Tewa origins, as well as style and quality of design (D. Levine 1990:180). Settlements proposed to have made these pots may have included not only indigenous settlements that experienced various admixtures of diverse ethnic groupings during reorganization after the Reconquista (John 1975; Gutiérrez 1991; Kessell 1995; James 1997) but also colonial settlements in which formerly captive indigenous groups were integrated and increased census counts of the *vecino* population (Frank 2000; Brooks 2002a; Rael-Gàlvez 2002). By the 18th century, potters from Tewa Pueblos, too, may have had diverse ethnic origins or been influenced by other Indian practices. Historic vessel forms at Santa Clara include those influenced by San Juan plain wares, as well as protohistoric types from Abiquiú and Tsankawi (Blair and Blair 1986:88).

It has also been noted historically that at least one ostensibly non-Tewa colonial settlement, Abiquiú—mother village to Casitas—sold pots that the settlers themselves made (Swadesh 1974:41). It is this reference to pottery made and sold by Genízaro women at Abiquiú, that Snow (1984:105) suggests as a solution to what may be in reality only a semantic issue. In other words, these women potters in a colonial village may have self-identified as Indian in other aspects of their identity. Carrillo (1997:65) also reduces the tension of dichotomous thinking by suggesting that people who lived in non-Pueblo Spanish colonial communities and who shared a common practice should be considered Hispanic, no matter what their origins. This demonstrates the case that the practice of calling any one potter "Indio" or "Hispano" may often serve to create confusion; in these communities, pottery making may have been a syncretic and situational practice in multiple social and economic contexts. As in other discussions problematizing discontinuous thought (Dawkins 2004) as potentially pigeonholing concepts, essentializing classificatory terminology handicaps anthropological and historical thinking about the nature of potting in these complex late-colonial-period situations.

Instead, I propose we follow the clues that Swadesh (1974:46) laid out regarding the ease with which communities on the northern frontier crossed boundaries of identity and status. Such crossings echo the way ethnoarchaeological studies have demonstrated how producers and consumers of material culture routinely blur boundaries between technology, function, and style (Foster 1948; Blair and Blair 1986; Dietler and Herbich 1989; Gosselain 1992; Kramer 1996; Stark 1998:4). In essence, it becomes necessary to change the question and the frame of reference to get at a discussion of how ceramic assemblage patterns can illustrate the recursive relationship between potter and consumer. As Stark suggests, it is necessary to avoid strict alignment with previous typologies and the concomitant dichotomizing models that oppose style and function in an attempt to embrace more holistic understanding of the variability that can be seen in the ceramic assemblage (Stark 1998:5). In the process, it is possible to depart from debates concerning the ethnic origins of particular historic ceramic types by "assigning as much weight to the discussion of technological systems as to the classification of the resulting artifacts" (Gosselain 1992:560).

Doing so directly challenges correlations between historic characterizations of identity and material practice and instead examines the various repertoires of colonial-era potters and compares them to each other during the several stages of the *chaînes opératoires*. In creating dialogues and negotiations around the production and flow of ceramic objects through their similarities in foodway performance, these suites of practices can be considered "marking compatibles" (Tsing 2005). Looking at these "repertoires of practice" allows us to avoid what Ann Stahl (2009) has warned is rhetoric that is a product of the minds of researchers far removed from the lived experiences of the people who inhabited Casitas.

As an example, red-banded brown and highly polished black wares are mutable categories, whose physical and social performances are compatible among multiple communities of practice. When I use the label "Red-on-Brown" or "Burnished Black" as a communicative device to spark recognition in the mind of southwestern ceramicists, I probably do not share their immediate correlation with a given potter's ethnic or other identity. Instead, I am trying to complicate the use of those terms. Rather than assign a particular ethnic affiliation for potters in the historically pluralistic 18th-century colony, I argue that foodways at Casitas have inherently diverse traditions of ceramic manufacture, use, and disposal that crosscut boundaries of ethnic affiliation and represent colonial potters and pottery users with syncretic communities of practice. Practice theory becomes usable for an archaeologist studying ceramic assemblages, especially in the myriad of ways that choices in the *chaîne opératoire* of ceramic production, use, and disposal can be quantified.

## Typologies and Historic New Mexican Pottery

We need not throw the baby out with the bathwater. In historical archaeologies of the Spanish colonial era in New Mexico, researchers have consistently documented the dominance of a familiar suite of ceramic types. Besides the ubiquitous decorated polychromes that have been assigned to specific pueblos of the Rio Grande, the many subvariants of polished red and black wares, red-on-browns, micaceous wares, and culinary plain wares occur frequently enough in large numbers across the former colony to surprise those who do not find them on colonial-era sites (Lambert 1981:228). A principal methodical organization for this project involved separating the ceramic assemblage into separate categories based upon generalized types rather than the specific types described below. This is because, as Carrillo has pointed out (1997:193), the analytical conundrum in typological descriptions of variation is how such typologies are completely dependent on how the ceramic types are defined. In discussing these historic wares, Warren (1979:27) succinctly opines that "recognizing and defining a type is never an end in itself. As a tool it can be used in the investigation of culturally related problems, and in time it becomes a word, or a term, by which the analyst may communicate certain concepts or ideas to listeners or readers." Expectations that valid typological classifications will not only account for all attributes but also be finite enough for indices of relevant cultural historical use is exactly why making everyone happy is "patently impossible" (Rice 1987:276).

Many of the sherds recovered from the loci at Casitas appear to match specific published type descriptions such as Carnué Plain (Dick [1964]

1968), Casitas Red-on-Brown (Dick 1968 [1964]); Kapo Black (Mera 1939); Powhoge Polychrome (Harlow 1973:31); Puname Polychrome (Mera 1939:18; Harlow 1974); and a type first described by Dick ([1964] 1968:81) as a subtype of Casitas Red-on-Brown, Casitas Polychrome. Other, similar formal types may be represented in the assemblage as well, such as Manzano Coarse (Hurt and Dick 1946); Plain Red "Brick" Ware (Toulouse 1949); Heavily Striated Plain (Kidder and Shepard 1936); Manzano Thin Red-on-Buff (Hurt and Dick 1946); Plain Red (Kidder and Shepard 1936); Tewa Red (Mera 1939); Manzano Burnished Black (Hurt and Dick 1946); Tewa Polychrome (Mera 1939); Ogapoge Polychrome (Harlow 1973); and Cimarron Micaceous (Gunnerson 1979). Micaceous wares could also be rough-sorted into groups similar to the thin-walled Petaca Micaceous (Dick [1964] 1968:85) and thick-walled, slipped El Rito Micaceous types (Dick [1964] 1968:83), but given the recent, excellent reformulation of a usable micaceous typology (Eiselt 2004), a closer examination of these groups may well result in a finer-grained sort into Petaca/Peñasco and El Rito/Vadito types.

At the heart of naming or using these types lurk the related assumptions about who made them and aspects of their identity that relate to the dichotomous tropes discussed earlier. The correlation between a type of pot and a type of person (Croucher and Wynne-Jones 2006) is precisely what I wish to avoid. These very disparities in typologies have been aptly identified as "the basis of one of the long and frustrating arguments in New Mexican colonial archaeology" (Cordell and Yannie 1991:106).

Rather, I wish to investigate the various repertoires of colonial-era potters in a way that attends to the interrelatedness of their products. In other words, aspects of making and using pottery that are shared among different geographic, ethnic, gendered, *casta*, or other groups of people may help them communicate other ideas about pottery, without necessarily practicing the full suite of one another's pottery practices. Such crosscutting relationships expose recursive, communicative roles between potters at various stages of the *chaîne opératoire* of production and use. For example, Red-on-Brown wares are mutable and shared compatible items among multiple communities that include potters living at Casitas Viejas (Dick [1964] 1968:84), Pecos (Kidder and Shepard 1936:281), and the Mission at Abó (Toulouse 1949:19).

From a practical perspective, people sitting across a table from each other may well have recognized not only how a red-banded buff flange plate related to other red-banded buff flange plates with respect to place of origin but also that similar vessels served similar functions in performing serving roles. Ring bases were made to be stable on flat table surfaces, the large concavity holding liquids as well as solids, and the flange itself could have supported pieces of tortilla or other food. From an archaeological perspective, analytical groupings (Table 2) of several related types allow for closer examination of other dimensions of production and use recorded in the ceramic assemblage at Casitas. These analytical groupings tie together or crosscut their roles as storage, cooking, and serving vessels. I sorted sherds in the assemblage into Culinary Plain, Red-on-Brown, Burnished Black, Polychrome, Smudged Red-on-Brown, Micaceous, and Micaceous-Slipped with this in mind. Being a lumper (rather than a splitter) makes sense via analogical reasoning. Imagine someone seated at a dinner table set with mid-20th-century Fiesta dinnerware. If some of the bright red-orange (and slightly radioactive!) plates of the original set were randomly replaced with pastel orange round platters with concentric rings toward the exterior margins, not much would seem amiss to the casual diner. And even those in the know might let their role at the table play out in the course of a meal with their hosts.

I also sorted potsherds in the Casitas assemblages for an evaluation of mean ceramic date (Table 3) of specific dated types, with cautious use of typologies for a limited number of identified specimens (NISP; also called Mininum Number of Items, MNI) (Orton 1993). The results agree well with proposed occupation periods of the site (Dick 1959; Speth 1963; Dick [1964] 1968; Quintana and Snow 1980; Carrillo 1997). Corroborating data include Quintana and Snow's (1980:48) report that Snow and Speth's unpublished test excavations at Casitas suggested to them an occupation originating AD 1750–1775. Moreover, the lack of post–Santa Fe Trail stoneware in surface or subsurface assemblages lends support to the site's major occupation having been before trade began with the American East in the first third of the 19th century.

## Choosing Clay for Making Pots

In an attempt to explore potential links between archaeological specimens and clay sources nearest to Casitas (Gosselain 1992:564), I identified and collected field clays using ethnographic information and with extraordinary assistance from Chris Gonzalez, Charles Carrillo, and Felipe Ortega (fig. 23). These samples were then processed by drying, grinding, and sieving to remove particulates larger than 0.1 mm. Test tiles of both processed and unprocessed field clays were created

Table 2. Ceramic types and analytical groups

| Ceramic type name | Analytical group |
| --- | --- |
| Carnúe Plain | Culinary Plain |
| Manzano Coarse Ware | |
| Plain Brick Ware | |
| Heavy Striated Pottery | |
| Casitas Red-on-Brown | Red-on-Brown |
| Manzano Thin Red-on-Buff | |
| Red Brick Ware | |
| Plain Red | |
| Casitas Red-on-Brown Polychrome | Red-on-Brown Smudged |
| Kapo Black | Burnished Black |
| Manzano Burnished Black | |
| Powhoge Polychrome | Polychrome |
| Tewa Polychrome | |
| Puname Polychrome | |
| Petaca Micaceous | Thin Micaceous |
| Peñasco Micaceous | |
| Cimarron Micaceous | |
| Vadito Micaceous | Slipped Micaceous |
| El Rito Micaceous | |
| Tewa Micaceous | |

to characterize various material properties and used fractionally for subsequent firing and refiring experiments. From these field clays, I made experimental vessels with various construction and finishing techniques, fired in various stacking orientations (nested or not), fuel types (e.g., bark, wood, and dung), and oxygen environments. By having these comparative examples of various processed and unprocessed clays, in different forming and firing regimes, I created a baseline of information for subsequent evaluations of paste and production categories.

For primary sorting under a binocular microscope, differences in paste and temper type were recorded and evaluated for uniqueness. At each observation of a new paste type, a mounted sample of the sherd

Table 3. Mean ceramic date, AD

| Type | Min | Max | Median | NISP | Factor | Mean ceramic date |
|------|-----|-----|--------|------|--------|-------------------|
| Casitas R/B | 1730 | 1850 | 1790 | 205 | 366950 | |
| Kapo | 1720 | 1760 | 1740 | 245 | 426300 | |
| Powhoge | 1750 | 1850 | 1800 | 70 | 126000 | |
| | | | | 520 | 919250 | AD 1768 |

Source: After South 1978.

exhibiting unique paste and temper characteristics was kept by affixing it sequentially to a cardboard strip, along with catalogue and provenience data (following Rye 1981:51). This comparative strip was used to evaluate the rest of the sample, in concert with binocular microscope sorting strategies that included sorting based on color and texture of paste matrix, as well as differences in the type, range, and relative proportion of mineralogical and lithic inclusions.

On average, two sherds per optical paste group and field clay (including those which were used as the comparative sample) were selected for petrographic analysis, resulting in the preparation of 28 thin section slides. The interior and exterior surfaces of each sherd selected was photographed before a 5 mm thick slice was taken from the sherd, parallel to the vertical axis of the presumed vessel using a diamond-edged saw. These samples were then vacuum-impregnated with a low viscosity epoxy resin before grinding and mounting to petrographic slides. Lapidary wheel reduction of the samples, via decreasing coarseness of grits, resulted in samples 0.03 mm thick. These samples were fitted with cover slips affixed with Canadian balsam, which can be removed should they require further processing in the future. The organization of the following analysis parallels what I consider to be less discursive choices made by potters, such as clay choice, to more recursive operations, including vessel sizes and shapes. The clearest evidence of differences between colonial pottery-making communities of practice comes from a principal stage in the ceramic material acquisition. Pastes groups defined by binocular microscope sort, then refined via thin section petrographic examination, were broken into nine categories and are interpreted as being from roughly different geological origins.

FIGURE 26. Sampled clay sources (*a*) Abiquiú; (*b*) Casitas; (*c*) Darst Hill; (*d*) La Madera Hill.

I also evaluated nonplastic inclusions and temper characteristics. While some potters may have preferentially selected clay sources for their immediate workability (Gosselain 1992:565), some may have added materials to the clay body to increase desired characteristics. Distinguishing characteristics of nonplastic inclusions include their mineralogy, size, shape, and regularity (Orton et al. 1993:139). Most important to this study is that I use these characteristics to distinguish between naturally occurring versus human-added tempers. After Rye (1981), I work from the assumption that particles within the clay body are naturally occurring if they show the rounded edges characteristic of natural erosion, exhibit a wide range of maximum dimensions, and are poorly sorted. Conversely, if nonplastics have sharp, angular edges that may be from crushing of raw materials and/or are well sorted, they may characterize temper additions to the clay (Rye 1981:52). These considerations are also part of the analytical paste groupings.

Looking at how tempers are represented within the assemblage reveals some interesting trends. For example, the presence of basalt temper is almost entirely limited to polychromes, suggesting origins from much farther south in New Mexico, in traditionally Keres Pueblo areas (Harlow 1974; Warren 1979). As argued in a Pueblo-only production model for historic northern New Mexican ceramics (Snow 1984), the majority of wares—if produced by potters living in Tewa pueblos—should contain volcanic ash or consolidated tuff, especially those types that characterize the plain ware traditions of the Española basin (Snow 1982; Olinger 1988). The idea of extreme conservatism of Tewa potters of the Española district in raw material selection is often contrasted with the "many changes in slip, paint, design, form and firing technology that have taken place within the Tewa ceramic tradition" (Habicht-Mauche 1993:60). Within the Casitas assemblage, polychromes and burnished black wares most closely meet these expectations for ash and tuff temper (fig. 27). Another trend is expressed in the paste groups most often associated with the Red-on-Brown and Culinary Plain types as well as in the site-specific type, Red-on-Brown Smudged, which researchers have previously argued suggest a non-Pueblo tradition (Hurt and Dick 1946; Dick [1964] 1968; D. Levine 1996). These coarse sand-tempered and untempered paste groups closely resemble clay sources local to Casitas (fig. 26) and the Upper Chama. These paste groups are also represented in the Burnished Black and Polychrome types in proportions that resemble ratios attributed to practices at other colonial frontier settlements (Dick [1964] 1968; Carrillo 1997). This complicates both models of production and suggests multiple locations, modes, and combinations of sources for the ceramics in circulation on the frontier.

These data suggest chains of supply wherein the potters making these vessels were located at various indigenous and colonial settlements and drew from more than one source of raw material. The types of vessels themselves, from simple Culinary Plain to highly ornate Polychromes, are present in all disposal loci across the site. This suggests that most households at Casitas had access to the full range of plain and micaceous wares. In contrast, the proportions of these types are not equally represented, nor are their constituent paste groups within each type. This suggests that people used these ceramics in different proportions of each type and that they were likely supplied by potters who were accessing different clay sources for their raw material. Some of these clay sources were local, others more distant, such as the Pliocene alluvial deposits in the Santa Fe Formation of the Española Valley (Olinger 1988:2). Although I assume nonlocal clay and temper resources reflect nonlocal pottery traded into the site in most cases, some raw clay may

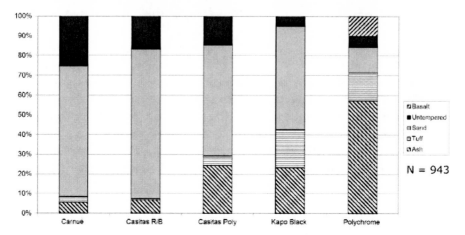

FIGURE 27. Distribution of nonmicaceous paste groups in most common types.

have been brought in as well. For example, Jicarilla Apache traded micaceous clay into colonial settlements (Eiselt 2006:333), and it seems likely that kin groups from Abiquiú gifted or traded clay from that mother village.

These results speak directly to archaeologists' observations that many of the common ceramic types in use in colonial New Mexico were clearly products of related temporal traditions (D. Levine 1990:180). Several people across the Casitas community were using polished black flange plates that looked quite similar in their form and appearance, especially from a distance (as in the earlier example, across a table during a meal). But the polished black wares were not all made from one type of clay, nor were the suite of polished black wares in any one disposal location (fig. 28) similar in their constituent materials (fig. 29). The more discursive aspects of final product forms are further discussed below, but it is worth noting here that the paste groups that constitute their proportional representation are themselves not correlated strictly along typological lines. In short, this is not a homogeneous assemblage by either type or paste.

These results beg the question of whether or not local or nonlocal potters who supplied the site were engaged in a classic form of resource

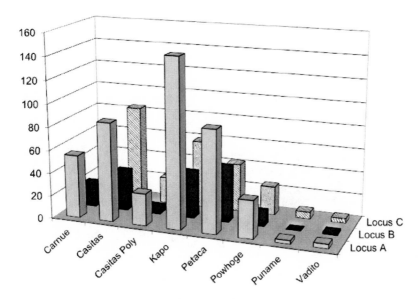

FIGURE 28. Ceramic analytical groups by disposal locus.

specialization (Rice 1991:262). Such specialization may have select use of particular resources in this stage of the manufacturing process. Alternatively, there may have been multiple potting communities accessing the same clay sources to produce a given type. This theme becomes evident through many stages of the ceramic production and challenges any attempt at characterization as a solely Indian village–based ceramic industry drawn from both precontact clay sources and manufacturing techniques.

This pattern of mixed resource use suggests that not all the pottery found in this colonial site was made by supposedly conservative Pueblo Indians. The situation is also more complex than an explanation of strictly Hispanicized potters would allow, since some of this pottery is either coming directly from potters based in Pueblo villages through trade or is being made locally by potters following a Pueblo *habitus* of temper use, sharing with Tewa potters a sense that ash is the proper temper to use. Using Burnished Black flange plates supplied to households at Casitas as an example, some potters preferentially

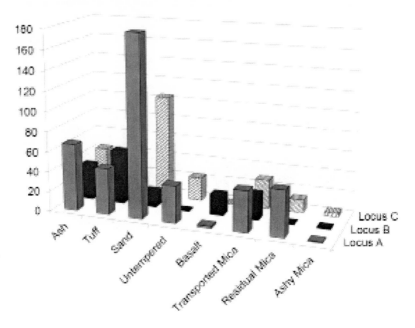

FIGURE 29. Ceramic paste groups by disposal locus.

used ash temper in the Tewa manner, while others used sand. The data might be interpreted as suggesting that these two groups were separate communities of potters or that they were similar but constrained by different local material choices. A third, much less likely scenario, is that two communities of potters were producing pottery at Casitas and one was accessing raw materials from Española basin sources. Regardless, these data draw a historically monolithic model of strictly Native American ceramic production into direct inquiry.

Just how different was the use and disposal of pottery made of various pastes across the site? The proportion of pastes present in the different midden contexts at Casitas confirm a statistically significant difference (fig. 30) in the way ceramics were distributed with respect to their raw material sources. Loci A and C were not significantly different in the proportion of pastes present, but both were significantly different from Locus B. Potters using materials from different sources supplied the households that contributed to the various disposal loci. Higher

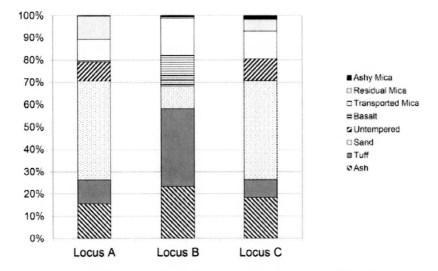

FIGURE 30. Differences in paste proportions by locus. All loci differ significantly by paste (χ2 = 203, df = 12, ρ < 0.01), as do comparisons between Locus A and Locus B (χ2 =158.5, df = 8, ρ < 0.01) and between Locus B and Locus C (χ2 = 128.5, df = 8, ρ < 0.01). Locus A and Locus C are not significantly different (χ2 = 9.381, df = 7, ρ = 0.226).

resolutions of paste group proportions at each locus confirm the depth and breadth of this difference. A statistical analysis of this difference of paste group representations among loci is needed to explicate local versus nonlocal sourcing, while accounting for differences in total numbers of sherds, or number of identified specimens (NISP) at each loci.

For most pastes, chi-square tests (Shennan 1997; Pallant 2005:288) indicate that there is a significant difference between Locus B and the other two loci, save for the micaceous wares. Micaceous pottery at Casitas appears with greater frequencies at Locus A than at Locus B, whereas Locus C seems to have a proportion of micaceous wares that resonate with both. This means that Loci A and B likely were supplied with more residual micaceous pottery or raw clay than Locus B, something that is closely associated (Eiselt 2006) with Jicarilla pottery manufacture in this part of the San Juan Mountains and found at the La Madera source (fig. 26). The only micaceous paste proportions between Loci A and B falling outside of significant values ($p < 0.01$) are those that represent micaceous-slipped wares, possibly from northern Tiwa sources, probably because of their limited representation across the site as a whole.

The question addressed by these statistical analyses is one of differences in chains of supply to the various households whose trash aggregated in the three disposal loci. In this sense, paste groups are proxies for sources of vessels that might otherwise look the same and serve the same functions. As shorthand geographic references, ash tempers come from Tewa areas, basalt from Keresan areas, and the untempered and coarse sand-tempered pastes are local to Casitas. To a lesser extent, these analyses compare the relative proportions of paste types to evaluate the likelihood that potters from a single community may have used multiple clay sources.

While Loci A and B are significantly different from each other, as are Loci B and Locus C, in the proportions of paste types, they are less so among micaceous pastes and ashy pastes (fig. 31). This relative proportion of pastes is borne out by a subsequent check of Locus A against Locus C pastes, as they are not statistically different except for in those micaceous paste groups (E and F) that occur in the assemblage in too few numbers for use in the test. Many of the materials used in the ceramics at Loci A and C were similar in proportion, but Locus B had a different kind of material profile.

The take-home message from statistical analysis of the ceramic assemblage is that the preponderance of plain ware ceramics disposed at Locus B were ash and tuff tempered, and most likely had southern origins in the Española valley. (As chi-square tests helped to establish differences in the nature of paste representation across Casitas, a higher-resolution test was needed to measure the differential presence of each of the paste types in each spatially segregated disposal locus. Pastes types were individually evaluated for their presence in comparison between disposal loci via statistical methods, including the Z-test. This nonparametric test is used to compare the proportions from two independent groups to determine if they are significantly different from one another. This calculates both one-tailed and two-tailed tests to evaluate the null hypothesis that the two proportions are equal. The two-tailed test result is more relevant, as a one-tailed test is used to determine if one proportion is greater [or lower] than another, as was observed.) For the other two loci, local untempered and coarse sand pastes dominate. Furthermore, basalt-rich pastes are almost exclusive to Locus B, particularly in the polychromes, suggesting a source near Keresan Pueblos, such as

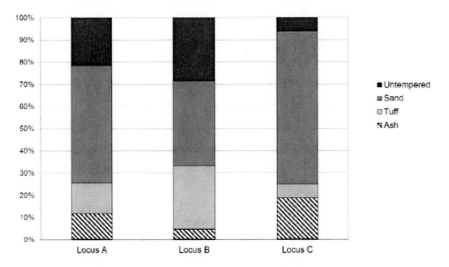

FIGURE 31. Difference in constituent pastes of Culinary Plain at each locus ($\chi 2 = 2.27E2$, df $= 12$, $\rho < 0.05$).

Zia, San Felipe, or Santa Ana, though historic, non-Pueblo sites in the Cochiti area are reported to have similar constituent basalts (Warren 1979:36). Households who contributed trash to Locus B were importing more ceramics from more distant, likely Pueblo sources than the more locally produced pottery at Loci A and C, even though the types were outwardly similar in appearance at all three loci.

A closer look at the grouping of paste categories reveals that not only were the various pastes differently distributed across the site, but they were also differently represented within the wares at each locus. As an example of this phenomenon (fig. 31), Culinary Plain vessels present in each locus in different proportions, but they were created with different materials in each. Statistically, the proportion of pastes making up the Culinary Plain sample at Locus C was significantly different than those in Culinary Plain at Loci A and B.

In summary, multiple households were supplied with and used similar-looking versions of a small range of simple vessels. Paste composition suggests that households were not getting these vessels in equal proportions from the same potters. The same is true for all analytical groups in the sense that multiple material sources were used to create the full suite of recognized types. This suggests multiple origins for vessels of each kind of pottery. Local and nonlocal clays were used to make pottery that had similar forms and surface presentations. So, in the example of someone using a Culinary Plain pot, they may have known of more than one community of potters creating vessels that looked similar. Access to Culinary Plain made from particular clays was not the same across the site, which meant some households had more access to imported pottery, while other households relied on local products. This strongly suggests that ceramics from the different household disposal sites were channeled through differential social mechanisms of both local and nonlocal production and exchange. In turn, this implies diversity rather than uniformity in the extended social networks of community households.

## Transformations of Clay into Tools

If some of the ceramics in use at Casitas were made from local materials and others from more distant sources, how might one track the practices shared by potters drawing on the same *habitus* of using those materials to form vessels? In other words, how are ceramics crafted within one community of potters? The preceding analysis of paste distributions must be contextualized by the way those pastes were transformed into vessels. The next stages in the operational sequence begin to translate the *habitus* of the ceramic producer to the consumer rather than solely being a reflection of potters' choice of material constituents. To some extent, the standards and preferences of the consumer determined potters' choices. How to examine the relationships between source and form?

In building these vessels up from the traditional pancake of clay at the base (Snow 1984:108), there were multiple potential choices that potters could have made in basic forming and finishing. Historical and archaeological data from the late colonial era document Spanish potters using wheels to throw pottery (Foster 1959; Curtis 1962; Lister and Lister 1976; Rodríguez-Alegría et al. 2003). Some knowledge of this likely made it to the northern colony via colonists who had visited or lived in urban Mexico, although no evidence (Rice 1987:129) of wheel manufacture was observed in the assemblage from Casitas. The majority of sherds from Casitas whose material signatures of construction were not obliterated or obscured by finishing suggest that potters who created the assemblage employed what archaeologists call the coil and scrape method (Shepard 1956:57). Bonding coils by direct pressure and then obliterating them with the use of a gourd scraper is common among Tewa potters (Peterson 1977:125; Blair and Blair 1986:97; Kramer 1996:71) and is in line with the dominant technological style in the Rio Grande region.

Table 4. Requisite characteristics for construction/finish designations

| Construction/ finish | Fracture patterns | Interior surface topography | Interior surface texture | Interior grain exposure | Inclusion orientation |
|---|---|---|---|---|---|
| Coil/Scrape | Stepwise | Semi-smooth | Fine parallel striations | Pulled grains, voids | Independent whorls |
| Paddle/Anvil | Laminar | Smooth | Sand-paper like | Equi-distant, compact | Parallel to surfaces |
| Pinch/ Drawing/Slab | Random | Lumpy | Grainy | Variegated | Random |

Source: After Rye 1981:59; Shepard 1956:183.

Similarly, molding and its related technique of paddle and anvil forming and finishing had multiple sources, including Mestizo traditions from Mexico (Foster 1948; Carrillo 1997:146), as well as Yuman, Piman, Shoshone, and certain Plains groups (Gifford 1935; Shepard 1956:185). Paddle and anvil techniques are also visible in the Casitas assemblage. A small number of pinched (8) or slab built (10) examples were also identified in the sample, mostly associated with irregular forms such as candlestick holders or *comal* fragments (Ewan 1991; Rodríguez-Alegría 2002).

While the analysis might have benefited from X-ray data regarding alternating densities in sherd walls (Rye 1981:69), experimental results with this method were mixed and abandoned. Instead, database entries list coil and scrape for sherds that exhibited stepwise fracture patterns (Pierce 2005:85), as opposed to laminar (Rye 1981:61; D. Hill 1984) or indeterminate fracture trends observed otherwise (Table 4). Observation of the parallel orientation or clustered whorls of asymmetrical or nonequidimensional paste inclusions (Shepard 1956:183) in the second round of microscope examination for paste sorts allowed me to modify database entries of construction type for sherds with not immediately identifiable construction methods. Shepard (1956:184) observed similar phenomena in the orientation of platy fragments of fine vitric ash temper at assemblages from Pecos.

Tracking the use of finishing techniques such as scraping or paddling is much more challenging throughout the nonmicaceous wares,

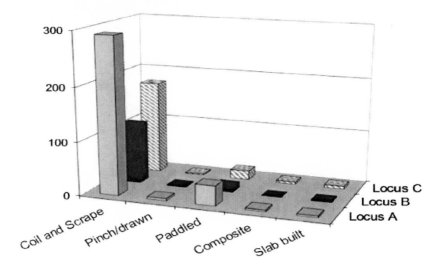

FIGURE 32. Construction and finish techniques by locus.

as potters often obliterated telltale surface features in the burnishing step that occurs frequently on these types. For the sample subset that retained some clues of construction and finishing techniques, the overall preponderance of coil and scraped vessels suggests that most potters who supplied Casitas used this technique for the nonmicaceous wares (fig. 32). Some vessels exhibited a mix of techniques (such as coil and scrape with convex molding) on a single sherd were recorded as composite. Such hybridity in forming techniques again complicates any simplistic attempt to separate Pueblo Indian from Hispanic–Mestizo pottery practices.

Likewise, the measured thickness of the vessels produced in various types is related not only to the range of choices for construction and finishing techniques of each vessel being produced but also to the size and function of the vessels. As a whole these attributes are linked to the potters making those choices. Because of the difficulties inherent in clearly identifying forming techniques, I relied on the quantitative evaluation of vessel thickness to relate community choices that influenced potters in the course of creating the different analytical groups (Table 2). The forming processes themselves are paramount to the thickness of construction, as relate to overall vessel weight-to-volume ratios. Such ratios are indices of vessel size and function, attributes which, in addition to the location from which the specimens originated (in this case, rim sherds), must be controlled for in statistical analyses to follow. This measure reflects the continuum of compromises (Rice 1987:227) potters balanced while creating everything from durable cups to large storage ollas, the functions of which are discussed below. The resultant modes of vessel thickness are significantly different by an analysis of variance (ANOVA, after Pallant 2005:231) by type (fig. 33). As Pallant describes (2005:229) the advantage of using this test is not only in how it tracks the changes in mean thickness with each independent variable of vessel shape, size, and analytical group/type but also in how it allows for evaluation of an interaction effect between the variables themselves: "An interaction effect occurs when the effect of one independent variable on the dependent variable depends on the level of a second independent variable" (Pallant 2005:229). So, given the categorical independent variables of locus, type, and form as well as the continuous dependent variable of thickness, the ANOVA test describes the relationship of locus and vessel type to the thickness of a given sherd in a range of forms. Although Puname-like polychromes and Slipped Micaceous sherds occur in numbers too small to use in ANOVA, the general trend expressed in this analysis is of plain wares significantly different than the thicker polychromes and the thinner, unslipped micaceous wares. Having obtained significant results for the interaction effects on thickness, follow-up tests on subsets of similar-sized and -shaped vessels within analytical groups explore this relationship further.

Smudged Red-on-Brown is significantly thinner than all of the plain wares ($p < 0.05$) as well as polychromes ($p < 0.01$). This is telling of its unique range of production and use influences at Locus C. A community of potters in Casitas created this variant of Red-on-Brown used forming techniques that resulted in a much thinner range of thickness, perhaps techniques more in line with those of similarly thin residual micaceous wares attributed to Jicarilla Apache production (Eiselt 2004). This attribute distinguishes it from other vessels in most iterations of vessel form and size observed from Casitas. As an example, the significant difference in the thicknesses of bowls (as the most populous vessel form) among the polychromes are apparent when plotted (fig. 34) by minimum and maximum thicknesses against their sample size and mean thicknesses.

Plotted this way, such a trend is more difficult, although not impossible, to see. When looking at such a large assemblage with seemingly close wall thickness tolerances exhibited across the types, most analysts

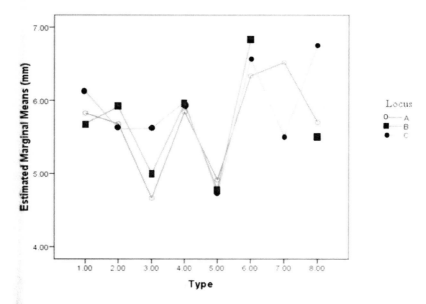

FIGURE 33. Estimated marginal means of thickness by type at each locus (X Axis Type codes: 1 = Culinary Plain; 2 = Red-on-Brown; 3 = Smudged Red-on-Brown; 4 = Burnished Black; 5 = Thin Micaceous; 6 = Powhoge Polychrome; 7 = Puname Polychrome; 8 = Slipped Micaceous).

probably would not be able to pick up on how thickness within a single analytical category varied uniquely across vessel types and sizes across the whole assemblage. The statistical method employed here can tease out data about thickness ratios of sherds related to the size and function of the pots that they came from. Having a separate source of data to correlate with rim diameters allows a check for whether or not potters who created the suite of polychrome bowls at Casitas were likely making them in different sizes and volumes. Otherwise, when rim sherds are of insufficient portions to faithfully record radius and circumference (Rye 1981:223), pot thickness-to-form ratio is a piece of information that makes multiple caliper measurements on each sherd worth the effort. Measuring thickness is useful to the archaeologist because it is one indication of form. Thickness in the final forming processes is arguably less a product of consumer preference for the potter than it is about how the pottery learned to make pots.

Demands of the consumer in part dictated the size of the final product. So does the workability of clay available, the suitability of stiffness

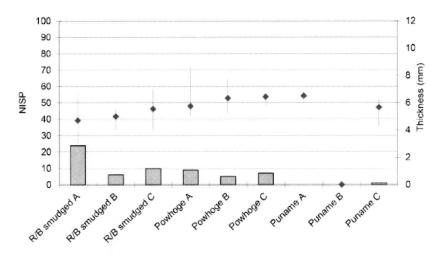

FIGURE 34. Polychrome bowl number of identified specimens (*lower solid bars*), minimum, maximum, and average thicknesses (*diamonds with variation*) by locus and type.

imparted by select tempers, and the pressures exerted on vessel walls by the forming and finishing practices of a particularly skilled potter (Rye 1981:60). All of these variables contribute to the vessel wall thickness. In the absence of whole vessels, knowing how to group and relate similarly thick sherds allows for a closer study of available evidence regarding forming and finishing.

In another example from Casitas, most of the plain ware types are much closer in their thickness profiles (fig. 35). This is a departure from the trend discussed above and suggests that plain ware vessels of similar size, in this particular form (bowls), are not being made by potters who create variation when forming the upper walls and rims of their vessels. The mental template shared in this case is much more tightly constrained than in the polychromes. Returning to the example of hemispherical Red-on-Brown bowls sitting on a table, such data suggest that consumer expectations for plain ware bowls demanded that they fall within parameters for regularity in thickness, perhaps for stacking, storage, or portion-size concerns related to individual serving vessels. Such constraints did not apparently apply to the thickness of polychrome bowls, as they exhibit greater diversity in thickness. This may be a result of potters supplying households who follow different foodways: those

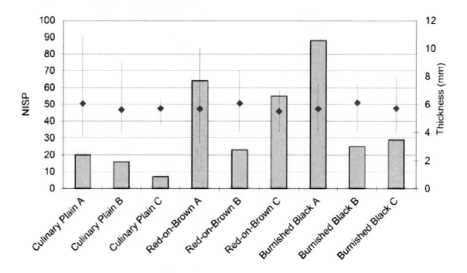

FIGURE 35. Plain ware bowl number of identified specimens (*lower solid bars*), minimum, maximum, and average thicknesses (*diamonds with variation*) by locus and type.

who use bigger bowls for communal food service and those who demand individually sized vessels.

Although vessel walls were likely continuously evaluated for their thickness (Blair and Blair 1986:97) during the construction sequence, one of the last things that occurred in the sequence of building operations before surface treatments like burnishing were added was shaping of the distal edge of vessels at the lip (fig. 36). As this is not as overtly characteristic of a vessel as its overall form or decoration (Shepard 1956:246), this allows for some measure of disengagement from the constraints of function and the dictates of consumer choice to which potters were responding. Rather, such features are more of a stylistic manifestation of the community of practice from which a potter learned her trade, a muscle memory of appropriate shape enacted in the last moments before the clay is left to dry to leather-hard. How potters did this probably did not affect the mechanical and technical suitability of a vessel. Such behavioral traces are idiosyncratic, something that a potter learned to do a certain way as part of a shared learning community. Lip forming can be described as a moment in which:

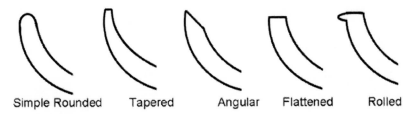

Simple Rounded    Tapered    Angular    Flattened    Rolled

FIGURE 36. Ceramic lip forms at Casitas.

no thinking or decision-making process takes place. Only a series of psycho-motor schemata are involved which are acquired during the learning process, gradually becoming deeply rooted through practice . . . the learning process, being the focus of close interaction between teacher and pupil makes possible the transmission of the psycho-motor schemata and their persistence from one generation to another. No other social pressure would seem to prevent the future potter from adopting any particular technological schema at any time. The procedure of acquiring the technique is alone responsible for its uniformity. (Gosselain 1992:570)

Across the site, lip forms are not equally represented; the difference is statistically significant between Loci B and C (fig. 37). This is a departure from the trend observed in paste distributions by locus described above, where Locus B was significantly different from both Locus A and Locus C. While the proportional use of paste materials was different between Loci A and B, these two loci are less different in the proportion of lip forms present in the assemblage. The statistical test takes into account sample size and relative proportions and suggests that the trend in difference at Casitas is less about access to different clays than it is about who trained the potters to make the various lip forms.

When paste groups are used to compare lip forms (figs. 38 and 39), distinct patterns of clay use emerge within the vessels with tapered and rolled lip forms. Sand and untempered paste groups dominate tapered lips on plain wares, suggesting that these forms are more closely associated with clay sources local to Casitas. In the micaceous wares, tapered rim forms are almost completely made from local micaceous pastes, which contain smaller mica plates with mixed lithic sand. Also distinct, the rolled lip forms are evenly split between only sand and ash tempers in plain wares, with ashy micaceous pastes from sources more distant from Casitas constituting the entirety of micaceous pots with rolled lips.

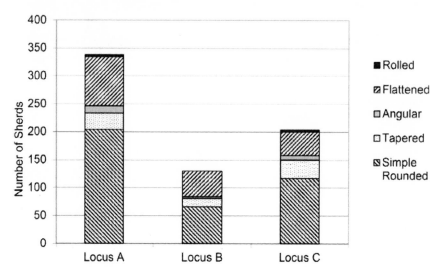

FIGURE 37. Lip form frequencies by locus. Overall, lip forms differ significantly across the site ($\chi2 = 11.591$, df = 4, $\rho < 0.05$), specifically between Locus
B and Locus C ($\chi2 = 11.591$, df = 4, $\rho < 0.05$). Locus A and Locus B are not
significantly different ($\chi2 = 7.424$, df = 4, $\rho = 0.115$), nor are Locus A and
Locus C ($\chi2 = 8.708$, df = 4, $\rho = 0.069$).

By contrast, simple rounded, angular, and flattened lips are not significantly different in what paste groups they are made from ($\chi2 = 5.977$, df
= 7, $\rho = 0.542$). These lip forms share similar constituent proportions of
the untempered and coarse sand-tempered pastes found in the Culinary
Plain and Red-on-Brown wares, as well as the fine sand and primary
micaceous clays found in the thinner-walled micaceous wares.

Simple rounded, angular, and flattened lip forms are made of a range
of pastes that, though proportionately more local to Casitas, are representative of the full suite of clay and temper types available to potting
communities in the northern Rio Grande (fig. 38). Potters who were
closely related to each other drew from clay sources available closer to
where they lived (Gosselain 1992:564). Such practices hint at processes
of translocation of learning and muscle memory that found potters who
drew from similar traditions located in places where they were making
pots from new and disparate clay sources.

The evidence points to crosscutting practices in clay and temper used
to make vessels with all varieties of lip forms except for in the tapered

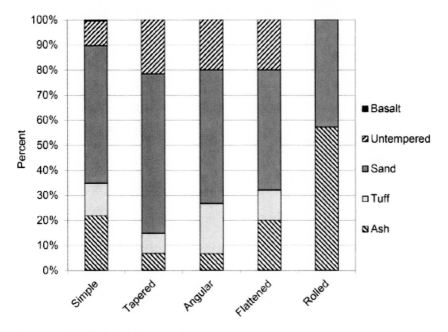

FIGURE 38. Lip forms by nonmicaceous paste groups.

and rolled styles. In the micaceous subassemblage particularly (fig. 39), the tapered rim forms resemble those ascribed to Apache and northern Tiwa potting communities (Eiselt 2004:538, 544), whereas the rolled lip forms more closely align with the poorly defined historic Tewa micaceous wares (Eiselt 2004:528). These lip forms' separation by paste groups is a further delineation between the communities of practice in which they not only learned to form pots of particular thickness and lip forms but also learned to gather "appropriate" raw materials.

## The Thermodynamic Art of Firing

A surface treatment such as high polish or vessel decoration pre-ceded firing and is the final step in the sequence of production. The most important contributions to color observed in fired clay are made by the carbon and iron composition of the clay. These constituents change color most dramatically to unaided observation, based on the firing duration, temperature, and atmosphere, allowing for measures of "how well a vessel is fired" if not exactly how (Shepard 1956:214). As the

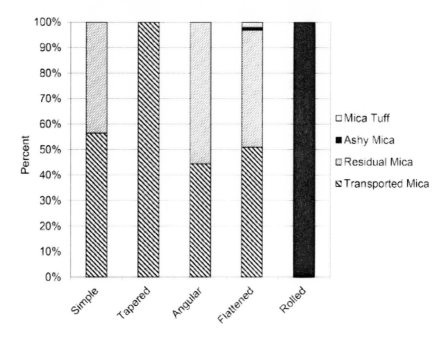

FIGURE 39. Lip forms by micaceous paste groups.

surface characteristics of the types present at Casitas are well described in the literature and discussed in relative frequency above, firing regimes are considered for their contributions to the distinct patterning of the assemblage. Data from my own experimental firing with multiple fuel sources, ethnographic accounts (Carrillo 1997:170), and from Anna O. Shepard's (1956:79) test results set a reasonable expectation for initial firing temperature of the Casitas pottery to between 500°C and 700°C.

I also conducted experimental refiring (after Shepard 1956:222) on a subset of the sample representing sherds from each paste group and type. This methodology involves iterative firing of small chips from the archaeological sherds in order to observe the temperatures at which the specimen changes colors. At that point, oxidation of minerals within the clay occurs at a temperature beyond that experienced by the vessel during its initial firing. I recorded surface and paste color changes on each refired sherd for each heating. Changes in paste color served as the primary measure of change, because surface treatments such as paint or slip do not always change color and are not as consistent between vessel types and forms in the same manner of paste.

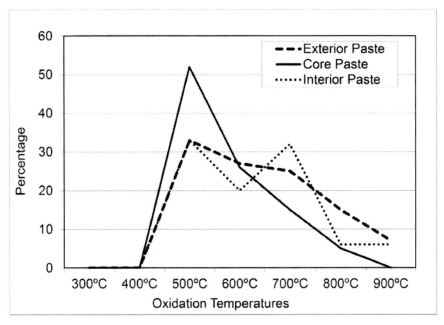

FIGURE 40. Refire temperature change profiles.

The results of the refiring experiment confirm that the majority of the sherds within the sample subset were fired to temperatures between 500°C and 700°C (fig. 40). Additionally, the differences between interior and exterior changes in color relate to the presence of firing cores with substantial carbon content that had not been burned out in the initial firing. The refiring therefore effected a change in color for these interior pastes at a much lower temperature than was required to change the paste fabric closer to the surface.

These results track well with the range of ethnographic clay sources, fuel choices, firing techniques, and firing durations observed in the northern Rio Grande by Shepard (1956:83). Her records for Tewa polished black and red wares, as well as polychromes from Zia and black-on-cream wares from Cochiti indicated that the lowest temperature of firing was 625°C. In her descriptions, Shepard describes higher temperatures but shorter firing durations for dung fuel (1956:78). I experimentally verified this effect by firing newly made vessels of old clay sources in both wood and dung fuel types, and I observed color ranges that closely matched archaeological specimens. Firing core thicknesses and colors, similar to the range of variation seen in the archaeological assemblage (fig. 41), were observed in the fired experimental vessels. Such close correspondence between refire temperatures suggests that vessels achieved similar maturation temperatures before circulation to users. Were they fired in similar thermal environments using comparable technology?

I tabulated firing profiles and paste color of various sherds from Casitas to code the range of oxidized and reduced colors following Rye (1981). Oxidation refers to the chemical process of a change in the oxidation state of iron and other elements, which results in a color change from firing. Another color change can occur through firing when carbon, such as organics included in the unfired paste, is burned off in the firing process. This can occur without iron achieving full oxidation. These two separate processes are different from that of reducing clays during firing. When oxygen is eliminated from the firing atmosphere of the pottery, free carbon atoms rob oxygen molecules within the clay body itself, reducing it to darker colors. Carbon may also be deposited on the surface of a vessel (smudging) by direct contact with burning fuels. These processes are more difficult to separate in open firings and can be achieved by smothering firing elements with dung. The resultant colors are a quick index to the process: orange or yellow paste often means a firing in an oxidizing atmosphere. Gray or black paste can be achieved by reduction, incomplete combustion of organics, smudging (carbon deposition), or some combination of these techniques.

Firing profile colors in the cross section are the result of different stages of firing and the extent to which oxidization or reduction penetrated the vessel's walls (Rye 1981:116). For vessels from Casitas, I recorded the different patterns of color banding observed in cross section of the sherds as codes describing the oxidation or nonoxidation of materials within the clay body. After Rye (1981:115), oxidation was recorded with a designation of "O," and carbon remaining within the clay body or affixed by other processes was recorded as "R."

In the case of Burnished Black vessels, ethnographic accounts describe the addition of manure at peak firing temperature to close off the supply of oxygen and deposit carbon on vessel surfaces and in the pores (LeFree 1975:63–65). Patterns of color in firing profiles can be a marker of not only firing atmosphere and temperature but also the addition of materials during or immediately after the firing process that fix carbon to the surface of vessels. The thickness of those alternating bands of color in cross section relate the rate of heating and cooling, also affected by the combustible content and tightness or looseness of stacked fuel materials.

Dung used to build masonry-like "walls" that mounded up and over firing vessels in practices described for Tewa potters (Kramer 1996:74) not only affixed carbon to the surface of those vessels but also changed the ratio of oxygen within the firing environment.

As noted above, colors observed in cross section of each sherd are different because of variability in firing duration, temperature, and atmosphere. For example, a black core with lighter margins such those found in some sherds labeled "ORO" implies that organic material in the clay was not completely burned out. Such a profile could be the result of a short, low-temperature firing. A dark core and light surfaces could be indicative of reoxidation after the vessel was blackened by carbon deposition that creates a thin layer of "natural" clay color parallel to the surface of the sherd; or reduction early in firing, followed by oxidation later in firing (Rye 1981:118). In contrast, vessels that were well fired, with a fully oxidized cross section, have more even paste color, with little to no apparent firing core.

As expected from the well-known description of the most common type of Burnished Black (Mera 1939), the largest proportion of smudged and reduced sherds within the plain ware categories did in fact belong to that type (fig. 41). The assemblage also exhibited a fairly even proportion of Burnished Black vessels across the firing core profiles, excepting the dual-toned "RO" category. This suggests that those Burnished Black wares that did not have the distinctive carbon-affixed "ROR" profile were still going through a smudging process to affix carbon to their surfaces but otherwise were fired in regimes similar to other plain ware pottery in the assemblage. The relative dearth of Burnished Black in "RO" profile counts speaks to the concentration of potters who avoided firing conditions that did not evenly reduce their Burnished Black pottery on exterior and interior surfaces, something uniquely controlled for in this analytical group.

Red-on-Brown sherds dominate "ORO" firing profile counts, with their distinct dark firing core. This suggests that this type was likely fired over shorter periods than types that exhibited fewer changes in color across their profiles. I was able to experimentally verify that high oxidation at the surfaces and lack of heat saturation through the clay fabric is concomitant with the firing temperature profiles observed by Shepard (1956:78). A low proportion of fire clouds on Casitas vessels attests to the control with which potters maintained protective buffers from fuels even as tricky to work with as dung.

The firing profile characterizations of micaceous wares at Casitas tells a story that perhaps has less to do with production of these vessels than

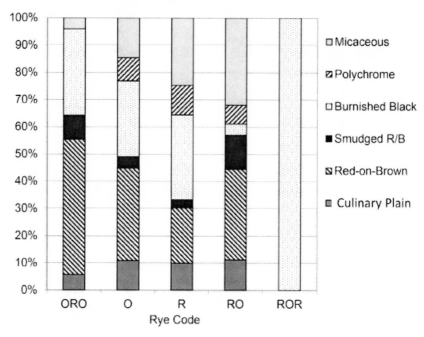

FIGURE 41. Carbon core profiles by type.

it does with their later use as cooking pots. While some carbon within these pots is well burned out by constant duty on hearths, the occurrence of two-toned firing profiles reflects the temperature gradient from outside the vessel to the interior closest to foodstuffs. For this reason, I collected data on firing cores that included interior versus exterior profile colors. In the preponderance of micaceous sherds that exhibit two-toned oxidation gradients, the lighter portion is closer to the exterior 93 percent, with the carbon-rich profile closer to the interior of the vessel. Only 7 percent of the two-toned sherds are oriented in the other direction. Carbon sooting, present on the exterior of many of the micaceous sherds, serves to reinforce their use as the workhorse cooking vessels of the Casitas hearthscape.

I also observed a second, bimodal distribution of these same two firing profiles across the vessel forms, suggesting a connection between the firing conditions of types that are represented in bowls (fig. 42) and some other, related strategy of firing. As discussed above, the relative proportion of two-toned firing profiles "RO" is evidence of incomplete oxidation or variation in temperature and atmosphere as a result of one

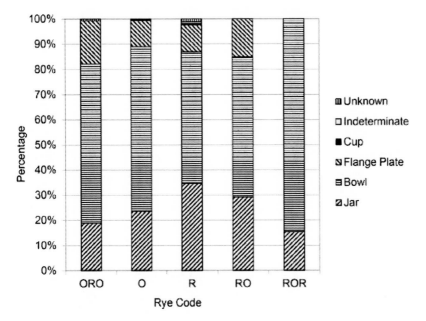

FIGURE 42. Carbon core profiles by form

side of the vessel having been differentially exposed to heat or oxygen (Rye 1981:117). If this gradient was not created by use as a cooking vessel, as in micaceous wares, then another source of such difference could have come from firing in an inverted position or differential heating by other means. These profiles types dominate the micaceous bowl forms and may indicate that bowls may have been stacked (Carrillo 1997:145) in the firing setting to achieve the heat or oxygen differential. I observed a similar effect in vessels during my experimental firing with field clays. Techniques such as stacking may reflect processes of surplus production and standardization (Orton et al. 1993:69) that resonate with the mold-made signature of vessels discussed above.

Taken as a whole, data regarding firing temperatures, durations, and settings strongly suggest that pottery produced for consumption at Casitas was created to meet certain well-patterned standards of color, size, and shape. Minimizing fuel required makes sense in terms of the economies of time and resources it would take individual potters to produce vessels for neighborhood use and exchange: a short firing time to achieve the buff fabric colors of nonsmudged plain wares, as well as the fully reduced surfaces of a Burnished Black. Stacking vessels facilitates firing batches of pottery, and protecting those not smudged from fire clouding. In what other ways is the standardization of pottery making important?

## Pots in Performance

The previous observations about steps in ceramic production focused on those traits whose properties may have been less conspicuous to household consumers. Comparing final ceramic products with household consumption patterns emphasizes the interrelatedness of their contexts. Community making and using these pots reinforced and shared practices that reflected foodway use, ceramic demand, and cultural identity. A cook like Eufemia would have just as carefully chosen her pottery as her ingredients for use in a feasting performance.

Typologies of colonial-era northern New Mexico vessel forms (Mera 1939; Harlow 1974; Blair and Blair 1986; Eiselt 2004) demonstrate that potters from different parts of the Tewa basin used similar vessel form patterns as part of a shared mental template. Similarly, ethnic Spanish and other colonial potters participated in maintaining a minimum repertoire of vessel forms throughout the Spanish empire (Lister and Lister 1976). These forms are loosely mirrored in the suite of vessel forms present at Casitas (fig. 43). I evaluated the size and shape of vessels in the sample by comparing diameter/circumference templates (Rice 1987:223) with profiles from archaeological reconstructions at other colonial sites (Dick [1964] 1968; Lister and Lister 1976; Carrillo 1997; Hanowell 2006). I aggregated these forms into simple categories: flange plate, cup, bowl, jar, olla, and indeterminate/other. Forms of the last category included rare examples of candlestick holders, comales, and cosmetic cupules (Carrillo 2006, pers. comm.).

Other potters within and outside of their own communities informed the skill of those who crafted what would later be a crucial part of foodway performance. As a result, vessels at Casitas were a mix of forms across the types (fig. 44) and show how pots engaged multiple stages of food storage, preparation, and consumption. Indeed, it is paramount to consider these functions within the ceramic assemblage, as it would seem that most manifestations of foodways in colonial sites were intimately related to the use of ceramics of particular forms (Harrington 1916; Cushing 1920; Gilbert 1970; Hughes 1977; Gilbert 1982).

Jars served as cooking and storage vessels (Henrickson and McDonald 1983:631–33) as noted ethnohistorically for *indio* people (Harrington 1916; Cushing 1920) as well as Spanish colonists (Lister and Lister 1976).

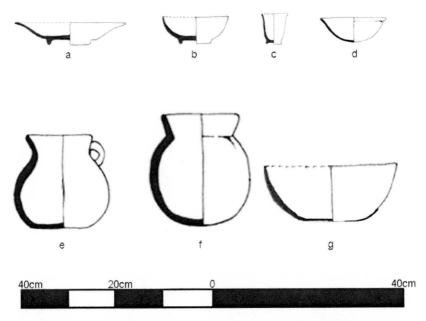

FIGURE 43. Reconstructed vessel forms from Casitas (adapted by author after Dick 1964; Lister and Lister 1976; Carrillo 1997; Hanowell 2006): (*a*) flange plate; (*b*) bowl (hemispherical); (*c*) cup; (*d*) bowl (escudillas); (*e*) jar (globular); (*f*) jar (olla); (*g*) bowl (large hemispherical).

One notable exception to the almost exclusive use of jars as cooking vessels comes from a Tewa account of using a large bowl filled with heated sand to pop corn (Blair and Blair 1986:100). Other jar uses such as the lime processing of corn shows up in the assemblage by noting distinct calcium carbonate rings in the upper necks of some jars. Calcium carbonate rings are likely related to the addition of lime to soaking corn kernels during the preparation of *nixtamal* (Gilbert 1970:5). Micaceous wares are the most represented by jars in the Casitas assemblage, corresponding with ethnohistoric accounts of their use as cooking vessels (Carrillo 1997; D. Anderson 1999; Eiselt 2004) as well as the cross-sectional heat gradient evidence described above. Jars are also a substantial portion of the polychrome vessels at Casitas. Large ollas for liquid carrying, storage, and presentation of contained goods was an enduring practice in indigenous and colonial New Mexico (Warren 1976:B38; Snow 1982:265), Iberian Spain (Curtis 1962:490), and other places in New Spain (Lister

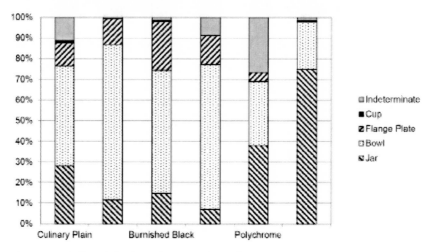

FIGURE 44. Vessel form proportions in each type across Casitas.

and Lister 1976:85). These practices were largely carried on in the Casitas context by Polychrome and, to a lesser extent, Culinary Plain vessels.

Individual-sized serving vessels such as flange plates, cups, and small bowls are concentrated in plain wares, though there is some evidence of this use for polychrome flange plates. The shapes, sizing, and presumed serving function of these vessel forms parallel those forms from other Spanish colonial regions (Lister and Lister 1976), other colonial-era New Mexican sites (Carrillo 1997:221–222), and mission sites in Mexico (Caywood 1950:85) and California (Hanowell 2006). Conversely, if Native American communities mostly used large bowls to share daily food (Elkins 2007) as well as during ritual feasts (Potter 2000) in pre-contact contexts, those practices can certainly have carried into colonial times (Rodríguez-Alegría 2005). In some cases, people may have helped themselves to food directly from preparation vessels. Historic accounts illustrate such practices more often to differentiate between the etiquette of "proper" colonial citizens and the lack of manners exhibited by *indios bárbaros* (Archibeque et al. 2000:303). Indeed, social prescriptions for eating at the table and from one's own vessel were strong enough in the upper echelons of Spanish colonial society to serve as a point of defamation in court for a Spaniard who would lower himself to eating on the floor with Indians (Rodríguez-Alegría 2005:557).

Types like Burnished Black and Polychromes are not distributed equally across the site (fig. 28). Noting this pattern is important for

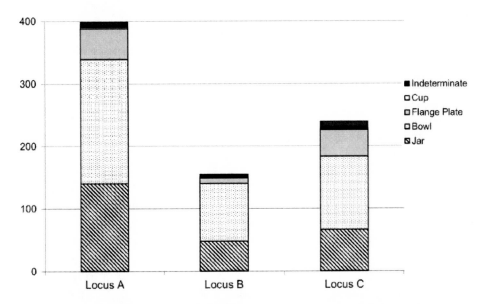

FIGURE 45. Differences in vessel forms by locus. Vessel forms differ significantly across the site ($\chi 2 = 25.56$, df = 10, $\rho < 0.01$), especially between Locus B and Locus C ($\chi 2 = 19.559$, df = 5, $\rho < 0.01$) but not between Locus A and Locus B ($\chi 2 = 8.650$, df = 5, $\rho = .124$). Locus A and Locus C are not quite significantly different ($\chi 2 = 10.878$, df = 5, $\rho = 0.054$).

discerning the significance of differences between vessel form distributions across the site. In this, paired chi-square tests allow for a better understanding of how these vessels were manifest at each disposal location in relation to each other. Overall, the occurrence of vessel forms is significantly different between disposal loci (fig. 45), with the difference between Loci B and C being the greatest. Given that Loci A and B are not statistically different in their proportion of vessel forms, by this measure the spatial pattern seen before in types holds true.

I was also able to discern a break in patterning between material signatures for those who made the pots and how those who were using them were distributed across the site. As distributions for vessel form do not occur statistically different for Loci A and B, the significant difference of their constituent pastes signals a disparity in supply for these households that might not have been as observable via the suite of vessels as performing vessels. Although it has been shown before that households that contributed to the trash accumulations at Loci A and B were doing so from different supply chains of pottery producers, they were simultaneously using similar suites of vessel forms.

Having seen how some households at Casitas Viejas used similar suites of vessel forms, it remains to investigate how closely related those vessels were within the disposal loci. At a higher resolution of analysis, the size of a given vessel form suggests use based on simple assumptions about volume, opening size, and accessibility. Large bowls can accommodate multiple people taking food, whereas small bowls offer less utility for such communal use. As (Pitts 2004:51) describes it, "particular strategies of communal consumption are likely [to have required] specific vessel forms to facilitate their enactment." Conversely, some practices strictly require certain forms for individual consumption (e.g., cups, flange plates). Additional factors, such as whether or not the vessel could sit stable on a table, may have restricted the number of people who could have access to it, as opposed to a similar pot sitting on the floor. Other foodway uses for similarly shaped but differently sized bowls may also be an issue. For example, some larger bowls may have served as dough bowls for making yeast-leavened breads (David Snow 2008, pers. comm.). It becomes apparent that interpreting uses of similar-shaped vessels within a given household is important to teasing out their role in the hearthscapes of Casitas.

Plain wares such as Culinary Plain, Red-on-Brown, and Burnished Black dominate the occurrence of serving vessels across the site (fig. 44). Taking plain ware bowls as the largest and most directly comparable subsample, I plotted frequency distributions of these bowls' diameters by both their mean diameter and range of variation (fig. 46). The point is to demonstrate not only what ranges of variation in size each analytical group exhibited but also where mean diameters and clustering of similar sizes within the bowls is made meaningful by sample size.

The relationship of bowl diameters to disposal loci is most clear in types that not only demonstrate tightly constrained ranges of sizes in a given locus but also trend similarly to other types within that locus. For example, the overall small size of Culinary Plain bowls at Locus A is comparable with the Red-on-Brown and Burnished Black bowl sizes at the same Locus. In fact, Burnished Black bowls are the most consistently smaller-sized bowls across the site, highlighting their use as principally individual serving vessels. In contrast, Locus B Culinary Plain and Red-on-Brown bowls are larger in general and much more so at the larger end of the range of measurements. This suggests that more of these types were used as larger bowls in household contexts. Locus C also exhibits some

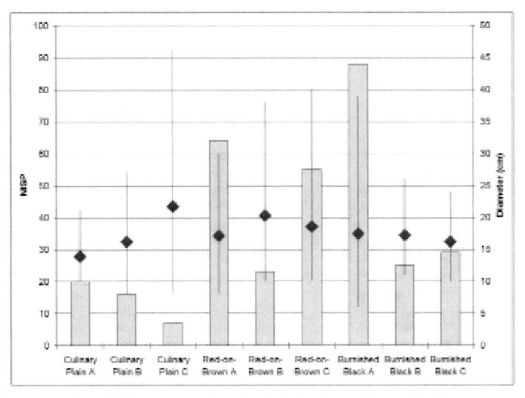

FIGURE 46. Plain ware bowls (*lower bars*), minimum, maximum, and average diameters (*diamonds with variation*) by locus and type.

trend toward larger Culinary Plain and Red-on-Brown bowls than Locus A, but less so than Locus B in Red-on-Browns and not at all in Burnished Black wares. Of the observed cut marks in the ceramic assemblage (35), all were located on plain ware bowls of smaller diameter (mean = 16 cm). These data suggest that the people who created Loci B and C used smaller sizes of Burnished Black serving bowls but also used greater numbers of larger Culinary Plain and Red-on-Brown bowls. Such trends are in contrast to the high proportion of imported pots in Locus B, which in turn suggests that these households were engaged in food presentations more aligned to precontact practices.

But just what foods might have been presented in dining performances using the elegant serving ceramics of Casitas? Many of those meals consisted of proteins contributed by animals raised or hunted by the families of the little *plazuela*. These ingredients are more closely investigated in the next chapter.

## A Process of Identity

The *casta* system of socioracial hierarchy experienced a typological collapse in New Mexico that reflected the importance of people of mixed or ambiguous ancestries in making the colony sustainable. Just as these labels did not work well for pigeonholing the people and behaviors of the colony, modern glosses such as "Hispanic" or "Indian" used by archaeologists or others labeling sites and cultural resources may also lack descriptive power and meaning for understanding the multiplicity of possible ways heritage could be experienced or enacted. These modern labels have been broadly applied to archaeological sites and contemporary communities in northern New Mexico. As scholars continue to wrangle with these concepts and to locate appropriate analytical frameworks, it is perhaps not surprising that policy makers continue to create racialized systems of legal inequity where stereotypes persist.

It is no small task to grapple with these issues. Yet the ceramic record at Casitas challenges archaeologists to evaluate some of the more common approaches for investigating identity on colonial frontiers. It is rarely satisfactory to look at the tangle of archaeological data in a simplified way, but it may prove useful to assess some of the material against a series of three models with divergent material expressions.

In the acculturation model, members of the Casitas community might have incorporated more or less of the material trappings of Spanish colonial society depending on how much they "bought into" the colonial ideals and associated identity aspects. By extension, the model of acculturation hypothesizes a dichotomous division of behaviors between Indian and Spanish identities. The presence of majolica equals Spanish identity, or an expression of Spanish identity. Similarly, the presence of polychrome pottery indicates Pueblo identity. That would mean that ceramic patterns should be visible as homogeneous among the three disposal loci. For a site labeled Spanish or Hispanic, the material correlates of behavior should, if not matching that of Seville or Mexico City, at least approximate the ceramic foodway behaviors at the capital of Spanish colonial New Mexico, Santa Fe (Bowen 1995; Snow and Bowen 1995). Simply put, this model tests the assumption that people who lived at Casitas "became more Hispano" via practices that mirrored Spanish culture. This does not preclude the possibility of coresiding "Spanish" and "Indian" cultural isolates. If indigenous people lived at the site, this model suggests that the ceramic signatures of their presence might also be located in a spatially distinct locus that mirrored Indian practices. Similarly at the larger scale, homescape practices should also align more or less strongly with one or the other of the categories that dichotomous labels imply. And if this would hold true, then overall the material patterns of those practices would be separable along the spectrum of pre- and postcontact idealized forms such as North African irrigation ditches versus ancestral Puebloan terracing.

In the second model, which hypothesizes creolization of material behaviors, household material culture, including ceramic patterns, at Casitas should exhibit hybridity of Indian and Spanish forms and/ or usage. Even so, such patterns should manifest as strictly differentiated between producer and consumer as a result of cultural mixing. For example, this may take the form of Indian food served in Spanish pottery, or vice versa, as interpreted at Spanish colonial sites in Florida (Deagan 1996). Characteristic or signal aspects of identity practice might be found in evidence for stages of artifact production, consumption, and disposal, similarly patterned among loci and within each independent material category. Most models of creolization posit a mixture of practices that are shared at the community level, with a commensurate level of resolution to see those patterns. Within material categories, this model would not expect practices to crosscut at these scales of behavior. If Casitas community behaviors included an "evening-out" of status differentiation and cultural practice in order to effect a unified Genízaro identity, as interpreted at San Jose de las Huertas (Rothschild 2003), then a similar homogenization of practices should be manifest in nearly similar deposits across the site. Homescape behaviors may also exhibit a blending of practices, but in ways parallel to foodway patterns, where practices "of European origin could be selected over aboriginal [practices] because of the greater prestige associated with the European in a mestizo milieu" (Deagan 1973:63).

In the third model posited by this volume, situational identity practices produce a plurality of identity-making behaviors that may crosscut choices between and within stages of production, use, and discard of multiple material categories involved in household foodways. Behavior that follows such a model may not closely parallel that from sites associated with either precontact indigenous societies or introduced European patterns but instead incorporate variable mixes of partially indigenous and European practices at different scales, and in different cultural settings. The disposal loci at a frontier site such as Casitas should exhibit not only intrasite diversity among the hearthscape assemblages but also intra-assemblage diversity in stages of the production, consumption, and/or use of artifacts within a material category such as ceramics. The material record of a Genízaro community that used strategies of situational identity practice would likely reflect differences in behavior at multiple temporal and spatial scales, including those at both the hearthscape and homescape.

In the end, the assumptions archaeologists make and patterns detected in the material record are always a constructed narrative that may or may not be recognizable to the communities who created them. Bits of broken pottery stand in testimony to the hard work, family meals, fiestas, daily staples, and traded luxuries that accumulated as part of life. Sometimes ceramic accumulation (the detritus of everyday behavior) were full of meanings tied to tastes and privileges, and sometimes they reflect less-conscious access and preferences. What the third model of situational plurality (varying identity behavior based on varying social situations) intends to do is to view these materials collections as remnants of the larger connections of everyday choices made, within and between inherited categories and/or reinscribed on a diverse range of stories. Artifacts, including ceramic choices, are part of the process of identity rather than a hallmark of identity.

The next chapter introduces important and intersecting lives of another sort in the historic Southwest: the role of introduced domesticated animals and wild game in everyday life. It takes an analytical approach to the sequence of operations by which a living animal might have become a meal produced for friends, family, important allies and perhaps enemies. Similar to the ceramic study, rather than just a listing of what animals were present or absent in the archaeological record, it becomes important to more closely tease apart what animal parts were used and how. My approach explores evidence for the use of animals in the foodways of multiple households and nuances how animal bodies and products might hint at different types of hearthscape performance.

# 5 /    Hearthscape Ingredients

## Grazing to Gravy

Within many archaeological sites, faunal remains are one of the most durable records of cuisine, and that was certainly the case at Casitas. Evidence from zooarchaeological analyses of meat, bone, and other animal ingredients from the hearthscape complement those of ceramic tools used to prepare and serve them. Perspectives on how animals played a part in cuisine (Gifford-Gonzalez 1993) are key to my research because the study of faunal remains and their taphonomic modifications reveal human behaviors and cuisine-related shared practices that would otherwise remain invisible in the historic record. The documentary record is generally silent on food preparation, probably because food practices were deemed unimportant or ordinary. Yet that very ordinariness is central to its archaeological utility and, if truly practiced by those considered unimportant, perhaps the most powerful argument for studying food. Faunal analysts such as Martha Binford (M. Binford 1979:247) some time ago argued against simple taxon lists that are interpreted to reflect resource constraints, and she encouraged researchers to explore behavioral differences illustrated by faunal remains at archaeological sites in historic New Mexico. Following this research path, more recent studies demonstrate the role of animal ingredients as they correlate to negotiation of relationships of power within colonial communities (Rodríguez-Alegría 2005). Rodríguez-Alegría showed how zooarchaeologists can investigate the dynamics of supply and demand that operated within past societies by studying how people used animals and their products to negotiate place and power in a frontier context.

My perspective on animal bones from Casitas tries to consider the entire sequence of operations through which a living goat browsing in the foothills was transformed by a series of choices and reductions into foods like a blood- and fat-rich gravy dripping from a serving of *panza de cabrito rellena* (stuffed kid's stomach) (Gilbert 1970:13) and an associated collection of bone fragments tossed into the household dump. This "grazing to gravy" approach anchors the material evidence for the use of animals in foodways at Casitas while permitting exploration of various practices shared during that series of choices. This chapter is an entry point to discerning how ingredients represented by animal products reflect "taste" and "choice" (Stahl 2002).

Archaeological study of evidence of routinized, daily behavior explores how taste (Bourdieu 1984) over time could change for both colonizer and colonized. Considering animals within Spanish colonial social relations, preferences reflecting Iberian culinary repertoires (Deagan 1973; DeFrance 1996) may subsume Islamic (Rodinson et al. 2001; Waines 2003), Jewish (M. Harris 1997), and other cultural influences. Similarly, studying animal remains in colonial sites presents opportunities to identify and explore indigenous influences between producers and consumers (McKusick 1982; Lang and Harris 1984; Baugh 1991; Mick-O'Hara 1992; Potter 1997; Sherman 2004; Wilson 2004; Pavao-Zuckerman and LaMotta 2007; Pavao-Zuckerman 2011).

At Casitas, study of animal remains in the archaeological record suggests that choices about portioning and modifying animal parts foregrounds the effects that different heritages had on patterns of culinary practice. To identify how dynamic relationships could crosscut historically understood identities, I needed to use an innovative approach to tease apart the differential use of animals across the site. During my study, I explored species and element frequencies to identify possible differences in taste and handling from each disposal locus at Casitas, as a way to distinguish cuisine-based choices.

We used a similar approach in previous work at the early colonial pueblo of Paa-ko, which contrasted Spanish and Puebloan foodways during a contact situation of the 17th century (Gifford-Gonzalez and Sunseri 2007). At Paa-ko, we theorized that means of self-identification likely fell along a spectrum, which probably affected expected outcomes of subsistence and culinary practice in this small community that has parallels to Casitas. Settlers at Paa-ko engaged in different economic activities at different times and events, crosscutting practices shared by multiple communities. Unlike Casitas, Paa-ko had at least two main eras of occupation, one precontact and another just before the Pueblo Revolt of 1680, with significant spans of occupation and far greater numbers of people living there in all likelihood (Lycett et al. 2004; Lycett 2005).

In contrast, Casitas is a small site, occupied for a short time, so the material record there was much easier to sample and yet had distinctly different depositional styles, practices, and constituent materials to compare at each locus. I recognize that heritage categories of cuisine can represent the extreme bookends of a spectrum of material outcomes. Yet there are also nuances of culinary practice. Not every action or portion of stew made within a small community in a colonial situation represents an "ethnic badge" for the cook or the person enjoying a warm serving of food.

Following a food systems approach (Gumerman 1997), my method of investigating Casitas's faunal assemblages considers the step-wise signature of past behaviors such as herding/hunting, butchering, apportioning, culinary preparation, consumption, and disposal in the three loci across the site. This aspect of hearthscape study parallels the ceramic analysis at Casitas and is richly informed by that work in the previous chapter. I use this approach to link human choices enacted on animal bodies to the ways that those actions were structured by both anatomical structures of the animals, and the environmental and social contexts of processing. Taxonomic representation of animals in the zooarchaeological assemblages of Casitas can be one proxy for species choices made in the primary acquisition stage of animal resource use. Were the animals taken in the field as game or perhaps culled from a herd? At the other end of the sequence of choices, disposal loci at the site can be a proxy representing the end result of human decisions about what parts of which species could be incorporated in various culinary repertoires.

Attempting a more holistic approach to the faunal remains at Casitas takes into account what was consumed, the labor and technology that went into the production and preparation of food, and how animals and their products were distributed and discarded (Gumerman 1997:105). Each step represents opportunities for expressing identity or other kinds of relationships between people in a group, or between groups. Past behaviors are structured not only by access to ingredients but also to the tools to process them (e.g., cutting tools and cooking vessels) and the context in which those ingredients might be used connect people (Family dinner? Neighborly hosting? Alliance-building feast?) .

## What Animals Were Part of Life at Casitas?

My assumptions about proximity to wild species, such as the close-ness of deer or elk, the intermediate distance of antelope, and the much greater distance of bison, are based upon the relationship of current and historic ranges of animals to Casitas and the Rito Colorado valley (Whitaker 1996). Most likely, deer and elk were locally available as noted by ethnographers (Harrington 1916), antelope were found in the open habitats of the expansive mesas and basins to the south and west of the Rito Colorado valley (Anthony 1928:535), and bison were accessible on wider plains far to the north and east (Almaráz 1994:75). These assump-tions work for the Rito Colorado valley because of its broken topogra-phy bounding its local geography and its long history of agricultural settlement. Their presence in the assemblage reflects direct acquisition via hunting forays or through trade. Carnivores such as cougars were not only located farther up the valley and in the foothills but were also dangerous to acquire. Further animal access opportunities are of course reflected by the full suite of European domesticates that were so central to the New Mexican economy (Simmons 1983). Livestock were sources of meat, as well as elements of agricultural economy, providing wool, milk products, and labor. Because of the northern frontier's isolation and the nature of its economy (Snow 1979; Snow 1981, Simmons 1983; Snow 1983), formalized locations for exchange were not likely the most power-ful factor structuring animal use.

Well before the colonial economy was established, distribution of large animals within precontact northern New Mexican villages was uneven and interpreted as a measure of varying aspects of social statuses (Potter 2002). Other aspects, such as ethnicity or *casta* status, were also important in species choice. Discursive aspects of animal use, such as taboo foods or animals with symbolic importance, likely changed the proportions of use of these species in culinary practices and, thus, the resulting midden assemblages.

Less discursive aspects of animal use were also important in the for-mation of the faunal assemblage. Inasmuch as social and anatomical constraints noted could have affected the choices made by individual human processors of animal resources, the nature of dismemberment and defleshing tactics and strategies (Gifford-Gonzalez 1993:185) likely reflected a product-focused approach to the animal portions as they would be incorporated into cuisine. This tension—requiring certain cuts of meat to produce the daily yet expressive medium of particular

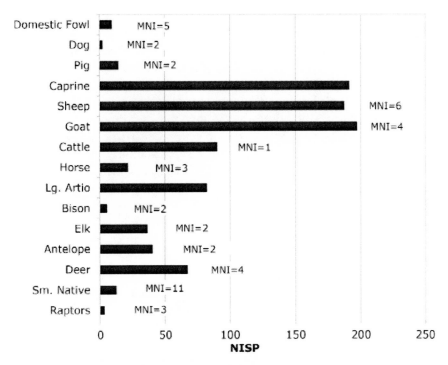

FIGURE 47. Animal species recovered from Casitas.

foodways, and the fact that access to different-sized animals presented different challenges and resulted in different physical outcomes—is resolved by studying the different choices made along various stages of the sequence of operations that constituted culinary practice at Casitas.

From the number of identifiable specimens (NISP), or 1,237 bones which could be compared to known species and elements at Casitas, the taxonomic representation shows a full suite of European-introduced domesticates, as well as a significant amount of wild fauna (fig. 47). Sheep and goat (caprines) dominate the domesticate count, although a significant number of cattle elements are also present. Almost full skeletal representations of bone elements are present for all three major domesticated food species.

Within the caprines, some of the specimens (189) identified to element, portion, and side could be attributed only to family, a common challenge to zooarchaeologists (Boessneck 1969; Prummel and Frisch 1986; Halstead et al. 2002). Ethnoarchaeological demonstrations by community partners from El Rito demonstrated that traditional butchery methods reduce those taxa for food in identical sequences of operations. In contrast, uses of fauna native to the immediate area were quite different for taxa including deer, elk, rodents, badgers, cougars, and certain raptorial birds. Groupings of bone from those animals suggest that full deer and elk skeletons were brought back to Casitas. Presence of deer and elk is unsurprising, given the mountainous terrain and proximity of forested area near the Rito Colorado valley. Other wild fauna identified in the Casitas assemblages include bison, tentatively (Balkwill and Cumbaa 1992) and antelope (Chorn et al. 1988), of which only the latter is represented by a fairly complete skeletal inventory. These animals would have come from farther afield than the immediate environs of Casitas and, if the identifications hold true against multiple other comparatives, would be compelling evidence for trade in to the village from more mobile groups in the region.

The dominance of domesticated animals at Casitas agrees with the documented historical reliance on European introduced species in the late-18th-century colonial agricultural economy (Simmons 1983; Snow 1983). Differences in handling (Gifford-Gonzalez et al. 2006:42) suggest that these species were exposed to the greatest amount of human processing, or at least that they were processed in quantities and via methods that allowed for higher rates of observation of cut marks and chops within archaeologically recovered bone (fig. 48). The idea is to get a snapshot view of how many modifications could be identified in the elements and for which animals those modification occurred at great frequencies compared to the rest of the assemblage. Carnivore modifications among taxa show the greatest difference, which may be related to how much more soft tissue was present in elements disposed of in butchery processes occurring closer to home instead of in smaller parcels brought back from a hunt. Discoloration related to thermal modifications such as burning show similar trends, as will be explored more below.

Closer examination of where and in what portions remains of animals were recovered from disposal loci across the site suggests a distinct and uneven distribution of taxa (fig. 49). By grouping the taxonomic counts into domesticate and wild species, the inequalities in the proportion of animal types used and discarded at each locus become even more apparent. It should not be surprising that in a late Spanish colonial–era New Mexican agricultural village, the remains of cow, sheep, and goats dominate the bones present in all of the disposal loci. It is interesting that Locus A is the only location where chicken remains were recovered

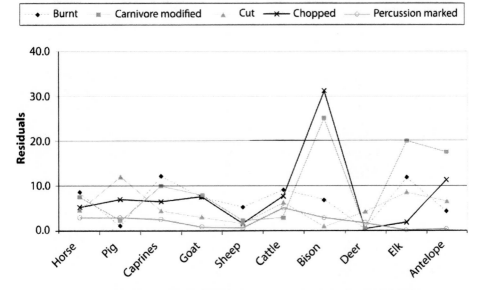

FIGURE 48. Differences in handling between taxa. Residuals are the difference between percent modified for a particular taxa and the average percent modified for all taxonomic categories.

and pig resources were found. To this day, swine rearing is a risky business in the high-altitude conditions of the Rito Colorado valley, and even successful local livestock operations report difficulties in keeping pigs happy and healthy (F. Martinez 2005). The potential for signaling belonging represented by having pork available will be discussed in the next chapter.

Inequalities in the proportion of animal types at each locus are more apparent with respect to acquisition of and access to wild species (fig. 50). All loci contain deer, elk, and antelope but only Loci B and C contain bison, a species that would not have been available anywhere near the Rito Colorado valley. Although limited in representation and with its own methodological difficulties to identify (Balkwill and Cumbaa 1992), bison was only one contributing animal to the bones deposited to Locus B. That disposal site contained the largest number of wild species across the board, including carnivores such as cougar and badger, which were absent at the other two loci. A further and potentially most notable taxonomic representation at Locus B is the nondomestic bird species. While turkey domestication was practiced in the Southwest before contact

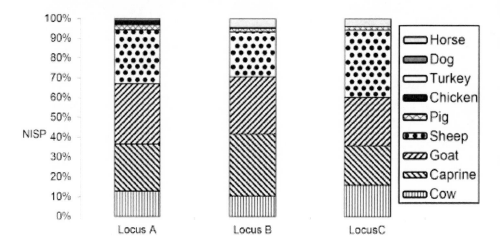

FIGURE 49. Domestic fauna proportions by disposal location at Casitas (nisp: Locus A = 219; Locus B = 283; Locus C = 176).

(Munro 2006; Speller et al. 2010), they could provide both meat and feathers. This was unlikely the case for predatory birds like raptors that occur solely in the deposit at Locus B. Overall, with respect to selection of native species, Locus B stands out as the most diverse subassemblage at Casitas and the only one with bird species, which are widely reported as important in precontact Pueblo ritual practices. The small numbers of fauna present are not as robust as a larger, longer-occupied site, but the hints that they give across the taxonomic ranges and distinct depositional distribution of wild animal remains compel me to at least compare their potential for meaning for the people who used and then disposed of them in such different places and ways.

## Creation of the Faunal Archaeological Record

When we take into account how those disposed-of animal bones eventually became the layered deposits recovered through archaeological excavation, observations of nonhuman bone surface modifications suggest that overall, the faunal assemblages were not subject to exposures that would have driven high incidences of destruction. I chalk this up to mostly to the short occupation leading to quick capping by adobe melt. Often, reuse of *vigas* (rough-hewn roof timbers) and other materials for new structures or relocating families means that unprotected

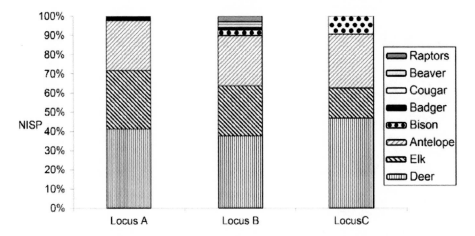

FIGURE 50. Wild fauna by disposal location (nisp: Locus A = 46; Locus B = 69; Locus C = 32).

adobe walls erode quickly (Bice 1993). A highly magnified look at the animal bones strongly suggests these processes, as a low incidence of root etching, combined with overall low rate of weathering (fig. 51) is consistent with excavation contexts of layered ash and adobe lenses in midden deposits.

Like borrow pits elsewhere in New Mexico (D. Levine 1990:170; Snow and Bowen 1995:4; Atkins 2001:116), the structure of an excavated feature that was capped by backfill episodes of alternating culinary waste and hearth ash probably also contributed to preservation of the archaeologically recovered faunal material. A similar trend was observed for the disused roomblock disposal loci, probably because of similar ash disposal and adobe melt processes. As there was little evidence of intrusive rodent disturbance, such as what occurs when pack rats or prairie dogs find their way into a site, the scant presence of rodents themselves (nisp = 9), even with the use of ⅛th-inch mesh and systematic flotation of samples, attests to a lack of bioturbation acting on the various disposal loci. In short, an analyst could hardly have asked for a better-preserved archaeological faunal assemblage. To further analyze the meaning of range of species within the disposed animal remains at Casitas, I first needed to consider the amount of human processing that went into creating the faunal refuse that occurred within each loci.

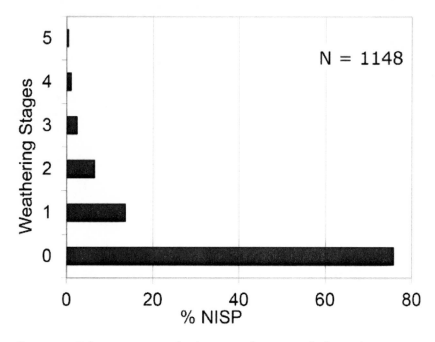

FIGURE 51. Behrensmeyer weathering stages for mammals, by % nisp.

## Animal Bodies Becoming Portions

Primary butchering is the first stage of processing following acquisition (Lyman 1994:300). This butchering takes into account factors such as the size of the animal, which affects patterns of field reduction and transport concerns (Perkins and Daly 1968; Lyman 1994:224). When an animal was killed close to home, transport considerations were likely less challenging an issue. Even so, the size of an animal probably still accounted for modes of primary butchering that rely on prostrate or suspended carcasses (Cope 2002:32). Long-standing Native American (Cushing 1920:397) and Iberian (Snow and Bowen 1995:1) pursuits like hunting would have simultaneously increased meat intake in frontier households while potentially constraining portions returning to the hearthscape (Faith and Gordon 2007). Butchering larger game such as deer and elk likely involved considerations of animal size, distance back to Casitas, the number of people in the party who could carry meat, whether they had a mule or other beast of burden with them, and how much time the hunters had to make their way home across a dangerous before dark.

Processes that occur during primary butchering include skinning (Lapham 2005), evisceration, and initial disarticulation (L. Binford 1978:48). These steps would reduce working or carrying weight, decrease the chance of contamination from stomach or bowel contents, and increase the portability of parcels of meat. Disarticulation usually occurs by cutting between the articular ends of bones, leaving bones largely intact (Lyman 1994:298). In the cases where people possessed heavy chopping instruments, they often severed some portion of the articular surfaces and traveled with a smaller detached segment while the bone from which it was detached remained behind. The tendency of several osteological elements to remain in close association during this stage is the result of "riders" created by tendons remaining attached (L. Binford 1978:50).

Secondary butchering (which may or may not have been subsequent to transport) is more likely to have taken place near to the place of consumption and discard at Casitas. This stage in the reduction sequence of animal bodies involved the apportioning of an animal and may be linked to processes of redistribution among household kitchens (Lyman 1994:300). Evidence of choices that people made in secondary butchering processes may be visible as different counts at each disposal locus at Casitas. Cuts of meat associated with the presence of certain elements, such as the larger muscle masses surrounding the upper femur, may well be what is reflected by higher occurrence of these elements in a given locus (Seetah 2006). The association of these meat portions with certain households may be one measure of status, but that assumes that we can link access to high-mass cuts of meat with control over the distribution of animal resources (Lyman 1987; Waguespack 2002). This association with status is not always true, though, as the presence of elements associated with high-mass meat portions of domesticates can show up in households at both ends of a socioeconomic spectrum, as has been seen in slave provisioning (Ferguson 1992:96). It is especially worth considering in this discussion just how much the equating of muscle mass with "high-quality" cuts (Crader 1990; Bowen 1995:8) ignores the fact that less fleshy portions are sometimes used to differentiate "taste" in various cuisines. For example, one interpretation about the metapodials and phalanges of pigs used in foodways of high-status houses in early colonial Pueblo and Cholula (Mexico) was that they were selected because of flavor preferences (Reynoso Ramos 2008:4) rather than by low-status consumers who could not afford fleshier bits.

A last sequence of modifications just prior to and during consumption can result in added butchering marks in what might be considered tertiary butchering (Lyman 1994:300). The specific form and modifications of animal end products resulting from this sequence are related to the culinary techniques and technology into which the butcher expects to introduce the meat and bone portions (Gifford-Gonzalez 1993). A cook who plans to roast the meat on the bone will need a different meat package than one who must reduce animal portions to fit chunks of meat into a stewing pot. Lyman (1994) conceptually supports these kinds of assumptions in that one should observe fewer marks on bones that were disposed of during the initial butchering process, whereas bones retained and transported into secondary and tertiary butchering contexts have the opportunity to undergo further processing and display additional marks.

Culinary techniques and technology are intricately linked to consumption of animals in cuisine even though the actual evidence for butchering can be left on bones at every step of reducing animal bodies into portions (Lyman 1994:297). At Casitas these included cut marks and chop marks. But other high-energy damages to bone, such as percussion notches and anvil marks, and in some cases, breaks occurring in the same location of an element without any percussion marks at all (Guilday et al. 1962) may be indicative of other processes such as bone marrow and grease extraction (Outram 2001; C. Sunseri 2015). Within the category of cut marks, the differential availability and access to stone or metal tools for people butchering animals far from the colonial supply lines should be considered. The availability of quality metal implements on the colony's frontiers was not a certainty (N. Thomas 2008), and evidence of stone tool use is found in association with a diverse cross section of colonial people, not only those called *Indio* but also those labeled *Vecino* (Moore 1992).

Bowen (1995:7–8) points out how in addition to (and sometimes subsumed within) considerations of those final butchering events, some analysts have tried to link considerations of nonbutchering culinary processing. Access to ingredients and the difference between who is preparing food versus who is consuming it may be as important to culinary processing as a singular identity aspect such as ethnicity (Smith-Lintner 2007:142).

Culinary techniques and technology are intimately related to previous butchering decisions. There is the potential for multiple people to be involved in successive stages of the *chaîne opératoire* of culinary practice such that the person who may have ultimately found themselves thickening the gravy with flour might not have been able to communicate to the person who butchered the goat that the new cooking pot had a more constricted opening (fig. 43) than other ceramic vessels and so required smaller pot-sizing of meat chunks. Just as the form and size of pots at Casitas likely structured the kinds of meat portions that were cooked inside of them, in each case analysts must recognize nuances in the ultimate dispositions of meat portions that structure the recursive relationships between producers and consumers.

## Transformations into Food

Evidence of thermal processing (Shipman et al. 1984), such as roasting or boiling, is a frequently underexplored aspect of culinary practice (Gifford-Gonzalez 1993). Instead of considering raw/uncooked dismemberment alone, it is important to look for the evidence of people having practiced butchering processes in which bones were heat-altered when left in the meat for roasts, stews, and oven cooking (Gifford-Gonzalez 1993:184). Associated heat-processing evidence may include pot polish on osteological elements (T. White 1992; Hurlbut 2000), as well as the pot-sizing of bones for insertion in ceramic vessels (Marshall 1990).

More intense stages in reduction of faunal materials may have involved grease rendering (Lyman 1994:279) for fats that have high caloric value essential to humans (Speth and Spielmann 1982), as well as marrow extraction from long bone cavities (Outram 2001; C. Sunseri 2015). Choices made in these stages of butchering were likely for meals that cook meat without bone left in. Stews that left bone in the meat, which extracts marrow and bone grease, were less likely to be followed by reprocessing of elements for grease and marrow. Observations show that people who mass-process marrow or bone grease strip off the meat first and freeze, dry, or immediately consume it (L. Binford 1978; O'Connell and Hawkes 1988; Yellen 1991; Enloe 1993). Marrow can then be extracted raw from the bones or the marrow roasted in the bone over a fire to be extracted when it has cooled and resolidified—a tasty treat to spread and enjoy in all its buttery goodness. In cases when marrow extraction is accomplished by direct heating of elements and breaking them into pieces, big fractures propagate along the shaft of long bones (L. Binford 1978:152–64). Other bone fractures related to cavity access, such as those on phalanges, may be related to the acquisition of nonfood products such as neatsfoot oil, the liquidity of which made it a useful light lubricant, as well as a metal, wood, and leather preservative (D. Levine 1985:64).

If sufficient processing in this stage results in enough long bone shafts, as well as spongy trabecular bone fragments, boiling may be further used to render bone grease. Grease rendering involves boiling of bone and skimming the fat off of the boiling water. Bone grease manufacture is incredibly labor-intensive and usually pursued by those who cannot otherwise obtain enough fat in their diet, either chronically or as the result of unusual nutritional stress (Outram 2001). This operation requires an appropriate container technology, which at Casitas was evidenced in the ceramic assemblage by the thermally efficient and shock-resistant sherds of micaceous vessels (D. Anderson 1999). In a settlement where sharing did not necessarily "smooth" inequalities in access to animals, evidence of bone grease production may reflect households that had less access to fats and fatty meats.

## Tool Marks and Burning

In evidence more proximate to the events of eating, I wanted to take a closer look at tool-related marks on the faunal assemblages. For example, chop marks can be organized into the same three stages of butchering: primary slaughter and dressing; secondary division of carcass sections; and tertiary reduction to household or pot-sized pieces (Rixson 1989:49). At Casitas, different tools were used to reduce animals into portions, although the cut marks were not evenly distributed throughout the assemblages. Comparing animal species, a relationship emerges between the number of specimens that exhibit any chop marks at all (Gruchy and Rogers 2002) and a high intensity of chop marks, which suggests heavy processing by chopping implements (fig. 52). Chopping separates one element or body segment from another, but it also propagates fractures through the bone (Seetah 2006). Following on our above discussion of grease production, such breakages can also be useful for marrow extraction and subdivision of elements into smaller pieces.

Z-score tests allow for an appropriate comparison of proportions between groups, while considering sample size (Shennan 1997; Pallant 2005). Figure 53 illustrates Z-score evaluations of the rates of chop intensity per disposal locus. The results demonstrate a significant difference (at a 90% confidence level) in chopping intensity between groups of chopped bone. Dissimilar chop mark intensities vary across the site's household loci. Cut mark intensities were different between Loci A and

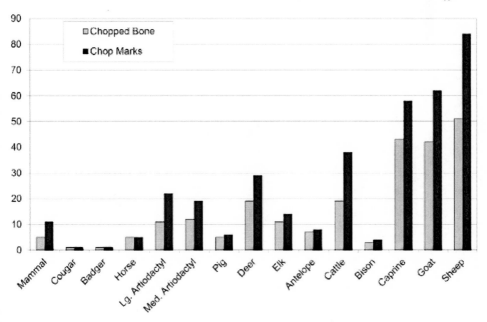

FIGURE 52. Taxonomic representation of chopped bone and chop mark intensity.

B (Z value = 4.375, actual confidence level 100%), between Loci B and C (Z value = 1.536, actual confidence level 93.8%), as well as between Loci A and C (Z value = 2.678, actual confidence level 99.6%).

Cattle, sheep, and deer all have greater frequencies of chop marks per chopped element than other species, yet the full suite of taxa at Casitas display the use of chopping in carcass subdivision. The only exceptions are the smaller birds and rodents that were more likely reduced by blunt disarticulation as one might do with a jointed piece of fried chicken today. If this sitewide behavior produced portions more likely to be processed by smaller tools, such as knives, then closer examination of cut marks is a logical next level of analysis.

Although equating cut mark frequencies with specific behaviors has been shown to be problematic (Lyman 2005), I wish to use the placement, cutting tool material, and probable functions to organize the relation of different observed tool marks to different taxa. Skinning traces are likely part of earlier processing sequences. At least for larger animals, the remainder of cutting activities is more likely related to later subdividing of animals into manageable portions. This may not hold true for smaller

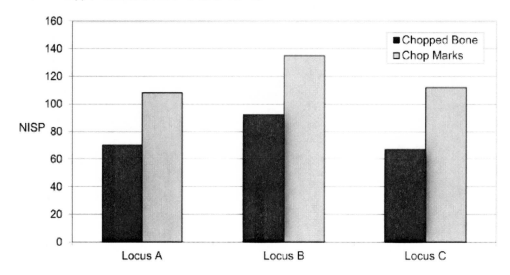

FIGURE 53. Chopped bone frequency and chop intensity by locus.

animals such as rabbits because of blunt disarticulation techniques, and roasting with skin still on the animal (Cushing 1920:594). If there was a lack of heavy chopping tools, cutting could have been used to segment carcasses.

Overall, caprine (goat and sheep), and deer specimens exhibited the highest proportion of metal to stone tool cut marks (fig. 54). Cuts on cattle and elk were almost evenly distributed between the metal and stone tool marks (Blumenschine et al. 1996; Greenfield 1999), whereas use of stone tools dominate the numbers of cut marks on horse remains. Medium and large skeletal artiodactyl (from hoofed animals) elements also bear a high proportion of stone tool cut marks. Although many of these specimens were reduced to pieces too small to identify to species, extrapolation by size suggests that stone tools were used to process more elk, cattle, deer, antelope, sheep, and goat than morphological analysis alone suggests. What might be even more telling is how cutting tool use was distributed among loci reflecting different households.

Organization of cutting tool use by locus is a complementary scale of analysis for considering how portions of animal protein were processed differentially by species among different consumers at Casitas (figs. 55 and 56). Stone tools seem to have been most significantly at work on processing caprines across the site, but especially on goats at Locus C (fig.

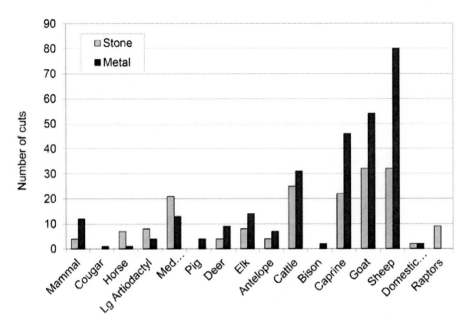

FIGURE 54. Evidence of metal and stone tool cuts on domestic and wild fauna.

56). Locus A exhibits minimal use of stone tools on wild species such as antelope and elk, as well as turkey. Stone tool use at Locus B is similar to Locus A on cattle elements, but Locus B stone cut marks stand out particularly in raptor and elk specimens.

Metal tool cut marks across the site again are concentrated on caprines, although at Locus B, a higher rate of metal cuts on cattle specimens stands out when compared to that of the other two loci. Metal cut mark frequencies on elk and caprine elements are also elevated for Locus B. At Locus C, metal cut marks outrank the other loci proportionately on deer and sheep elements.

As a whole, all three of the disposal loci display evidence for intensive processing of caprines with cutting tools. Stone cut modifications on cattle are generally similar, but in Locus B, metal tool signatures differ markedly, exhibiting higher cut mark frequencies on elk and cattle than the other two loci. Loci A and C are quite similar in their cutting tool evidence, except that at Locus C, metal tool cut marks are higher proportionately for deer, and stone tool cut marks are much higher proportionately for goat.

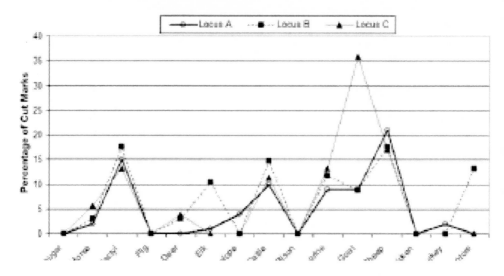

FIGURE 55. Taxonomic representation of stone tool cut marks by locus.

Systematic fracturing of long bone shafts and epiphyses for marrow extraction is often differentiated from pot-sizing processes by characteristic, multiple chopping on larger bones to consistently reduce the maximum length to some size requirement. Otherwise, increased percussion marks on bone relate to breaching the marrow cavity to access marrow or reduce osteological component maximum dimensions in a manner that increases surface area to volume ratios for grease processing. At Casitas, the same taxa that display the highest rates of chops and cuts have the highest rates of percussion marks, measured by number of observations per element (fig. 57).

The rate of processing by percussion (including hammerstone, anvil, and counterblow) displays noticeable difference across the disposal loci. Percussion mark incidence demonstrates statistically significant differences between Loci A and B (at the 90% confidence interval; Z value = 1.564, actual confidence level 94.1%) and between Loci A and C (Z value = 4.375, actual confidence level 92.9%). Loci B and C are not significantly different in the rate of percussion marks on elements (Z value = 1.468, actual confidence level 53.1%).

Such rates of percussion are related intimately to the fragmentation rates recorded by size grade across the site (fig. 58). Avoiding lower-counted species (NISP of less than 5), loci across the site demonstrate a significant difference in size grade frequencies ($\rho = 0.0001$). Although

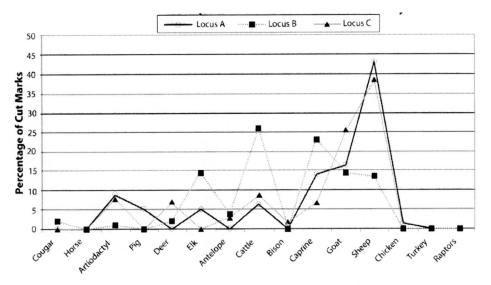

FIGURE 56. Taxonomic representation of metal tool cut marks by locus.

Loci A and B are not significantly different in fragmentation modalities ($\rho$ = 0.696), Loci B and C are significantly different ($\rho$ = 0.0001), as are Loci A and C ($\rho$ = 0.001).

If the size of assemblage specimens at Locus C significantly differs from Loci A and B, it parallels the differences in deer cut mark patterning, as well as general food utility. High rates of processing characterized by the small size of assemblage specimens at Locus C echo intensified nutrient extraction seen at other colonial sites, such as those seen south of Casitas in the Cochiti area (Hunter-Anderson et al. 1979:72). It is likely that not all fragments of bone were deposited into the three disposal loci directly following culinary processing. Study of other Spanish colonial sites (M. Binford 1979:255; Schutt 1979:196) suggests that deposition of smaller bone pieces into or near the hearth in the room was a process that was spatially distinct from the discard of bone fragments used in bone grease rendering (Chapman et al. 1977:189).

At Casitas, burned bone is present across the site, but higher burning temperatures, as evidenced by changes in color through browns to black and then grey/white (Shipman et al. 1984) are not evenly distributed among the disposal loci. The degree to which the faunal material at each locus exhibits these color changes is dramatic in difference at Locus C (fig. 59).

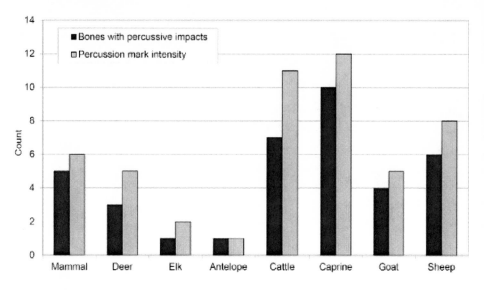

FIGURE 57. Percussion-marked bone by taxon.

Bone color differences among the loci are significant at a sitewide scale ($\rho$ = 0.02), though much more so between Loci B and C ($\rho$ = 0.009). Differences between Loci A and B, and Loci A and C were not significant ($\rho$ = 0.265 and 0.097, respectively). It may be that some bones were not as highly burned because they were boiled in stews in ceramic pots and thus not exposed directly to flame or high heat. Observations of uneven, laminar patches of bleached, spongy-looking bone (Roberts et al. 2002) on elements that otherwise have completely smooth cortical surfaces often occur in association with what I identify as "pot polished" bones, those having smoothed/abraded surfaces at opposing ends of the element. Whether or not the specimens recorded with analytical notes for "boiling" or "pot polish" can actually be ascribed to those behaviors, it is likely that a combination of factors would have had an effect on their color and structure.

## How Was Meat Portioned and Consumed?

To compare the spatial representation of anatomical segments, elements of cattle, deer, and sheep, the most common specimens in the assemblage were plotted as % MAU (minimal animal units) (figs 58 to

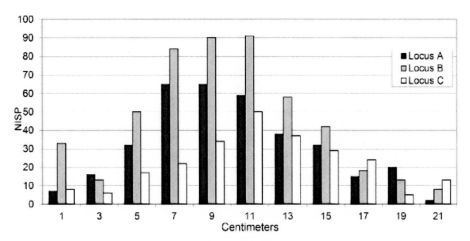

FIGURE 58. Distribution of faunal specimen sizes by locus.

60). When compared with nutritional indices that include osteological elements remaining in close association as "riders" (L. Binford 1978:50), some commonly articulated elements were combined in the plots but not counted twice (M. Hill 2001:71). These elements were plotted as anatomical regions including axial: mandible (MND), atlas plus axis (AT-AX), posterior cervical vertebrae (C3–7), all cervical (CE), thoracic vertebrae (TH), ribs (RI), lumbar vertebrae (LU), and sacrum (SA); forelimb: scapula (SC), humerus (HM), radio-ulna (RD), metacarpals (MC), and metacarpals plus carpals (MC-CA); and hind limb: innominate (IM), innominate plus sacrum (IM-SA), femur (FE), tibia (TA), tibia plus tarsals (TA-TR), and metatarsals (MT). Phalanges (PH) were separately plotted.

At Locus A, remains associated with the axial skeleton (except the mandible) are extremely underrepresented in comparison to limbs or other appendages. In the case of sheep, though, more vertebrae are present (fig. 60). Skeletons of cow and sheep have more forelegs present in Locus A (represented by humeri, radio-ulnae, and metacarpals), while hind limbs are more represented by deer skeletons.

At Locus B, more axial skeletal portions are represented than at Loci A and C, especially mandibles and cervical vertebrae of domesticates (fig. 61). Cow and sheep again are primarily represented by the presence of forelimb body regions; deer hind limb representation is far greater at this locus.

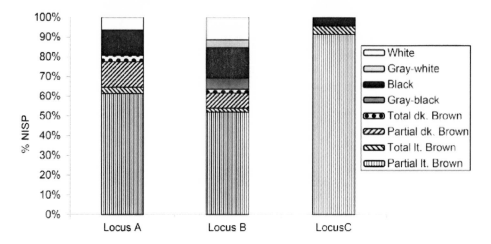

FIGURE 59. Distribution of burning by locus (nisp: Locus A = 31; Locus B = 52; Locus C = 23).

At Locus C, the axial skeleton is again underrepresented in comparison to the appendicular skeleton, again with the exception of mandibles and in this case the rib units of deer (fig. 62). Except for the scapula, forelimb body regions are more represented by cow and sheep than deer at this locus, especially in comparison to the other two loci. Similarly to Locus A, Locus C hind limb representation of deer and cattle appear in higher numbers than sheep.

Summarizing the differences in handling at these disposal loci, caprine axial elements dominate Locus A; Locus B has some of all three species (cattle, caprine, and deer); and Locus C has the greatest relative proportion of deer axial elements. Locus B differs from the other two loci in its relatively lower proportions of cattle hind limbs, suggesting heavy meat-bearing portions. Sheep and cattle dominate forelimb regions for both Loci A and B, but deer is well represented. This is not the case for Locus C, which has more deer hind limb portions than sheep, and fewer sheep portions overall than the other two loci. A generalized perspective of the three disposal loci suggests less emphasis on beef portions from the largest muscle groups at Locus B, while Locus C seems to have had less mutton in the culinary refuse. Reconsidering chapter 4 discussions of trends in pottery at Locus C as seen in the ceramic analysis, the presence of higher-quality ceramics at Locus B seems to be complicated by a

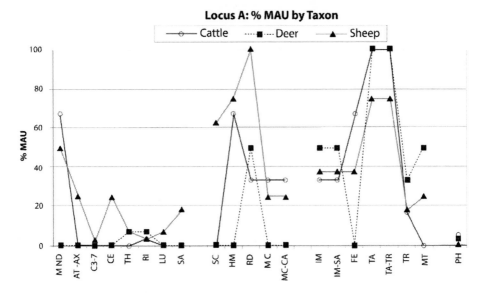

FIGURE 60. Locus A skeletal element abundance profiles (nisp: cattle = 28; deer = 19; sheep = 59).

lower frequency of high-status cuts of meat, if based on what in the later American West is considered normative European portions (Schulz and Gust 1983; Szuter 1991).

How might these differences in the use of different animal portions be explained? The nutritional utility indices are quantified comparisons of the nutritional yield of various elements of body segments. Zooarchaeologists use these indices to investigate the motivations for human selectivity in using different portions of an animal (L. Binford 1978; Metcalfe and Jones 1988; Madrigal 2004). At Casitas, such patterns may indicate that some people consistently ate more nutritious cuts of meat of the same species than others. As nutritional utilities have not been created for every animal, analysts are forced to use proxies. I used Lewis Binford's (1978:73) grease utility values for sheep and deer, as well as caribou values in place of cattle to approximate the sparse graze of region. I compared meat weight, kilocalories, meat return, marrow return, and combined meat and marrow return indices (Madrigal 2004:748–51) across the three species. Finally, I compared ranked values of food utility index across loci and the same species (Metcalfe and Jones 1988:498) by

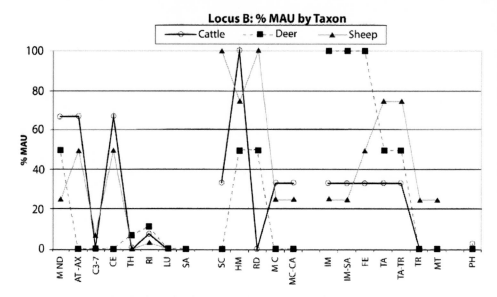

FIGURE 61. Locus B skeletal element abundance profiles (nisp: cattle = 29; deer = 26; sheep = 64).

Spearman's rho, or rank order correlation, that take into account the different sample sizes reflected in each subassemblage (Faith and Gordon 2007).

These statistics suggest that while cattle and sheep grease was important across Casitas, deer had more general utility as food or as a source of marrow. Locus A may have been choosing cattle and sheep for marrow return as well. Locus B marrow returns were significant for both sheep and deer. Finally, Locus C does not indicate concern with marrow returns at all but has an elevated significance with regard to the relative importance of the general food utility of deer. This patterning in relative animal body segment use across the loci, when considered against other types and scales of material evidence elsewhere in this study, highlights how household networks of access and/or taste differentially accessed a diverse array of species and also used portions of them in different ways.

## Hearthscape Evidence in Dialogue

The size and anatomy of animals structured the way in which animals were butchered and apportioned, which in turn affects the archaeological

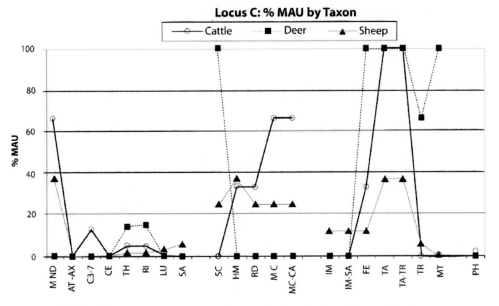

FIGURE 62. Locus C skeletal element abundance profiles (nisp: cattle = 28; deer = 15; sheep = 60).

record. Sheep and goat elements may have more complete anatomical representation in a given disposal loci than proportionately larger animals, such as cattle, for reasons that have to do with the amount of meat contained by an individual animal. In other New Mexican colonial sites, the faunal remains recovered reflected that because cattle were so much larger in size, butchering events resulted in shared portions among several households (Atkins 2001:116). The trade value and husbandry demands of the suite of introduced domesticates directly affected different colonial groups' access to them. For example, shepherds and household heads would have had different degrees of control over how pastoral livestock were used. Breaking each step down further, differential access is reflected by species choices that stemmed from varying New Mexican social and occupational roles—household head, captive laborer, shepherd, or descendant of groups who might have had different ideas about what portions were most tasty or fit specific culinary arts, such as Pueblo or nomadic mountain or Plains peoples (Brooks 2002a). Such differences in turn may well have affected proportions of introduced domestic versus indigenous wild animals (Reitz and Cumbaa 1983; Reitz 1991; Ávila et al. 2004) present in the site. This may manifest in distinctly different provisioning chains as well, as subsequent differences in the presence of wild versus domesticated species (Haecker 1976:111) at each of the disposal loci. Social relationships of trade also affected which nonlocal animals were acquired and consumed.

In the past, scholars of Indo-Hispano northern New Mexico have argued that close kin relations linked families who lived around little fortified *plazuelas* like the one at Casitas (Swadesh 1974; Van Ness 1991). Differences in ceramic and faunal assemblages (and thus foodways) between distinct disposal loci make any notion of a homogeneous community problematic. Within the larger grouping of colonial citizens, smaller categories of group identities such as Genízaro were perhaps not as unified as historical sources might suggest. There is little doubt that Casitas represents a satellite of the famously Genízaro outpost of Abiquiú and was positioned in the Rito Colorado valley as part of a larger set of tactical decisions. Concurrent with those strategies, but at smaller scales and in daily practice, identity and status differentiation among lower *casta* people appears to have manifested along lines that colonial elites might not have imagined. For those who lived, raised families, and died at Casitas, internal politics and cross-cultural fluency were dynamics that played out differently on hearths around the central courtyard than they did on scales that united them in the goal of keeping possession of their land grant by accommodating royal decrees about settlement structure.

Fauna from three archaeological disposal loci suggest that settlers at Casitas were making full use of the animal resources available to them locally and, importantly, additional species through trade. The exchange of such animal products may have been advantageous to maintaining social transactions along a continuum of values (Spielmann 2002:202), and those relationships appear to be corroborated by the presence of fine Tewa and Keres Pueblo pottery as well as colonial table settings at Casitas. In a settlement likely established and headed by Genízaros, and within that ostensibly homogeneous category, faunal and ceramic data suggest that substantial differences existed in household levels of "Hispanicization," wealth, and relations with other Native American groups.

Archaeological evidence from the hearthscape of Casitas suggests that animal consumption and use of ceramics were embedded in a complex of meanings that complicates simple categorizations of identity for those who lived there. As a heritage resource located close to its contemporary descendant community, the narratives of identity performance and linkages to hearthscapes of the past are potentially laden with meanings related to current struggles for self-determination. In turn, identity labels ascribed by government agencies, institutions, and researchers referring to the documentary and archaeological records often neglect and affect those struggles. Ceramic and faunal data, studied as multiple lines of artifact and spatial evidence, suggest the inhabitants of Casitas tried to inhabit a middle ground of existence. In these borderlands, homogenization and sole identification with the colonizers may have been a serious liability. Trade, even with the ostensible enemy, and use of local animals and clay were likely essential to survival.

# 6 /    Historical Archaeology of a Place beyond Labels

So who lived at Casitas? The answer to that question is more complex than labels such as "Hispanic," "Casitas," or even "Indo-Hispano" might allow. There is no doubt that the families who peopled this outpost on the frontier did so with the help of deep connections in both Indian and Spanish colonial communities. Those connections were reflected in practices that contributed to the archaeological record at Casitas in varied ways. I conducted my research of the material residues of past lives at Casitas necessarily with the intent of teasing apart how people expressed their affiliation with diverse communities of practice at different but complementary scales of actions and contexts. Representations of identity were embedded in processes of creating meaning and articulated within local communities as well as larger colonial and indigenous societies. By bringing different artifact analyses together, it becomes easier to see that the families who lived at Casitas brought different kinds of cultural expertise to both hearthscape and homescape levels of community life.

I theorize identity as an array or complex of possibilities, of which elements may be variably mobilized in different contexts and at various scales of social performance. Daily practice, as lived in household and cultural memory, is represented through the material record of foodway routines of kitchen and hearth. Localized patterns of behavior, represented by hearthscape foodways reconstituted from the dispoal loci of Casitas, exemplify archaeological manifestation of household-scale practice (*habitus*). At a larger scale of analysis, homescape practices in the Rito Colorado valley were integral to negotiating the survival of a colonial buffer settlement. Study of the larger-scale homescape gives a nuanced representation of a pluralistic community identity on the frontier. After considering these interconnected scales of study, I think the citizens of Casitas were neither fully creolized nor did they fully retain their precolonial identities. Rather, their association was fluid. They effectively used their identity, including material expressions of identity, on a situational basis. Expressions of community membership have to remain fluid in a warzone.

## Foodways Stages of Production and Consumption

I compared hearthscape behaviors—stages in foodways production and consumption—across faunal and ceramic assemblages in order to show how results of analyses from each inform the other. I wanted to consider a broader examination of hearthscape behaviors as composites within each disposal locus, as they reflect intrasite differences within the households. The main goal of my analysis of hearthscape foodways is to link middle range interpretive methodologies with expectations for divergent choices in the stages of production, use, and discard of ceramic and faunal procurement, production/reduction, use, and disposal by households at Casitas. These culinary materials reveal the agency people from this community demonstrated in the interplay between colonial identity expectations and local identity practices. Analyses of two kinds of foodways evidence also shed light on relationships between producers and consumers.

### Raw Materials

In the procurement of materials, the sources for clay and animal resources (as evidenced by paste composition and taxonomic lists) suggest that people at Casitas obtained both local and distant resources. Ceramic data suggest that pottery was made from diverse raw materials, including both local and nonlocal clay and temper constituents (pastes), built into similar outward forms and surface presentations (wares). These are linked to the fabrication stages. A closer look at the grouping of paste categories suggests that the various clay and temper mixes were differently distributed across the site, and that pastes were also variably represented within the wares at each locus. For example, Culinary Plain vessels were present in different proportions in each locus. Technological analysis reveals that Culinary Plain vessels at each of those loci were built using dissimilar proportions of the diverse raw materials. Specifically, the proportions of plain ware pastes at Locus A and Locus C were significantly different than those in Locus B, with far more local untempered and sand-tempered clays present in those two subassemblages. Culinary Plain vessels at Locus C are even more extreme in this trend, with the highest proportion of sand-tempered pastes at the site. This contrasts with the high proportion of ash- and tuff-tempered pastes in pottery at Locus B, which characterizes products made from Española basin material sources and suggests that people in this household were more often supplied by potters distant from the Rito Colorado valley.

Put more simply, Casitas residents living in different parts of the site used pottery that was supplied by potters who were accessing different clay sources for their raw material. Paste group distributions strongly suggest that pottery at each locus of Casitas was acquired through different social networks of both local and extralocal production and exchange. Some of these networks may have relied upon supply relations instituted in the colonial period, but others may have had deeper, more indigenous roots.

This ceramic raw material evidence speaks directly to Snow's (1984:93) observation that many of the common ceramic types in use in colonial New Mexico were the products of related potting traditions. But the Casitas evidence does not locate the origins of any one type of clay-temper combination within a single ethnic classification, such as sand-tempered clay's oft-reiterated ascription to Hispano potters (Dick [1964] 1968; D. Levine 1990; Carrillo 1997). Instead, each of the types of pots used at Casitas were made by both local and nonlocal potters, with pastes that others have interpreted as both Indian and Hispanic. With the exception of Puname Polychrome, no single ware category is made from only one source of clay, or even from closely related clay and temper mixtures. Ceramic types at Casitas were not homogeneous in source. This begs the question of whether or not potters supplying households at the site were engaged in resource specialization (Rice 1991:262), selectively using particular clays, or if multiple communities of practice accessed different clay sources to produce a given type.

Another way of looking at this, in terms of how such pottery would have been a part of household-scale life, is to see these pots in terms of gradients along a continuum of acceptable social performance. Although not identical, they were compatible tools for people preparing and serving cuisines, with subtle differences that would have marked those who used them as belonging to similar communities of practice.

Such compatibilities would have variably accomplished similar tasks, such as their role in crosscutting variable household relationships to diverse communities of potters. For example, the Burnished Black vessels at Locus B were of more highly polished, more completely smudged ash- and tuff-tempered varieties than those at Loci A and C. Locus A contained greater amounts of Burnished Black wares than the other two loci, but not all Burnished Black pottery in Locus A was as "Kapo-fancy" in finish or made of the ashy pastes much as in the same forms of pots at Locus B. Locus C also contained Burnished Black vessels of all paste types, in versions that were probably just as functional, if perhaps not as "presentable" because of their less-reduced surface colors and coarser burnishing. It is plausible that a member of any of these households at Casitas would have recognized the generally similar style of such vessels, as manifest in table and kitchen settings across the site. I posit that the potential was high for such outward quality in final products to serve as diacritical markers for outside observers (guests) to distinguish different household connections to potters.

Loci A and C carry on this trend toward divergence in quality within the micaceous wares. All loci seem to have used their micaceous jars in cooking, reflected by sooting and differentials in carbon profiles across the sample. Large, plate-like, fully micaceous paste groups (as opposed to those that were mica-slipped) are more strongly represented at Loci A and C than at Locus B, where pastes of ash temper with finely divided mica and mica slips dominate. The former may represent either cooking pots made locally using imported or traded residual clay or pottery obtained from itinerant Jicarilla Apache potters (Eiselt 2006). The latter ash-tempered, mica-slipped vessels were probably imported from Tewa pueblos. Thus, while each echoed similar ideas about what made a good cooking pot, they reflected distinct networks of acquisition and possible technical preferences related to performance. Similarly, although each disposal locus contained polychrome vessels, only Locus B had any significant proportion made with basalt temper. Because it has the lowest proportion of local sandy and untempered clays and the greatest percentage of ash, tuff, and basalt pastes, Locus B seems to have been supplied by greater quantities of extralocal pottery, particularly pottery likely to have been from Keres and Tewa Pueblo sources. This internal diversity of composition exists despite the fact that each locus contains almost identical suites (if not proportions) of vessels in type and form. This theme of difference-but-comparability manifests itself through many stages of the ceramic assemblages. These findings call into question models

of monolithic colonial Pueblo ceramic industry based on strictly traditional clay sources for specific types. As well, the diversity of fabrication
methods and links to varied indigenous traditions—Pueblo, Apache,
and other—evidenced at Casitas calls into question models of a separate, *hispano*-specific ceramic industry. This study demonstrates the relevance of technological ceramic analyses for amplifying and modifying
hypotheses proposed by pioneering studies of pottery production.

Animal remains at Casitas are a mix of domestic and wild fauna comparable to other colonial New Mexican assemblages. Almost the full
suite of domesticates found in the middens of Santa Fe (Bowen 1995) is
present at Casitas. But the dominance of sheep and goats over cattle is
more similar to proportions of taxa from more peripheral *vecino* settlements (A. Harris 1967; Haecker 1976; Ferg and Johnson 1984; Atkins and
Gastoni 1997). Unlike at Santa Fe, wild artiodactyl remains are similar to
those found at the early colonial Pueblo site of Paa-ko (Gifford-Gonzalez
and Sunseri 2007).

Casitas is distinct from most Pueblo sites (e.g., Lang and Harris 1984)
in the low proportion of rabbits and jackrabbits, which formed a core
source of protein intake in precolonial Pueblo cuisines. The dominance
of Old World domesticates at Casitas corresponds with similar heavy
reliance documented in the late-18th-century colonial agricultural economy (Simmons 1983). Domestic fauna are dominated by caprine (goat
and sheep) specimens, in more or less complete skeletal representation.
The element representation of local wild fauna at Casitas might suggest
chance encounters of wild game by herders, perhaps younger or lower
*casta* family members (Swadesh 1974), who supplemented provisions at
Casitas with wild animals happened upon in the field.

Nonlocal bison and antelope portions, heavily modified for use as
food (as opposed to processed for hide production), also appear in the
assemblage. These species would have been encountered farther from
Casitas, with antelope more frequent in open habitat outside the small
intermontane valley systems of the southern San Juan Mountain ranges,
and bison occupying the Plains. These species came from different places,
but acquisition of both benefitted greatly from communal hunting.
Although occasional hunting parties may have forayed through hostile
territory, another scenario is possible: these species entered some Casitas
households as traded portions of meat from nomadic groups. Such interactions, documented in regional folktales and oral histories (Rebolledo
and Márquez 2000), would have depended upon more situation-based
affinity relationships than imagined in earlier, dichotomized Spanish and

Indian paradigms. These interactions may have drawn upon the complex individual histories of Casitas persons and families. In other words, differences in proportions of each species among Casitas households offer another archaeological window to the diversities within Casitas culinary repertoires, which themselves reflect divergent lives and histories.

While cow, sheep, and goat remains are dominate fauna in all disposal loci at Casitas, Locus A alone contains pig and chicken remains. Interestingly, it is also the only locus to be completely devoid of horse and bison remains. Locus B, on the other hand, is unique in the diversity of wild taxa present in its subassemblage. It is the only disposal location that contains wild carnivores as well as birds of prey. Locus C, though lacking most of those wild species, shares the presence of bison with Locus B.

Like the diversities apparent in ceramic pastes in this small village, residents' uses of various wild and domestic taxa may reflect membership in more than one community of practice, as evidenced by their species choices and acquisition strategies. Similar parallels manifest in practices that tie production to consumption, implying that foodway preferences of more than one consumer group structured the production and consumption of those products.

## Production Practices Related to Consumption

How were the behaviors of pottery and meat suppliers structuring and being structured by the desires and tastes of households at Casitas? The foregoing discussion of raw material acquisition must be contextualized in relation to how those materials were transformed into attractive or useable vessels and edible or appropriate meals. These next stages in both operational sequences relate the *habitus* of producers (potters and home butchers) to that of consumers (cooks and eaters) in ways that suggest how demand (Costin 2000:396) may have crosscut stages of production and use. The *chaîne opératoire* approach examines intermediate transformations between source and form.

Plain wares are significantly different than the polychromes and the micaceous wares in their construction, finish, thickness, lip form, and firing. Variation within each ware category and their distribution across the site suggests that multiple individuals and communities of practice contributed differently to each of these production variables. Construction methods evidenced mostly coil and scrape, though some vessels exhibited a composite of techniques, including coil and scrape with convex molding. These latter practice may reflect a Mexican Indian technique introduced to historic New Mexican potting communities (Foster 1948; Warren 1979; Carrillo 1997), but see Snow (1984:108). Finishing techniques obliterated so much evidence of forming techniques that other analytical methods were pursued to explore the common practice of vessel wall construction. This archaeological evidence demonstrated a hybridity in pot production methods.

As potters created vessels for use at Casitas, embodied behaviors were manifest in variables such as thickness and lip form that suggest certain nondiscursive learning communities of practice. Thickness is related to potters' forming techniques (Shepard 1956:185), as well as overall size and performance characteristics required by consumers (Rice 1987:227). In the case of plain ware bowls, the fact that there are no significant differences in thickness across the types and disposal loci is evidence of the unique constraints that potters and consumers communicated about these serving vessels. Such evidence is in contrast to the range of thickness of polychrome bowls, which presumably were not made to be as consistent in stacking, storage, handling-weight, or portion-size attributes. Lip forms similarly crosscut plain ware categories, suggesting that multiple potting groups, though using different clays, had similar habits in their execution of final forming practices. Only Locus C departs from the sitewide trend in evenly proportioned lip forms, largely because of tapered lip quantities. Tapered and rolled styles of lip were distinguished by concentration in only two micaceous paste groups from different geographic locales. Ocate and Peñasco pottery with similarly tapered lip forms and large mica plates like those found in the Casitas assemblage have been attributed to Jicarilla and Picurís sources, respectively (Eiselt 2006). These classifications are complicated, even in the best typology of micaceous wares available. Jicarilla Apache sites in the El Rito and La Madera area are at the heart of this confusion, as noted in the potential need for type revisions as "El Rito and Abiquiú samples have not been compared to good Jicarilla collections from this area" (Eiselt 2006:521). Rolled lip forms, on the other hand, match up with the ashy and ash-tempered with finely divided mica pastes and mica slips of the northern Rio Grande Pueblo sources, including those that also have similar lip forms. Such selectivity is not seen in other pottery types at Casitas and relates the disparate practices of people who produced the micaceous wares in the assemblage. Perhaps this is related to the cooking role that such vessels filled across the northern borderlands. What these lip forms demonstrate is that the diversity of potting communities evidenced in the plain wares was greater than that of those who made the cookware-centric micaceous pots. As lip forms are usually interpreted as less varying because of habitual behaviors in final forming techniques, their presence in multiple paste groups suggests that potters shared practices despite using different raw materials. Overall, trends in thickness and lip forms crosscut spatial distributions at Casitas as well as geologic origins of materials. But the communities of potters making these ceramics were differentiated by cooking versus plain wares, something picked up on by the households who differed in their selection of micaceous ware providers.

Firing temperatures and profiles suggest that potters who created the Casitas ceramic assemblage pursued multiple sources of fuel acquisition and varied techniques of arranging vessels in their fires. Hot, short firings predominate, with control of heat gradients and smudging coverage for Burnished Black wares. Gathered fuel for firing—wood from common, *ejido* lands associated with grant communities, versus dung from corrals (Carrillo 1997:168)—shows some aspects of the organization of labor in pottery making, suggesting forms of nonclay working labor performed by potters or people in addition to the potters themselves (Costin 2000:391). Firing core evidence, exhibited as consistently oriented color gradients across their firing cores, suggests a standardization of vessel size, shape, and possibly stacking of plain ware bowls in the assemblage. Although not developed by quantitative means here, spalled, unsooted, and apparently unused wasters (Rice 1987:179) of micaceous and Culinary Plain pots, when considered with the presence of local clays in both types, may support near-site production sources for some of the ceramic material at Casitas. Abraded sherds predominantly in Loci B and C, whose working edges exhibit the same radii of curvature as vessel interiors, may be further evidence of on-site potters who abraded rough inner surfaces of unfired vessels to smooth and even them out (Haecker 1976:110). Taken as a whole, ceramic production techniques reflecting forming practices and processes hinting at standardization resulted in a tightly constrained set of final products that satisfied multiple households' demands for culinary tools.

The ways that steps in the ceramic production sequence related to the physical and social roles of pots were paralleled by how varying identities were expressed through the handling of food ingredients. Subsequent uses for these hearthscape tools can be seen in the ways in which whole animals were reduced into meat ingredients. The use of chopping tools at Casitas varied widely among the three disposal loci. Those portions themselves may be more telling of the transformation of animals into household-level meat resources.

Spatial differentiation of portion representation showed that among the three disposal loci at Casitas, axial, hind limb, and forelimb sectioning crosscut the communities of practice reflected in species choice. With regard to axial portion representation, Locus A continues in adherence to domestic caprines, while Locus C's underrepresentation of caprines is in some part made up by deer ribs. Locus B is exceptional in the amount of axial resources present, especially in livestock. Compared to the other loci, the Locus B household was likely served by cooks who may have known well how to "cook the spinal column with red chile and season it right" (Gilbert 1982:42). Perhaps this was a matter of taste or, in part, a compensation for not receiving as many of the large meat cuts associated with the hind limb portions of domesticate animals. Locus B lags behind Loci A and C in that respect, particularly in how much less hindquarter beef is evidenced by faunal remains there. When considering forelimb anatomical portions, the trend of Loci A and C track more closely to each other than to Locus B. Mutton portions at Locus C are reduced with respect to the other loci, a trend that in both hind- and forequarter portions is accompanied by a concomitant increase in venison. In general, it would seem that the Locus C household was more closely aligned with the practices of people who deposited animal remains at Locus A. This follows from the kinds of animals and the portions that were chosen for their respective cuisines. Where there were shortfalls in mutton, it appears that the Locus C household closed the gap with the use of venison. Such practices of supplementing domestic fauna with wild species have been seen elsewhere in the Spanish colonies and strikes an interesting balance between the "Santa Fe–like" suite of domesticates at Locus A and the diversity in wild species at Locus B.

Processing of these animal resources into meals continued on ever-decreasing portions of meat and bone. The cut marks left on faunal elements relates prior butchery practices at Casitas to later, finer-scale practices of culinary processing and consumption. As with other aspects of animal use at Casitas, data must be interpreted in the context of a preponderance of caprine remains. In the case of cut marks, intensive processing of sheep and goat portions is evidenced across the site, with Locus C exhibiting a higher relative incidence of stone tool use on these animals. Metal tool use at Locus B is seen at high rates in cattle and elk, contrasting stone tool cut marks on wild cervids (deer) at the same locus. The combination of metal tool cut marks on animals from farther afield and use of stone tools on much of the domestic fauna suggests a complex history, perhaps of multiple actors, for these foods. A lack of quality metal tools in the northern provinces was common (Moore 2005) and could be problematic for sedentary and vulnerable frontier outposts like Casitas. On the northern frontier, the true *ricos* were part of the alliances of nomadic groups with the best horses, knives, guns, and surpluses of livestock and captives to trade (Blackhawk 2007). Perhaps more than for butchers and cooks among nomadic raiders, cooks processing meat at Casitas may have compensated for lack of good metal edges by using stone tools. Shortfalls of mutton at Locus C were paralleled by greater use of stone tools for butchering.

Differences in the provisioning, processing, and consumption differences among the three disposal loci at Casitas produces a more textured perspective on how cuisine may have reflected and crosscut status across the site. Households such as that at Locus C approximating the dominantly domestic animal diet of Santa Fe compensate for the frontier situation by using replacement animals or stone tools to process portions. But at least one set of consumers at Locus B—despite having had access to domesticated animals—appears to have included more wild species not seen in the other two loci, while cutting with a higher proportion of metal tools. Such diversities in food portions, tools, and animal species used at Casitas complicates how cuisine was actually experienced by people who lived there, making problematic any assumption of Indian versus Spanish identity, as well as assumptions of cultural homogeneity.

## Use and Disposal

The previous discussions of choices made during sourcing and production focused on how decisions made by potters and home butchers may have related the products of their labor to the tastes of household consumers. As a researcher, my question is that now that I know *what* kinds of pots and animal portions went *where* at Casitas, can I relate that to how these items were used within the household contexts? Evidence of use and disposal behaviors on the hearthscape emphasizes the interrelatedness of tool and ingredient choices and how they built and rebuilt communities via reflexive processes of taste and demand.

In the ceramic assemblage these processes include how vessel forms tied the community of potters to those who used their products in making hearth-scale decisions. Potters from various communities, and perhaps ethnic groups, created vessels that were a crucial part of foodway performance. Evidence from forming to firing shows that potters were not only informed by their own communities of pot-making practice but also by the other potters who were producing pottery for colonial consumption. As a result, vessels at Casitas were a mix of forms across the types. Plain wares dominate the occurrence of flange plates, cups, and small hemispherical bowls across the site. Archaeologically, micaceous wares are more strongly represented by jars, corresponding with ethnohistoric accounts of their use as cooking vessels. Polychromes, too, seem to have filled traditional roles as storage jars. But even among these categories, some overlap occurred, such as micaceous flanged bowls or cosmetic vessels and Culinary Plain cooking pots. Use wear evidence, such as sooting, cutlery marks, or banded lime deposits, was not observed frequently enough to include statistical analyses of patterning. Consider though that utilitarian performance characteristics were only a small part of how ceramic vessels were engaged in the social creation and re-creation of foodways at Casitas. Ceramics used in the hard work of preparation, as well as the sensory performances of presentation and consumption of cuisine, were part of a process of communication (following Skibo and Schiffer 2008:26). Vessel holding capacity and accessibility of contents were interarticulated with their users' conspicuous ability to possess examples of a range of pots that exhibit indigenous and colonial forms, as well as hybrid in-betweens.

Within a category of vessel form, hemispherical bowls, the sample demonstrates a large proportion of single portion–sized vessels. These vessel forms specifically draw from the suite of vessel types associated with serving meals on Iberian and colonial Spanish tables. They relate to the cultural shift from shared serving vessels to individual servings for each person at the table. Flange plates and small bowls occur across the assemblage but are concentrated in Culinary Plain, Red-on-Brown, and Burnished Black types. Smaller vessel forms such as these diverge from the communal eating and feasting vessels and practices of indigenous Pueblo people, which focused on larger, irregularly sized communal bowls. Pueblo food sharing in such vessels is reflected in long sequences of large bowls in the archaeological record. The practice of sharing was "a metaphor for interdependence and interconnection as a way of understanding [Tewa] relationships to each other" (Cajete 2004:110). Conversely, smaller colonial vessel forms have been explained as representing in colonial contexts "the growing custom of individual rather than communal dishes and served as an all-purpose eating vessel for liquids as well as solid foods" (Lister and Lister 1976:72). Only Locus B shows any trend in bowl sizes that might be related to the practice of eating together. While this is another independent line of evidence suggesting stronger indigenous affinities of this household, Locus B also has a high proportion of individual serving vessels in colonial forms.

Deetz discussed a similar change in orientation as part of the Georgian Order (Deetz 1977); in the era of the Bourbon reforms in Spain, a parallel process of increasing emphasis on the individual was well under way. Other reformulations of relationships between the individual and the collective, such as those happening in the Church (O'Hara 2009), were experienced by people in New Spain. These trends parallel how shifts in culinary behavior occurred along a continuum within the community of Casitas.

Individual serving practices reinvigorated the late-18th-century colonial elites' preoccupation with distinguishing between different classes and *castas* (Katzew 2004:112). If colonists were forced to share their settlements, households, and even their tables with people of lower *casta* designation, they certainly did not have to eat out of the same vessels with them and may have expected more choice portions of whatever cuisine was being produced in their kitchens. Such attitudes are reflected by representations of neatly stacked, individually sized colonial household vessels in period art (Katzew 2004:24). They are also strongly suggested by the faunal assemblage at Casitas in how the ingredient choices were portioned for household consumption. What other ways might shifts from collective to individual culinary practices be archaeologically observed within a small community of ostensibly homogeneous and related settlers?

Bone evidence for the size of servings consumed in Casitas households was different enough among disposal loci to suggest that cooks were sizing elements not only to fit cooking pots and serving plates but also to extract differing amounts of nutrients. For example, Loci B and C exhibit similar intensities of percussion processing of bone, smashing them open in similar proportions. Both Locus A and Locus B differ from Locus C in how small those fragments ultimately were. High rates of processing characterized by small bone pieces at Locus C echo data from other colonial sites interpreted as having intensified nutrient extraction from a constrained suite of animal resources (Hunter-Anderson et al. 1979:72). Furthermore, these differences parallel those also observed for the presence of supplemental venison and its general nutritional utility at this locus. Locus C folks may have been poorer than the Locus A household, even though they may have been striving to put together a similar Hispano way of life, at least when the need arose to do so.

Nutritional utility comparisons suggest that while cattle and sheep may have been important sources of bone grease across Casitas, overall leaner deer portions had more utility as sources of marrow and meat at Locus C. The Casitas data somewhat diverge from observations by analysts of other Spanish colonial New Mexican faunas, where "even in times of famine, they did not or could not completely adopt Pueblo cuisine, which emphasized deer and small mammals" (Trigg 2004:231). The heavy selection for beef and mutton at Locus A is very much in keeping with the domesticate-based cuisines of colonial society of New Spain, perhaps nearly to the extent of domestic "meat glut" behaviors of colonial Mexico (Ávila et al. 2004). The taste for sheep and deer marrow suggested for the Locus B fauna in both wild and domestic species is not paralleled in the seemingly poor Locus C, where the fauna contains few high-return marrow bones. This is in keeping with the Locus C house-holds' attempts at approximating cuisine seen in the colony center, but not having the means to replicate it because they were less in control of animal resources than their neighbors. Locus B, though not having eaten much rabbit, was getting the marrow bones, while Locus C was perhaps making bone grease, certainly a mark of less access to fats in the form of marrow and/or body fats.

Bison remains in Locus B, as well as in Locus C, seem to indicate a general trend of wild animal use not shared by Locus A practices. More-over, horse butchering and cooking evidence in these two loci reveal taboo-breaking behaviors in which Locus A contributors do not partici-pate. On the other hand, pork consumption, evidenced only at Locus A, is a prescribed (rather than proscribed) practice. Pork and its culinary transformations are a quintessentially "Spanish" meat, the consumption of which was used to signal Christian practice in Reconquista Spain and its New World holdings because it was taboo to Muslims and Jews (M. Harris 1997; Kunin 2001; Hordes 2008). Such practices may also be con-textualized by the fact that in New Spain, Jews were the first to receive the formal sentence of burning at the stake (Ebright and Hendricks 2006:107). Given the genetic evidence for Jewish heritage at the northern edge of the colony (Wheelwright 2008), there is some reason to believe that regions that far north meant refuge for more than one kind of fugi-tive and opportunities to reinvent oneself. With this pull came brutal pushes, such as the famous witchcraft trials reported to the Church from Abiquiú which could not have escaped the attention of anyone living on the frontier, certainly not relatives at Casitas.

In other cases, foodway choices may be understood by how ingredi-ents from the initial realm of choices were omitted from human con-sumption. A notable nonfood animal use practice can be found in the avifauna. These raptor remains were exclusive to Locus B, and other wild carnivores in this midden suggest that at least part of the animal use contributing to that assemblage was a result of continued precolonial indigenous practices. Raptors in the assemblage are distinguished from other species by the type and frequency of anthropogenic modifications in represented elements. From the shallow and frequent cut marks along feather attachment areas, it seems plumage access factored highly in the use of these bird remains, something that suggests continuation of pre-contact Pueblo ritual practices.

## Hearthscape Trends across the *Plazuela*

Overall, foodway evidence from Casitas complicates yet provides depth to discussions of appropriate cuisine choices for colonial people in New Mexico. Trigg's (2004:234) discussion of Spanish colonial culinary choices is informed by the historically defined "moral imperatives" of reproducing Spanish foodways. From such a perspective, only famine could force proper *vecinos* to eat foods associated with Pueblo (Trigg 2004:236), or worse, *indio bárbaro* cuisines. But in acknowledging how foods closest to those from Spain were desirable because of their symbolic connection with the upper classes of colonial society, Trigg opens the door to consideration of how wealth and status may have created differences between individual households' cuisines (Trigg 2004:238) that can be seen archaeologically.

At Casitas, material evidence suggests that hearthscape foodways were negotiations of status on many levels and in several dimensions, even according to other "moral imperatives." For example, Locus B's repeated digression from Spanish conventions may not necessarily have been behavior as *los de abajo*, such as Locus C. Rather, such practices may have been in accordance with other indigenous rules of behavior, which Locus B may have scrupulously followed. In terms of the households that contributed to the deposition of culinary refuse at each disposal loci, many crosscutting and syncretic practices were evidenced. In the Locus A borrow pit, plain ware serving vessels were smaller and more consistent in size and shape than at the other loci. Along with micaceous cooking wares, these vessels came from a variety of potters but were more tightly constrained in their final characteristics than at other loci, suggesting less diverse networks of supply. Within these vessels, cuisines based largely on domestic livestock were served, including the only instances of pork. Again, networks of material access seem constrained, as evidenced by the lack of bison at Locus A. The sense of a strong adherence to Santa Fe–style colonial *habitus* pervades the use of foodway-related material at Locus A. Compared to the other two loci, it may not have had as much of the nicest polished wares, or even come in second place in the diversity of animals used, but the use of ceramics suggests table settings of matching, individual serving vessels and cuts of meat. What is conspicuously absent from Locus A are horse and bison remains—the former, potentially abhorrent to consume (Rabasa 2000; Beebe and Senkewicz 2001); the latter, demonstrative of ties to erstwhile enemies of the Plains (Spielmann 1991). A concomitant attention to taboo to that which led to consumption of specifically non-Jewish food at Casitas seems to have reinforced prohibitions against use of horse and wild carnivore remains at Locus A in ways not seen elsewhere in the site.

Locus C evidence parallels the themes read from Locus A but may be at some lower economic index. Domestic animal presence is similar to Locus A, but the portions of animals used by contributors to Locus C consistently indicate less breadth and depth to diet than in more diverse neighboring loci. People who created this disposal locus did not incorporate pork or wild carnivores but shared in some aspect of horse and bison consumption with Locus B. These eating practices were enacted with a similarly sized and proportioned suite of ceramic vessels as Locus A, but more of them were made from local clay sources. In fact, on-site production of pottery at Casitas is in greatest evidence at Locus C, as suggested by the various by-products of ceramic production, as well as some traits of standardization. If Snow is right about pottery production being a low-status endeavor in New Mexico, this locus seems the best candidate to support such interpretations. It is certainly not the most "Indian"-like in its foodway practices.

Locus B is interesting because of the diversity of the ceramic and faunal assemblages in this midden. Among the numerous geographic origins for its pottery, Tewa-basin producers largely factor, but so do micaceous wares from both northern and southern protohistoric sources. Potters from more than one community of forming and firing practice contributed pots made from similar or identical paste groups. These pots were present in vessel sizes for both individual portions and larger communal eating styles, the latter of which were more common at Locus B than at the other two loci. Given the use of horse as food, the predilection for wild game, and the great breadth and depth of pottery sources and functions at this locus, it would be hard to categorize the behaviors evidenced at Locus B as aligned with *vecino* tastes described elsewhere in the colony. The greater use of metal tools in subdividing protein-rich animal portions as well as flavorful axial elements, the high quality of smudging and polish on serving vessels, contrasts with the greater use of slipped micaceous pots (the second-best kind for beans) and less use of domesticate hind limbs and forelimbs. These differences complicate interpretations about status at Locus B. This is in contrast with behavior that has been interpreted as that of wealthy colonists maintaining Spanish foodways to differentiate themselves from less affluent households (Trigg 2004:238).

These are tentative interpretations at best, given the small sample sizes in such a short occupation, small site such as Casitas, yet they are tantalizing nonetheless. In a Spanish colonial world in the grip of the Inquisition, and with what would become infamous witch trials occurring in Casitas Viejas's mother village of Abiquiú just to the south (Ebright and Hendricks 2006), the prescription of pork and proscription of horse at Locus A could uniquely reflect some affinities most closely paralleled by assemblages from colonial deposits at Santa Fe (Bowen 1995; Snow and Bowen 1995), while those of Locus B and C potentially demonstrate fewer concerns with elite tastes than alignments with indigenous practices of the north.

Such interpretations are difficult to apply to sites far from Santa Fe. On the northern frontier, nomadic groups were powerful brokers of alliance and trade (Blackhawk 2007). Perhaps the people who contributed to the Locus B subassemblage were able to mobilize many interconnected aspects of similarity with a range of frontier indigenous people. Such strategies may have served to elevate their social status in ways reflected in the diversity of materials at Locus B.

As the material evidence at these loci suggests, practices paralleling single group identities were not a sitewide phenomenon at Casitas. Not only were foodways practices different between loci, but they were also varied in how syncretic combinations within and between various stages of production and consumption materially manifested in the archaeological world. A culturally homogeneous creole model does not hold up against the complex ways that this single community engaged aspects of practices associated with different traditions. Although Swadesh (1974) and Van Ness (1991) have argued that close kin relations linked families who lived around the little fortified *plazuela* at Casitas, the differences between distinct disposal loci problematize any notion of a homogeneous corporate community. Within the larger grouping of colonial citizens, smaller categories of group identities such as Casitas were perhaps not as uniform as historical sources might suggest.

There is little doubt that this site represents a satellite of the Casitas outpost of Abiquiú and was positioned in the Rito Colorado valley as part of a larger set of strategies. Concurrent with those strategies, occurring at smaller scales and in daily practice, identity and status differentiation among lower *casta* people was enacted along lines that colonial elites might not have imagined. But for those who lived, raised families, and died at Casitas, internal politics and cross-cultural fluency were dynamics that played out differently on hearths around the central courtyard than they did on scales that united them in the goal of keeping possession of their land grant.

## Tactical and Engineering Perspectives on Homescape Practices

At the largest scale of analysis, I have used a landscape approach that follows Bourdieu's (1977) analogy of language acquisition. Such an approach focuses on specific grammars of spatial pattern and how multiple material vocabularies could have crosscut and built tension and relations with each other. As applied to the Rito Colorado valley, this approach departs from the structurally determined constraints of a single scale or context. In this case, the broader frameworks include what I call the tactical homescape and the engineered homescape. GIS analysis is central to understanding the Casitas homescape in both aspects, but I employed different methodologies to explore material expressions, suited to specific research questions regarding defense and hydrodynamic function.

The historic northern routes of entrance into the tactical homescape were located such that it was very likely raiding groups could be spotted well in advance by people living at Casitas. Viewshed analyses also suggests that the vastly superior agricultural position of Sapawe would have made it an almost equally effective vantage point, if monitoring northern entries was prioritized. A cost surface study suggests that what might have been more important to settlers at Casitas was an ability to withdraw from the southern end of the Rito Colorado valley at a location that made flanking maneuvers from mounted raiders less effective against a rear guard. In combination with what appears to be a more marginal agricultural location, such tactics reinforce the interpretation of greater emphasis placed on opportunities to successfully execute a retreat southward to other settlement locations along the Rio Chama.

This proximity to and probable use of these lines of retreat have social ramifications in regards to the masculine notions of *vergüenza*, or shame (Valdez 1979, qtd. in Rodriguez 2006:100). Relying upon other landholders for succor, subordinating one's labor or military status to others, was not valorized in adult male status. Placing one's community in the debt of another undermined the expected equality between independent landowners, a serious breach of social equity that very much played upon masculine *vergüenza*. Different perspectives informing such retreats might derive from studies of protohistoric Tewa aggregation and dispersion. These non-Spanish predecessors in the borderlands landscape regularly "abandoned" sites as they used kin connections to temporarily relocate for social and environmental reasons (Anschuetz 2007). This worldview resonates with multiple indigenous perspectives on homescape, where belonging implicitly connects movement with life (Anschuetz and Merlan 2007:138). In tactical perspective, the differences and synchronicities between Spanish and Tewa worldviews may have built tensions not only between settlers and colonial administrators but perhaps also within the extended Upper Chama community itself. There are definite and multilayered differences in cultural practice at the hearthscape, as seen in Casitas foodways. Potential intercommunity tensions about the tactical homescape may have found resolution at the larger scale of practices visible in the material signature of hybrid engineering endeavors.

Both settler and indigenous colonial people relied heavily on the productive nature of New Mexican field systems. In land grant communities, those attachments were intimately connected with colonial mandates for settlement. Hydrological modeling of known and historical *acequias*, in conjunction with an analysis of Pueblo agricultural space, suggests that irrigation was not practiced near Casitas in a way that was completely sanctioned or understood within Spanish colonial parameters. Although settlers were supposed to have established irrigation agriculture as part of the process of taking possession of the land grant, at Casitas they could not have actually gotten water into those required ditches by colonial techniques alone. This required a different amalgam of strategies. The only other example of successful farming to precede the buffer settlement in the Rito Colorado valley is found in the array of archaeological features associated with farmers from Sapawe pueblo. In fact, the site of Sapawe represents a prime location for colonial communities to have settled. The apparent decision to not use this site, unlike what was common in other colonial settlements in the Rio Arriba, may have been motivated by more nuanced understandings of the cultural landscape of the valley. This suggests that a mixed composition of settlers made decisions about where Casitas would be located. Characterization of topography in and around hydrological and agricultural features by high-resolution sampling suggests that linear irrigation features near Casitas were located in places almost identical to those where the Sapawe community practiced non-*acequia* techniques.

From such closely matching characteristic topographies, it appears that people at Casitas may have used "dry farming" technologies (Anschuetz 2001), similar to those once used by ancestral Tewa people at Sapawe, to bring water into their community. This most visible, intentional hybridization of technologies would give the appearance of *acequia* usage to any cursory observation by colonial administrators, but it drew upon much older, deeply rooted understandings of sustainable agricultural processes in the Tewa basin. Such means of "hiding in plain sight" from colonial invigilation may have also required some reorganization of traditional *acequia* leadership roles, such as *mayordomos* and *comisionados,* to account for missing components of a formalized and transposed, Moorish-derived irrigation system (Rodriguez 2006).

Communal efforts evidenced by homescape features are by nature less amenable than those at the hearth to understanding and interpreting intersecting cultural practices. Archaeological data strongly suggest that people with differing suites of cultural expertise, as reflected in hearthscape practices, contributed to the homescape in ways that combined both traditional Pueblo and Spanish practices in unique, syncretic ways. How those and other roles played out among the households at Casitas may have had much more to do with how these large-scale, public negotiations of community status articulated with hearthscape-level performances of identity.

## Complicating Identity on the Frontier by Putting Scales in Dialogue

There is no simple label of "Spanish" or "Indian" that can adequately encapsulate the lived experiences of the Casitas community. This is partly because, as described above, communities in the northernmost realms of 18th-century Spanish colonial New Mexico were populated by a diversity of people with heritages from Europe, Africa, indigenous Mexico, Southwest Pueblo, Plains, and other nomadic Native Americans. As a means of institutionalizing elite paranoia over this multiplicity of people, the *sistema de castas* was used to enumerate colonial people. This classification scheme has been keenly described as a "cognitive and legal system of hierarchically arranged socioracial statuses created by Spanish law and the colonial elite in response to growth of population in the colonies" (Chance and Taylor 1977:460). In an out-of-the-way branch of the Spanish empire, people of mixed ancestries became the keystone of New Mexico, and despite colonial officials' attempts to maintain the elaborate Spanish *casta* system of hierarchy, historical records testify to two centuries of Nuevo Mexicano renegotiations of their statuses and attached social stigmas in that system. Most illustrative of these phenomena, historical accounts (Kessell 1979; Gutierrez 1991; F. Levine 1999) contain tantalizing suggestions of the expression of varying social identities by communities and individuals known as "Casitas."

These famous frontier fighters were colonial citizens and, in the context of New Mexico, were ostensibly detribalized and ransomed Native Americans raised in Spanish homes (Chavez 1979; Magnaghi 1994). Casitas settlers would have had to rely upon more than simply the scattered and vulnerable colonial military outposts to survive in these dangerous areas (Brinkerhoff and Faulk 1965). Economic, political, and corporeal survival depended upon flexibility in dealing with all of the cultural groups that were, at least militarily, evenly matched in the borderlands (Twinam 1999; Brooks 2002a). Casitass, by their position in colonial society, were placed at the edge of the colony, but at the center of the cross-cultural negotiations among their enemies and kin along the frontier.

Historical archaeological evidence suggests that the cultural identity of those living at Casitas was not homogeneous, neither totally Spanish nor totally Indian. Nor can it be simply explained as a creolized community. The label of "Casitas" requires a finer-grained perspective on what ranges and mixtures of practice persons bearing this designation may have enacted. Ceramic, faunal, and landscape records do not exhibit a series of material signatures concomitant with expectations for one group or the other. Behavior evidenced by the three disposal loci at Casitas was anything but homogeneous across the site. An argument could be made that a creolized community identity is manifest in the material record of people using indigenous tools and materials in affectations of European identity. But if creolized households did constitute the population and behavior of the Casitas community, they did not do so similarly among the three loci explored archaeologically. For example, at Locus A and Locus B, a cursory observation might suggest that largely Spanish or Indian practices were enacted respectively by the different households. Only by teasing apart decisions made about foodway materials does it became apparent that both loci departed from the consumption practices of Spanish or Indian cuisine; instead, they drew from multiple relationships among the various stages of production of foodways. In order to survive, residents of Casitas had to be familiar with Spanish cuisine, Indian cuisine, and, if circumstances required it, a blending of the two.

A single practice might draw its roots from one or another tradition of precontact behavior, but information on this heritage of practice would be lost were it evaluated at coarser-grained temporal or spatial scales of analysis. It is the nature of situational identity to mobilize different suites of behavior, each resonant with practices that are the target of particular performances or behaviors for appropriate audiences. In a situation like that of the buffer settlement at Casitas, settlers brought different levels and aspects of cultural expertise to hearth- and homescape performances. In doing so, a single community could draw deeply from various experiences in order to successfully interact with the diverse groups that surrounded them on the frontier.

Imagine the fortified door at Casitas as it was occupied in the late 18th century. Depending on who came to knock (or pound) on it, a different set of cultural fluencies might have been advantageous to the community inside. If it were a colonial administrator, being able to sit them down at a table set with pork-rich *posole* in individual Spanish-style serving vessels might have been seen as a gracious prelude to a brief walk with the *mayordomo* along a select portion of what appeared to be an *acequia* system. If a group of Pueblo pilgrims on their way to visit Sapawe stopped in with a gift of a decorated polychrome vessel, it might have been best to have had a meal together on the floor, discussing how the Casitas community might contribute to the next dance at San Juan. Given the limited tactical capacity of the small *placita*, a good set of relations with much more heavily defended Pueblos would have served the community well. This may also have been the case when limited retreat from the site of Casitas could be spent with friends and kin outside of colonial centers, without administrators fully apprised of how long possession of the land grant had been given up in the interests of survival.

It may have been very difficult for any single household to perform all such interactions with equal measure of competence. But at the landscape scale, different expertise and worldviews were essential in creating a working agricultural system that was also embedded within a more communal sense of place. A community that could integrate multiple households with varying levels of cultural expertise likely had the greatest advantage in the fluid circumstances of the frontier. Historical accounts of Casitas families taking full advantage of blended experiences across diverse colonial circumstances illustrate how such practices may have worked. The archaeological record accounts for how less-illustrated genres of community practice played out at many levels to help a tiny village survive and prosper on the frontier.

Taken together, foodways and landscape data suggest that situational identity practices enabled Casitas to be a middle ground between indigenous nomads to the north and the sedentary Pueblo and Spanish colonial villages to the south. The link between situational practice and the concept of middle ground is a defining characteristic in both tangible and intangible aspects of identity performance and place-making. Richard White (1991:10) describes how such a characteristic interaction may be formulated for the colonial encounter:

> On the middle ground, diverse peoples adjust their differences through what amounts to a process of creative, and often expedient, misunderstandings. People try to persuade others who are different from themselves by appealing to what they perceive to be the values and practices of those others. They often misinterpret and distort both the values and practices of those they deal with, but from these misunderstandings arise new meanings and through them new practices—the shared meanings and practices of the middle ground. (R. White 1991:10)

If occupancy of this middle ground operated in a way similar to other frontier situations, then the social efficacy of such physical and social locations may well have affected the balance of power while materially conveying a new social order. Examining foodways and cultural landscape production exposes practice-structured dispositions managing the organization and use of these differently scaled, yet related social arenas within the middle ground of colonial frontiers. For some people, tension on the frontiers mirrored the situational expression of old traditions and newly reformulated identities.

In the case of northern New Mexico, culture contact occurred along a frontier among nomadic Native Americans, Pueblo Native Americans, Hispanic colonists, or Hispanicized captive and client groups (Brooks 2002a; Rothschild 2003). For many actors in such fluid circumstances of conflict and collaboration over land, resources, and captives, cultural heritage was not a fixed, unitary identity but rather a situational one. Different aspects of one's multiple heritages could be invoked at different times to defuse potentially dangerous or unstable situations by asserting a prior personal attachment among potential antagonists, as has been eloquently demonstrated by historians (Brooks 2002a, 2002b; Rael-Gàlvez 2002), and with this study, reinforced and made more nuanced by the inclusion of the archaeological record.

For Casitass, changing attachments were created and re-created by social practices that enacted and demonstrated affinities to the more militarily strong raiding nations surrounding them (Barth 1969; Bourdieu 1977; Bentley 1987). Because of their intimate links to the everyday practices of life, community landscapes and cuisine—here introduced as the concepts of homescape and hearthscape—are valuable investigative tools for tracing these dynamics of culture contact and negotiation, especially in colonial situations where people had so much at stake in occupying a middle ground during cycles of extreme violence. At Casitas, creation of the middle ground happened in a time and place of both danger and opportunity, populated by families who otherwise would have more deeply experienced the dimensions of their lower social status. The diverse frontier community of Casitas took advantage of their situation to reinforce the bonds between different groups of people and their land. By doing so, they stood fast in the middle ground.

# Epilogue: Protecting a Guardian of the Frontier

Just as the colonial settlers were aware of how the landscape they entered was very much in play for their indigenous friends and foes, historical archaeology at Casitas is an endeavor that takes place in the context of contemporary preservation challenges. Such issues place Casitas as part of a living history for communities living in the Rito Colorado valley. Working from this perspective, the El Rito community demands respect for the opportunities it affords to archaeologists and historians who work with the materials from Casitas and for its continuing role as a vanguard of frontier heritage and memory. This role has been validated by generations of people since the final days of occupation.

The fact that there is any standing architecture at Casitas at all testifies to long-lived cycles of restorative plastering events and restraint in removing timbers from the chapel, which probably lasted as a wholly standing structure until the late 19th or early 20th century (fig. 63). During the Great Depression, scores of people living in a huge camp between Casitas and modern El Rito strained their backs and calloused their hands in hard labor to preserve the Rito Colorado landscape from flooding and erosion. Forest Service efforts at the simple, yet deceptively complicated bureaucratic task of erecting a solid fence and curating as many artifacts as possible from various excavations are a testament to their perseverance in protecting the site. More recently, a community-based history (Gonzalez 2001) of the valley conducted in relation to the establishment of a secular cemetery near present El Rito (Anschuetz et

FIGURE 63. Standing adobe walls at Casitas.

al. 2001) includes an effort to take account of the preeminence of Casitas in the cultural history of the valley.

My own research at Casitas is deeply informed by these independent historic preservation efforts in the Rito Colorado valley. Although some of these projects were archaeological, historical, ethnographic, or architectural studies undertaken to comply with legally mandated historic preservation requirements, an ongoing active protection of the site is still part of daily life for the El Rito community. Community members, teachers, and activists have all done more than simply express interest in this project. They have pointedly encouraged me to make information available to more than a few academics with access to grey literature, academic journals, or dissertation databases. Requests and suggestions have included not only guest presentations in community forums related to control of former *ejido* common lands but also projects that integrate archaeological data and interpretations into local community college and K-12 curricula, as well as the fledgling community library. More than one local educator endorsed the potential of tying research related to Rito Colorado valley archaeological landscapes, developed as hard skills (e.g., GPS and total station mapping projects), into initiatives for developing respect for local heritage in the current generation. These creative ideas and motivations are indicative of how local advocates are proud of their cultural heritage and look for ways to reinvigorate celebration and respect for it as one means to buffer their communities from the spreading urban problems that plague today's youth.

As a new generation comes of age and important *abuelos* (living libraries of information about the traditional lifestyles, foodways, and land management) pass on, many northern New Mexicans see now as a crucial time for revival of community history and education about heritage. The dream of college-bound children, armed with the kind of education that would bring them back to northern New Mexico as consultants for other land grant communities, is an important related goal. Today's youth will be the ones to protect the rich cultural heritage across the entirety of the valley.

No signage or interpretive works describe the site standing silently at the entry to the Rito Colorado valley behind its low, modern fence line. Nonetheless, contemporary pot hunters who have been found on the site have hastily dropped their spoils when confronted with local community concerns about site preservation. Sometimes these concerns are expressed by on-site researchers such as myself; other times they have been demonstrated by community members on horseback, who have been observed to almost magically materialize when a nonlocal vehicle or group wanders too far onto the site. Whether on horseback, in four-wheel-drive vehicles, or on foot, members of the local communities of El Rito and Placitas are often found in this region of the Carson National Forest. All have been forthcoming with their desire for protection and interpretation of the site and its already excavated assemblages, though very few opine that more excavation would be well received. From first-hand experience, I can attest to the watchful eyes of those who are suspicious of anyone "poking around" near the Casitas site. Frequent phone calls to the El Rito ranger station to confirm visitors' intentions are proof of deep commitments to protect Casitas from looters. As if in some form of retirement from its long tenure as the protector of the Rito Colorado gateway in the north, the adobe ruins of Casitas and its surroundings have deservedly enjoyed various forms of active protection since the earliest days of standing watch on a challenging frontier.

## New Directions for Future Research

One unexamined hypothesis for the location of Casitas lies in its connection to a lesser-studied aspect of colonial economic infrastructure in the Rio Chama area. Like its mother site, Abiquiú, Casitas was located in close proximity to (almost on top of) a clay source. Such location preferences may be connected to ceramic production as a premeditated aspect of economic sustainability strategies for land grant communities. Several other Indo-Hispano sites in northern New Mexico have close proximity to clay sources (Charles Carrillo 2007, pers. comm.). An additional complex of site features lends itself to this hypothesis, such as the near-surface geology of the Rito Colorado directly west of Casitas. Such subsurface "bottlenecking" of the surface flow of water creates an unusable floodplain for agriculture, while simultaneously exposing Pleistocene lake deposits of clay from erosion banks. Genízaro sites such as Casa Colorado del Sur, San Jose de las Huertas, and the colonial settlement near the Pueblo site of Kuapa may be investigated for local, subsurface geological characteristics to compare with the Abiquiú and Casitas situations. Sampling of nearby clay sources and petrographic comparison with archaeological ceramics from these sites could greatly inform this line of inquiry.

Another future research focus may allow me to better understand the nature of ritual homescape, or *espacio sagrado* in the Rito Colorado valley as it relates to regional practices. Analysis of individual attributes of this aspect of homescape, such as sanctified land or dwellings (Fowles 2004), processional space (Rodriguez 2002), or attached outdoor areas (Robin and Rothschild 2002; Kidder 2004) may expose practice-structured dispositions toward managing the organization and use of these large-scale social arenas. Any investigation of place created in the Rito Colorado valley must first recognize the "big-site" (Anschuetz 2007) ritual anchor represented by the ruins of Sapawe pueblo. Ethnohistorical accounts relate archaeological site visitation and collective recognition of a number of sacred points on the landscape, including Sapawe, by Tewa villagers (Harrington 1916; Ortiz 1969). Associated with this site are numerous stone shrines dotting the valley floor in an array that centralizes Sapawe. Severin Fowles (2004) points out that ethnographic accounts can be confusing regarding a systematized spatial logic to their distribution (Parsons [1929] 1974), but it is clear that such landscape-marking and ritual practice involving shrines occurred across northern

New Mexico and is crucial to maintenance of ties to the supernatural world (Ortiz 1969; Basso 1996).

It is not much of a stretch to posit that the Rito Colorado valley encapsulated aspects of a sacred homescape, centered upon the large Pueblo of Sapawe, before the first colonists ever set foot in it. Perhaps because of their potency, it was these very homescape-marking elements that were to be among the first targeted by colonial ecclesiastics. In the account of the alcalde mayor of Abiquiú, during the infamous witchcraft trials of the 1760s, a Devil-possessed woman identified symbols of idolatry that needed to be exorcised and destroyed. One of the idols identified was "a powerful stone located in an ancient ruin of an Indian pueblo near the ranch that belonged to [Juan José] Lobato" (Ebright and Hendricks 2006:192). The ruin referred to is none other than Sapawe in the Rito Colorado valley. After a protracted program of exorcism, shrines in the area, such as the Stone Lions of Bandelier National Monument, as well as petroglyph panels, still show defacement by Fray Juan José Toledo.

But how successful was the attempted isolation of people in the Upper Chama from the influences of the ancestral Tewa world? Sylvia Rodriguez writes that generations later, "key foci in the sacralized cultural landscapes of aboriginal, historic, and living populations" remain shared and that for both Indian and Hispanos alike, these included "the same hydrological, techno-economic, and symbolic kinds of locale: springs, lakes, streams, ditches, reservoirs, fields, buildings, burial grounds, and shrines" (Rodriguez 2002:15). Such continuities are powerful reminders of the depth and breadth of influence that pluralistic frontier communities had on creating an enduring suite of northern New Mexican identity traits that remain cogent to this day.

## Archaeology and Preservation as Memory, Performance, and Political Action

This study of homescape and hearthscape cultural processes on the farthest northern frontier of Spanish colonial New Mexico challenges implicit assumptions about power dynamics related to the creation and maintenance of a buffer settlement. What appeared to be, at first glance, a bold program of colonial frontier defense and agricultural systems has been reconstructed by historical archaeological investigation to have been something subtly different, yet an equally encompassing example of human experience in the northern borderlands. Perhaps this variant from the prescribed colonial landscape stems from the indigenous Tewa world in which it was set. The presence of a major Tewa site in the heart of the valley settlement structure only reinforces the connections between the ancestral landscapes associated with the agricultural practices that precluded a strictly colonial irrigation technology. Tensions within household practices at the heart of this community set the stage for any number of constant reappraisals of social status, based not only on ethnic heritage but also on wealth and class. Synthesizing these lines of investigation builds upon recent studies of culture contact, further exposes how various modes of identity and expressions of community membership correlate or crosscut each other, and situates different aspects of historic identities in tension with each other. In doing so, the nature of historic identities in northern New Mexico is also complicated.

In the development of homescape and hearthscape concepts, I draw very heavily from practice theory and landscape phenomenological perspectives as they become bound in recursive lived experiences and community memories. If archaeologists interpret these through analysis of material residues, then we explicitly develop theoretical entanglements, reframing historicized imaginations of identity (e.g., colonial elites' paranoia evidenced by their creation of the *sistema de castas* fantasy) with the actual practices of peoples who are inadequately described by any simple label. Performances and behaviors are central to the project, centering attention on practices of identity as appropriate to context and allowing for material expressions of identity to be investigated as situational, contingent, and changing. As an historical archaeologist working with (semi)static records of the past, being able to evaluate different performative aspects of material culture through different, interrelated temporal and spatial scales is crucial to interpreting situational identity performance at the scales of household and village life. This, too, teases out the multiple, intersecting aspects of identity performance in this dynamic period.

Although individual lives of the nonelite are less visible, individualized categories of behavior can be brought to some resolution through differences in social realms of material life. For example, animal encounters and field-dressing practices of an adult shepherd in mountain pastures leave archaeological traces different from the trapping and blunt disarticulation of near-site crop-pest rabbits by a child close to the irrigated fields and adobe plaza. Alcaldes and other administrators visiting the fortified plaza of the communities on the frontier saw the architecture and features of the Crown's land grant from quite a different perspective than that of those visitors who might recognize petroglyphs and sacred viewsheds as integration within a Native American landscape.

Perhaps they are not entangled in readily visible ways, but the connections between the tone of the narrative attempted here and different forms of ethnographic literature run in currents that affect daily, contemporary aspects of Genízaro history and themes. Historians may point out that other perspectives on colonial life do not necessarily valorize or situate Genízaro stories as critical to historical engagements with life in northern New Mexico. As any story from the past, some of them also celebrate the resilience and innovations of these frontier communities in ways that do not ring true with ears tuned to critical nuance. I especially appreciate those community mentors and scholars who point out how complex and nuanced these narratives are in context. In my evaluation of historical context, I try to consider both difficult memories and celebrations of frontier life. The latter have been less frequently visited in light of how many Genízaro descendants today, especially community elders, learned to whisper their native heritage in shame of recognition of their captive and compromised trajectories as colonial citizens. I think this project begins to reframe frontier agency, so that noncaptive kin groups recognize Genízaro military and political prowess within their colonial context, and Genízaro descendants are provided one more set of records to decide for themselves if such work assists in reclaiming Indo-Hispano heritages as core to community survival.

Most importantly, these narratives articulate with contemporary concerns about the preservation of heritage resources that speak to the community's diverse heritage, much in defiance of dichotomous schema such as "Indian" or "Hispanic." In this sense, it has been the community itself, along with dedicated cochampions like their local Forest Service archaeologist and allied villages and community networks, that has driven protection measures for the cultural resources of the Rito Colorado valley. Without such protection, my reconsideration of the flexible and situational expression of multiple identities within a colonial settlement would have been more obscured by neglect or more severe looting.

Ultimately, it is this level of engagement that has allowed me to explore the linkages between the heritage concerns of local communities to practices embodied by their predecessors' differential participation in the processes of creation and transformation of physical space. Nowhere has this been more direct than in today's struggles for self-determination and litigation over management of land and water resources. Archaeological analyses refute outsider interest groups' notions of some "primeval wilderness" to which they would like to see *ejido* land "restored." Such attempts to appropriate rural Indo-Hispano homescapes have been interpreted locally as having "disturbing parallels to racial purity and cleansing" (Matthews 2008:2). Yet resurgent community-based activism and scholarship (Dunbar-Ortiz 2007; Correia 2013; Ebright 2014) buoy new trajectories for Indo-Hispano solidarity and sovereignty. Communities like El Rito and Abiquiú are partnering with archaeologists, historians, linguists, artists, and others as they confront old challenges and take up new, decolonizing endeavors. Like the original Casitas community, much negotiation will occur in marking place from space. When one considers the multiplicity of possible choices that a community must have made to situate themselves on both challenging physical and social landscapes, it is impossible to not admire their ability to synthesize so much information successfully and translate those choices into making and keeping a home in such a complex place.

# References

Adler, Michael A., and Herbert W. Dick, eds. 1999. *Picuris Pueblo through Time: Eight Centuries of Change at a Northern Rio Grande Pueblo*. Dallas TX: William P. Clements Center for Southwest Studies, Southern Methodist University.

Almaráz, Félix D., Jr. 1994. "An Uninviting Land: El Llano Estacado 1534–1821." In *Spain and the Plains: Myths and Realities of Spanish Exploration and Settlement on the Great Plains*, edited by R. H. Vigil, F. W. Kaye, and J. R. Wunder, 70–89. Niwot: University Press of Colorado.

Anderson, Duane. 1999. *All That Glitters: The Emergence of Native American Micaceous Art Pottery in Northern New Mexico*. Santa Fe NM: School of American Research Press.

Anderson, Jay. 1971. "A Solid Sufficiency: An Ethnography of Yeoman Foodways in Stuart England." Ph.D. dissertation, Department of Folklore and Folklife, University of Pennsylvania, Philadelphia.

Anschuetz, Kurt F. 1998. "Not Waiting for the Rain: Integrated Systems of Water Management for Intensive Agricultural Production in North-Central New Mexico." Ph.D. dissertation, Department of Anthropology, University of Michigan, Ann Arbor.

——. 2001. "Soaking It In: Northern Rio Grande Pueblo Lessons of Water Management and Landscape Ecology." In *Native Peoples of the Southwest: Negotiating Land, Water, and Ethnicities*, edited by L. Weinstein, 49–80. Westport CT: Bergin and Garvey.

——. 2007. "Room to Grow with Rooms to Spare: Agriculture and Big-Site Settlements in the Late Pre-Columbian Tewa Basin Pueblo Landscape." *Kiva* 73, no. 2:155–72.

Anschuetz, Kurt F., Esperanza Gonzalez, Tessie Naranjo, and Susan Smith. 2001. *Data Treatment Investigations of ar-03-02-0296/0543 (la 89391/la 118494) within the Proposed El Rito Cemetery Association Special-Use Permit Parcel, El Rito Ranger District, Carson National Forest, Rio Arriba County, New Mexico.* Santa Fe NM: Rio Grande Foundation for Communities and Cultural Landscapes.

Anschuetz, Kurt F., and Thomas Merlan, eds. 2007. *More Than a Scenic Mountain Landscape: Valles Caldera National Preserve Land Use History.* U.S. Department of Agriculture, Forest Service, Rocky Mountain Research Station, Fort Collins CO.

Anschuetz, Kurt F., Richard H. Wilshusen, and Cherie L. Scheick. 2001. "An Archaeology of Landscapes: Perspectives and Directions." *Journal of Archaeological Research* 9, no. 2:157–211.

Anthony, Harold Elmer. 1928. *Field Book of North American Mammals.* New York NY: Putnam.

Archibeque, Benino, Conception Archibeque, José Gurulé, Pedro Gurulé, Magdalena Gallegos, Patricio Gallegos, and Lou Sage Batchen. 2000. "Clotilde and Francisca: The Story of an Indian Raid." In *Women's Tales from the New Mexico WPA: La diabla a pie,* edited by T. D. Rebolledo and M. T. Márquez, 298–308. Houston: Arte Público Press.

Atkins, Nancy J. 2001. "Valencia: A Spanish Colonial and Mexican-Period Site along NM47 in Valencia County, New Mexico." *Museum of New Mexico Archaeology Notes of the Office of Archaeological Studies* 267:109–16.

Atkins, Peter, and M. Gastoni. 1997. "The Maltese Food System and the Mediterranean." *Geojournal* 41, no. 2:127–36.

Ávila, Ricardo, Rodolfo Fernández, and Guillermo Gómez. 2004. "Meat Gluttons of Western Mexico." *Estudios del Hombre* 18:105–25.

Balkansky, Andrew K., Gary M. Feinman, and Linda M. Nicholas. 1997. "Pottery Kilns of Ancient Ejutla, Oaxaca, Mexico." *Journal of Field Archaeology* 24, no. 2:139–60.

Balkwill, Darlene, and Steven L. Cumbaa. 1992. *Guide to the Identification of Postcranial Bones of Bos taurus and Bison bison.* Ottowa ON: Canadian Museum of Nature.

Bancroft, Hubert Howe. 1889. *History of Arizona and New Mexico.* San Francisco CA: History Company.

Barth, Fredrik, ed. 1969. *Ethnic Groups and Boundaries: The Social Organization of Culture Difference.* Bergen, Norway: Universitetsforlaget.

Basso, Keith. 1996. *Wisdom Sits in Places: Landscape and Language among the Western Apache.* Albuquerque: University of New Mexico Press.

Baugh, Timothy G. 1991. Ecology and Exchange: The Dynamics of Plains-Pueblo Interaction. In *Farmers, Hunters, and Colonists: Interaction between the Southwest and the Southern Plains,* edited by K. Spielmann, A., 107–27. Tucson: University of Arizona Press.

Beebe, Rose Marie, and Robert M. Senkewicz, eds. 2001. *Lands of Promise and Despair: Chronicles of Early California, 1535–1846*. Berkeley CA: Heyday.

Beekman, Christopher S., Phil C. Weigland, and John J. Pint. 1999. "Old World Irrigation Technology in a New World Context: Qanats in Spanish Colonial Western Mexico." *Antiquity* 73, no. 280:440–47.

Benes, Jaromir, and Marek Zvelebil. 1999. "A Historical Interactive Landscape." In *The Archaeology and Anthropology of Landscape: Shaping Your Landscape*, edited by P. J. Ucko and R. Layton, 73–93. London: Routledge.

Bentley, G. C. 1987. "Ethnicity and Practice." *Comparative Studies in Society and History* 29:24–55.

Bice, Richard A. 1993. "Earth to Earth—An Abandoned Hispanic Adobe Village." In *Archaeology, Art, and Anthropology: Papers in Honor of J. J. Brody*, 9–21. Albuquerque: Archaeological Society of New Mexico.

Binford, Lewis R. 1978. *Nunamiut Ethnoarchaeology*. New York ny: Academic Press.

Binford, Martha R. 1979. "Spatial Patterning and Content Variability in Four Historic Faunal Assemblages." In *Archeological Investigations in Cochiti Reservoir, New Mexico*, 4 vols., edited by J. V. Biella and R. C. Chapman, 247–68. Vol. 4: *Adaptive Change in the Northern Rio Grande Valley*. Office of Contract Archeology, Department of Anthropology, University of New Mexico, Albuquerque.

Blackhawk, Ned. 2007. "The Displacement of Violence: Ute Diplomacy and the Making of New Mexico's Eighteenth-Century Northern Borderlands." *Ethnohistory* 54, no. 4:723–56.

Blair, Mary Ellen, and Laurence R. Blair. 1986. *Margaret Tafoya, a Tewa Potter's Heritage and Legacy*. West Chester PA: Schiffer.

Blumenschine, Robert J., Curtis W. Marean, and Salvatore D. Capaldo. 1996. "Blind Tests of Inter-Analyst Correspondence and Accuracy in the Identification of Cut Marks, Percussion Marks, and Carnivore Tooth Marks on Bone Surfaces." *Journal of Archaeological Science* 23, no. 4: 493–507.

Boessneck, Joachim. 1969. "Osteological Differences between Sheep (*Ovis aries* Linné) and Goat (*Capra hircus* Linné)." In *Science in Archaeology*, edited by D. R. Brothwell and E. S. Higgs, 331–58. London UK: Thames & Hudson.

Bolton, Herbert E. 1921. *The Spanish Borderlands: A Chronicle of Old Florida and the Southwest*. New Haven ct: Yale University Press.

Bourdieu, Pierre. 1977. *Outline of a Theory of Practice*. Cambridge UK: Cambridge University Press.

———. 1984. *Distinction: A Social Critique of the Judgement of Taste*. Translated by R. Nice. Cambridge MA: Harvard University Press.

Bowen, Joanne. 1995. *Seventeenth Century Faunal Remains from Santa Fe's Downtown Historic District*. Santa Fe NM: Santa Fe Archaeological Review Committee.

Bower, Jennifer L. 2006. "Forced Adaptations? Possible Effects of Cultural

Practices on the Skeletal Development of Sheep and Goats in El Rito, New Mexico." Senior honors thesis, Department of Anthropology, University of California, Santa Cruz.

Boyer, Meghann. 2002. *Report on Soil Tests of Agricultural Features in the Rito Colorado Valley.* Santa Fe NM: St. Michaels High Senior Thesis Review Board.

Briggs, Charles L., and John R. Van Ness, eds. 1987. *Land, Water, and Culture: New Perspectives on Hispanic Land Grants.* Albuquerque: University of New Mexico Press.

Brinkerhoff, Sidney B., and Odie B. Faulk. 1965. *Lancers for the King: A Study of the Frontier Military System of Northern New Spain, with a Translation of the Royal Regulations of 1772.* Phoenix AZ: Arizona Historical Foundation.

Brooks, James F. 2002a. *Captives and Cousins: Slavery, Kinship, and Community in the Southwest Borderlands.* Published for the Omohundro Institute of Early American History. Chapel Hill: University of North Carolina Press.

———. 2002b. "Violence, Exchange, and Renewal in the American Southwest." *Ethnohistory* 49, no. 1:205–18.

Brown, Carolyn, and Jane Robertshaw. 1973. "Casitas: A Plaza of the El Rito Valley (NMCRIS 48655)." Colorado Springs: Colorado College.

Bustamante, Adrian H. 1989. "Españoles, Castas, y Labradores: Santa Fe Society in the Eighteenth Century." In *Santa Fe: History of an Ancient City,* edited by D. G. Noble, 65–78. Santa Fe NM: School of American Research.

———. 2001. "'The matter was never resolved': The Casta System in Colonial New Mexico, 1693–1823." In *Native Peoples of the Southwest: Negotiating Land, Water, and Ethnicities,* edited by L. Weinstein, 203–22. Westport CT: Bergin and Garvey.

Cajete, G. A. 2004. "A Pueblo Story for Transformation." In *Learning toward an Ecological Consciousness: Selected Transformative Practices,* edited by E. O'Sullivan and M. M. Taylor. New York NY: Macmillan.

Carrillo, Charles M. 1997. *Hispanic New Mexican Pottery: Evidence of Craft Specialization 1790–1890.* Albuquerque NM: LPD Press.

Casella, Eleanor Conlin, and Chris Fowler. 2005. "Beyond Identification." In *The Archaeology of Plural and Changing Identities,* edited by Casella and Fowler, 1–10. New York NY: Kluwer Academic.

Caywood, Louis R. 1950. "Hispanic Pottery as a Guide in Historical Studies." *For the Dean: Essays in Anthropology in Honor of Byron Cummings on His Eighty-Ninth Birthday,* 77–97. Santa Fe NM: Hohokam Museums Association and the Southwestern Monuments Association.

Chance, John K. 1978. *Race and Class in Colonial Oaxaca.* Stanford CA: Stanford University Press.

Chance, John K., and William B. Taylor. 1977. "Estate and Class in Colonial Oaxaca: Oaxaca in 1792." *Comparative Studies in Society and History* 19, no. 3:454–87.

Chapman, Richard C., Jan V. Biella, Jeanne A. Schutt, James G. Enloe, Patricia J. Marchiando, A. Helene Warren, and John R. Stein. 1977. "Description of Twenty-Seven Sites in the Permanent Pool of Cochiti Reservoir." In *Archaeological Investigations in Cochiti Reservoir, New Mexico*, edited by Chapman, Biella and S. D. Bussey, 119–336. U.S. Department of the Interior Contract No. CX700050431 (UNM proposal No. 101–82) for U.S. Army Corps of Engineers. Vol. 2: *1975 Field Seasons*, F. J. Broilo, principal investigator, general editor. Office of Contract Archaeology, Department of Anthropology, University of New Mexico, Albuquerque.

Charlton, Thomas. 1976. "Contemporary Central Mexican Ceramics: A View from the Past." *Man* 11, no. 4:517–25.

Chavez, Fray Angelico. 1979. "Genizaros." In *Handbook of North American Indians*, edited by W. C. Sturtevant, 198–200. Vol. 9. Washington DC: Smithsonian Institution.

Chorn, John, Barbara A. Frase, and Carl D. Frailey. 1988. "Late Pleistocene Pronghorn, *Antilocapra americana*, from Natural Trap Cave, Wyoming." Special issue, *Transactions of the Nebraska Academy of Sciences*, no. 177.

Church, Minette Carrier. 2001. "Homesteads on the Purgatoire: Frontiers of Culture Contact in 19th Century Colorado." Ph.D. dissertation, Department of Anthropology, University of Pennsylvania, Philadelphia.

———. 2002. "The Grant and the Grid." *Journal of Social Archaeology* 2, no. 2: 220–44.

Clark, Bonnie J. 2005. "Lived Ethnicity: Archaeology and Identity in Mexicano America." *World Archaeology* 37, no. 3:440–52.

———. 2011. *On the Edge of Purgatory: An Archaeology of Place in Hispanic Colorado*. Lincoln: University of Nebraska Press.

Clifford, James. 1997. *Routes: Travel and Translation in the Late Twentieth Century*. Cambridge MA: Harvard University Press.

Comaroff, Jean. 1996. "The Empire's Old Clothes: Fashioning the Colonial Subject." In *Cross-Cultural Consumption: Global Markets, Local Realities*, edited by D. Howes, 19–38. London UK: Routledge.

Comer, Douglas C. 1996. *Ritual Ground: Bent's Old Fort, World Formation, and the Annexation of the Southwest*. Berkeley: University of California Press.

Cope, Carole. 2002. "The Butchering Patterns of Gamla and Yodefat: Beginning the Search for *Kosher* Practices." In *Behaviour behind Bones: The Zooarchaeology of Ritual, Religion, Status and Identity*, edited by S. J. O'Day, W. Van Neer, and A. Ervynck, 25–33. Oxford UK: Oxbow.

Cordell, Linda S. 2004. "Discussion: Rio Grande Village Formation in the Late Coalition Period." *Proceedings of the Society for American Archaeology, 69th Annual Meeting*. Montreal QC.

Cordell, Linda S., and Vincent J. Yannie. 1991. "Ethnicity, Ethnogenesis, and the Individual: A Processual Approach toward Dialogue." In *Processual and*

*Postprocessual Archaeologies: Multiple Ways of Knowing the Past*, edited by R. Preucel, 96–107. Carbondale: Southern Illinois University Press.

Correia, David. 2013. *Properties of Violence: Law and Land Grant Struggle in Northern New Mexico*. Athens: University of Georgia Press.

Costin, Cathy Lynne. 2000. "The Use of Ethnoarchaeology for the Archaeological Study of Ceramic Production." *Journal of Archaeological Method and Theory* 7, no. 4:337–403.

Crader, Diana C. 1990. "Slave Diet at Monticello." *American Antiquity* 55, no. 4:690–717.

Croucher, Sarah, and Stephanie Wynne-Jones. 2006. "People, Not Pots: Locally Produced Ceramics and Identity on the Nineteenth-Century East African Coast." *International Journal of African Historical Studies* 39, no. 1:107–24.

Curtis, Freddie. 1962. "The Utility Pottery Industry of Bailén, Southern Spain." *American Anthropologist* 64, no. 1:486–503.

Cushing, Frank Hamilton. 1920. *Zuni Breadstuff*. New York NY: Museum of the American Indian, Heye Foundation.

Cusick, James G., ed. 1998. *Studies in Culture Contact: Interaction, Culture, Change and Archaeology*. Carbondale: Southern Illinois University Press.

Dawkins, Richard. 2004. *The Ancestor's Tale: A Pilgrimage to the Dawn of Life*. Boston MA: Houghton Mifflin.

Deagan, Kathleen. 1973. "Mestizaje in Colonial St. Augustine." *Ethnohistory* 20, no. 1:55–65.

———. 1996. "Colonial Transformation: Euro-American Cultural Genesis in the Early Spanish-American Colonies." *Journal of Anthropological Research* 52, no. 2:135–59.

Deetz, James. 1977. *In Small Things Forgotten: The Archeology of Early American Life*. New York NY: Anchor.

DeFrance, Susan D. 1996. "Iberian Foodways in the Moquegua and Torata Valleys of Southern Peru." *Historical Archaeology* 30, no. 3:20–48.

Deutsch, Sarah. 1987. *No Separate Refuge: Culture, Class, and Gender on the Anglo-Hispanic Frontier in the American Southwest, 1880–1940*. Oxford UK: Oxford University Press.

Diamond, Jared. 1999. *Guns, Germs, and Steel: The Fates of Human Societies*. New York NY: Norton.

Dick, Herbert. 1959. "Notes from Excavations of ER-5 (LA 917)." USDA Forest Service, El Rito Ranger District, Carson National Forest, El Rito NM.

Dick, Herbert W. (1964) 1968. "Six Historic Pottery Types from Spanish Sites in New Mexico." In *Collected Papers in Honor of Lyndon Lane Hargrave*, edited by A. H. Schroeder, 77–94. Papers of the Archaeological Society of New Mexico. Santa Fe: Museum of New Mexico Press.

Dietler, Michael. 1998. "Consumption, Agency, and Cultural Entanglement: Theoretical Implications of a Mediterranean Colonial Encounter." In *Studies in Culture Contact*, edited by J. G. Cusick, vol. 25, 288–315. Carbondale IL: Center for Archaeological Investigations.

Dietler, Michael, and Ingrid Herbich. 1989. "*Tich Matek*: The Technology of Luo Pottery Production and the Definition of Ceramic Style." *World Archaeology* 21, no. 1:148–63.

Domínguez, Fray Francisco Atanasio. (1776) 1956. *The Missions of New Mexico, 1776: A Description*. Translated by F. A. Chavez and E. B. Adams. Albuquerque: University of New Mexico Press.

Druc, Isabelle C. 2000. "Ceramic Production in San Marcos Acteopan, Puebla, Mexico." *Ancient Mesoamerica* 11, no. 1:77–89.

Duff, Andrew I. 2002. "Interaction, Migration, Ritual, and a Transformed Social Order." Chapter 8 of *Western Pueblo Identities*. Tucson: University of Arizona Press.

Dunbar-Ortiz, Roxanne. 2007. *Roots of Resistance: A History of Land Tenure in New Mexico*. Berkeley: University of California Press.

Ebright, Malcolm. 1994. *Land Grants and Lawsuits in Northern New Mexico*. New Mexico Land Grant series. Albuquerque: University of New Mexico Press.

———. 2014. *Advocates for the Oppressed: Hispanos, Indians, Genízaros, and Their Land in New Mexico*. Albuquerque: University of New Mexico Press.

Ebright, Malcolm, and Rick Hendricks. 2006. *The Witches of Abiquiu: The Governor, the Priest, the Genizaro Indians, and the Devil*. Albuquerque: University of New Mexico Press.

Eiselt, B. Sunday. 2004. "Historic Micaceous Pottery Production and Raw Material Procurement in a Southwestern Horse Nomad Society: The Jicarilla Apache of Northern New Mexico." *Proceedings of the 69th Annual Meeting of the Society for American Archaeology*. Montreal QC.

———. 2006. "The Emergence of Jicarilla Apache Enclave Economy during the 19th Century in Northern New Mexico." Ph.D. dissertation, Department of Anthropology, University of Michigan, Ann Arbor.

Elkins, Melissa Anne. 2007. "Serving up Ethnic Identity in Chacoan Frontier Communities: The Technology and Distribution of Mogollon and Puebloan Ceramic Wares in the Southern Cibola Region." Master's thesis, Department of Anthropology, Washington State University, Seattle.

Ellis, Florence Hawley. 1963. *Sapawe Preliminary Report*. Albuquerque: University of New Mexico Maxwell Museum of Anthropology.

Enloe, James G. 1993. "Ethnoarchaeology of Marrow Cracking: Implications for the Recognition of Prehistoric Subsistence Organization." In *Bones to Behavior: Ethnoarchaeological and Experimental Contributions to the Interpretation of Faunal Remains*, edited by J. Hudson. Carbondale: Southern Illinois University Press.

Ewan, Charles R. 1991. *From Spaniard to Creole: The Archaeology of Hispanic*

*American Cultural Formation in Puerto Real, Haiti.* Tuscaloosa: University of Alabama Press.

Faith, J. Tyler, and Adam D. Gordon. 2007. "Skeletal Element Abundances in Archeofaunal Assemblages: Economic Utility, Sample Size, and Assessment of Carcass Transport Strategies." *Journal of Archaeological Science* 34, no. 6:872–82.

Ferg, Alan, and Paul C. Johnson. 1984. "Historic Archaeology on the San Antonia de Las Huertas Grant, Sandoval County, New Mexico." *Casa Papers*, no. 3:68–82.

Ferguson, Leland. 1992. *Uncommon Ground: Archaeology and Early African America, 1650–1800.* Washington DC: Smithsonian Institution Press.

Flint, Richard, and Shirley Cushing Flint. 2003. *The Coronado Expedition: From the Distance of 460 years.* Albuquerque: University of New Mexico Press.

Foster, George M. 1948. "Some Implications of Modern Mexican Mold-Made Pottery." *Southwestern Journal of Anthropology* 4, no. 4:356–70.

———. 1959. "The Potter's Wheel: An Analysis of Idea and Artifact in Invention." *Southwestern Journal of Anthropology* 15, no. 2:99–119.

Fowles, Severin M. 2004. "The Making of Made People: The Prehistoric Evolution of Hierocracy among the Northern Tiwa of New Mexico." Ph.D. dissertation, Department of Anthropology, University of Michigan, Ann Arbor.

Frank, Ross. 1998. "Demographic, Social, and Economic Change in New Mexico." In *New Views of Borderlands History*, edited by R. H. Jackson, 41–71. Albuquerque: University of New Mexico Press.

———. 2000. *From Settler to Citizen: New Mexican Economic Development and the Creation of Vecino Society.* Berkeley: University of California Press.

Gaffney, Vincent, and Zoran Stančič. 1991. *gis Approaches to Regional Analysis: A Case Study of the Island of Hvar.* Ljubljani, Slovenia: Univerza Ljubljani, Znanstveni Institut.

Gifford, Edward W. 1935. "Pottery-Making in the Southwest." *American Anthropologist* 37, no. 1:535.

Gifford-Gonzalez, Diane P. 1993. "Gaps in Zooarchaeological Analyses of Butchery: Is Gender an Issue?" In *From Bones to Behavior: Ethnoarchaeological and Experimental Contributions to the Interpretation of Faunal Remains*, edited by J. Hudson, 181–99. Occasional Papers. vol. 21. Carbondale: Center for Archaeological Investigations, Southern Illinois University at Carbondale.

Gifford-Gonzalez, Diane, Kenneth Gobalet, and Jean C. Geary. 2006. "Vertebrate Faunal Remains: Environment, Subsistence, Taphonomy, Historical Ecology." In *Archaeological Investigations at ca-sma-18: A Study of Prehistoric Adaptations at Año Nuevo State Reserve*, edited by W. Hildebrandt, R. M. Farquhar, and M. Hylkema. Davis CA: Far Western Anthropological Research Group, Albion Environmental, University of California Santa Cruz, California Department of Parks and Recreation.

Gifford-Gonzalez, Diane P., and Jun Ueno Sunseri. 2007. "Foodways on the Frontier: An Early Colonial Pueblo." In *We Were What We Ate: The Archaeology of Food and Identity*, edited by K. Twiss. Occasional Papers, Annual Visiting Scholar Conference. Vol. 34, K. C. Twiss, general editor. Carbondale: Center for Archaeological Investigations, Southern Illinois University at Carbondale.

Gilbert, Fabiola Cabeza de Baca. 1970. *Historic Cookery*. Las Vegas NM: La Galeria de los Artesanos.

———. 1982. *The Good Life: New Mexico Traditions and Food*. Santa Fe: Museum of New Mexico Press.

Gonzalez, Esperanza. 2001. "History of El Rito Community." In *Data Treatment Investigations of ar-03-02-0296/0543 (la 89391/la 118494) within the Proposed El Rito Cemetery Association Special-Use Permit Parcel, El Rito Ranger District, Carson National Forest, Rio Arriba County, New Mexico*, edited by K. F. Anschuetz, vol. *Challenge Cost-Share Grant among the El Rito Cemetery Association, the Carson National Forest, and the Río Grande Foundation for Communities and Cultural Landscapes* (Challenge Cost-Share Grant No. R3F2-99-CCS-003 9 [RGF 113]). Rio Grande Foundation for Communities and Cultural Landscapes, Santa Fe NM.

Good, David 1984. *The Economic Rise of the Habsburg Empire, 1750–1914*. Berkeley: University of California Press.

Gosselain, Oliver P. 1992. "Technology and Style: Potters and Pottery among Bafia of Cameroon." *Man* 27, no. 3:559–86.

Grace, R. 1990. "The Limitations and Applications of Functional Analysis." In *The Interpretative Possibilities of Microwear Studies*. In *Proceedings of the International Conference on Lithic Use-Wear Analysis*, edited by B. Gräslund, H. Knutsson, K. Knutsson, and J. Taffinder, vol. 14, 9–14. Uppsala, Sweden: Societas Archaeologica Upsaliensis.

Greenfield, Haskel J. 1999. "The Origins of Metallurgy: Distinguishing Stone from Metal Cut-marks on Bones from Archaeological Sites." *Journal of Archaeological Science* 26, no. 7:797–808.

Gruchy, S., and T. Rogers. 2002. "Identifying Chop Marks on Cremated Bone: A Preliminary Study." *Journal of Forensic Science* 47, no. 5:1–4.

Guilday, J. E., P. W. Parmalee, and D. P. Tanner. 1962. "Aboriginal Butchering Techniques at the Eschelman Site (36 La 12), Lancaster County, Pennsylvania." *Pennsylvanian Archaeological Bulletin* 32:59–83.

Gumerman, George. 1997. "Food and Complex Societies." *Journal of Archaeological Method and Theory* 4, no. 2:105–39.

Gunnerson, James H. 1979. "Southern Athapaskan Archaeology." In *Handbook of North American Indians*, edited by A. Ortiz, vol. 9, 162–69. Washington DC: Smithsonian Institution.

Gutiérrez, Ramón A. 1991. *When Jesus Came the Corn Mothers Went Away*. Stanford CA: Stanford University Press.

Haas, Lisbeth. 1995. *Conquests and Historical Identities in California, 1769–1936*. Berkeley: University of California Press.

Habicht-Mauche, Judith A. 1993. "Tribalization, Trade, and the Rio Grande Classic Tradition." Chap. 4 of *The Pottery of Arroyo Hondo Pueblo, New Mexico*, edited by J. Habicht-Mauche. Santa Fe NM: School of American Research.

Haecker, Charles M. 1976. "Modes of Subsistence and Level of Technology of the Eighteenth Century Spanish Settlers on the Rio Puerco." Master's thesis, Anthropology, Eastern New Mexico University, Portales.

Halstead, P., P. Collins, and V. Isaakidou. 2002. "Sorting the Sheep from the Goats: Morphological Distinctions between the Mandibles and Mandibular Teeth of Adult *Ovis* and *Capra*." *Journal of Archaeological Science* 29, no. 4:545–53.

Hämäläinen, Pekka. 2008. *The Comanche Empire*. New Haven CT: Yale University Press.

Hammond, George P., and Agapito Rey. 1953. *Don Juan de Oñate, Colonizer of New Mexico, 1595–1628*. Albuquerque: University of New Mexico Press.

Hanowell, Benjamin D. O. 2006. *Heirlooms of Utility and Domesticity in a Transitional Old Town San Diego: An Analysis of the Mexican Pottery Recovered in the Excavations on Block 408 in Old Town San Diego State Historic Park, California*. San Diego: California State Parks

Harlow, Francis H. 1973. *Matte-Paint Pottery of the Tewa, Keres and Zuni Pueblos*. Santa Fe: Museum of New Mexico Press.

———. 1974. *Historic Pueblo Indian Pottery: Painted Jars and Bowls of the Period 1600–1900*. Santa Fe: Museum of New Mexico Press.

Harrington, John Peabody. 1916. *The Ethnogeography of the Tewa Indians*. Bureau of American Ethnology 32nd Annual Report of the Bureau of American Ethnology to the Secretary of the Smithsonian Institution. Washington DC: Government Printing Office.

Harris, Arthur H. 1967. "The Vertebrate Fauna from LA 591." In *Cochiti Dam Salvage Project: Archaeological Excavation of the Las Majadas Site, la 591, Cochiti Dam, New Mexico*, vol. 75, 38–39. Santa Fe: Museum of New Mexico Press.

Harris, Marvin. 1997. "The Abominable Pig." In *Food and Culture: A Reader*, edited by C. Counihan and P. Van Esterik, 67–79. New York NY: Routledge.

Henrickson, Elizabeth F., and Mary M. A. McDonald. 1983. "Ceramic Form and Function: An Ethnographic Search and an Archeological Application." *American Anthropologist* 85, no. 3:630–43.

Hill, David V. 1984. "An Analysis of Voids in Ceramics." *Lambda Alpha Journal of Man* 16, no. 1:7–34.

Hill, Jonathan D. 2002. "Just About the Pottter's Wheel? Using, Making, and

Depositing Middle and Later Iron Age Pots in East Anglia". In *Prehistoric Britain: The Ceramic Basis*, edited by A. Woodward and Hill, 143–60. Prehistoric Ceramics Research Group Occasional Publication no. 3. Oxford UK: Oxbow.

Hill, Matthew Glenn. 2001. "Paleoindian Diet and Subsistence Behavior on the Northwestern Great Plains of North America." Ph.D. dissertation, Department of Anthropology, University of Wisconsin, Madison.

Hordes, Stanley M. 2008. *To the End of the Earth: A History of the Crypto-Jews of New Mexico*. New York NY: Columbia University Press.

Horvath, Steven M. 1977. "The Genízaro of Eighteenth-Century New Mexico: A Re-examination." *School of American Research Discovery* 1:25–40.

Hughes, Phyllis. 1977. *Pueblo Indian Cookbook*. 2nd ed. Santa Fe: Museum of New Mexico Press.

Hunter-Anderson, Rosalind, James G. Enloe, and Martha R. Binford. 1979. "LA 10114." In *Archaeological Investigations in Cochiti Reservoir, New Mexico*, edited by J. V. Biella, 55–73. U.S. Department of the Interior Contract No. CX702960151 (UNM proposal No. 101–127B) for U.S. Army Corps of Engineers. Vol. 3: *1976–1977 Field Seasons*, F. J. Broilo, principal investigator, general editor. Office of Contract Archaeology, Department of Anthropology. Albuquerque: University of New Mexico Press.

Hurlbut, Sharon A. 2000. "The Taphonomy of Cannibalism: A Review of Anthropogenic Bone Modification in the American Southwest." *International Journal of Osteoarchaeology* 10, no. 1:4–26.

Hurt, Wesley R., and Herbert W. Dick. 1946. "Spanish-American Pottery from New Mexico." *El Palacio* 53, no. 10:280–312.

Ingold, Tim. 1993. "The Temporality of the Landscape." *World Archaeology* 25, no. 2:152–74.

Inizan, Marie-Louise, Michael Reduron-Ballinger, Helene Roche, and Jehanne Tixier. 1999. *Technology and Terminology of Knapped Stone*. Translated by J. Feblot-Augustins. Meudon, France: Cercle de Recherches et d'Etudes Prehistoriques.

Jackson, Robert H. 1999. *Race, Caste, and Status: Indians in Colonial Spanish America*. Albuquerque: University of New Mexico Press.

James, Steven R. 1997. "Change and Continuity in Western Pueblo Households during the Historic Period in the American Southwest." *World Archaeology* 28, no. 3:429–56.

Jimenez, Petra F. 1972. "Methods of Obtaining Title to Property under Spanish Law." In *Land, Law and La Raza: A Collection of Papers Presented for Professor Theodore Parnall's Seminar in Comparative Law*. Albuquerque NM: UNM School of Law.

John, Elizabeth A. H. 1975. *Storms Brewed in Other Men's Worlds*. Lincoln: University of Nebraska Press.

Jones, Oakah L. 1979. *Los Paisanos: Spanish Settlers on the Northern Frontier of New Spain.* Norman: University of Oklahoma Press.

Katzew, Illona. 2004. *Casta Painting: Images of Race in Eighteenth-Century Mexico.* New Haven CT: Yale University Press.

Kessell, John L. 1979. *Kiva, Cross, and Crown: the Pecos Indians and New Mexico, 1540–1840.* Washington DC: National Park Service.

———. 1995. *To the Royal Crown Restored: The Journals of Don Diego de Vargas, New Mexico, 1692–1694.* Albuquerque: University of New Mexico Press.

———. 2013. *Miera Y Pacheco: A Renaissance Spaniard in Eighteenth-Century New Mexico.* Norman: University of Oklahoma Press.

Kidder, Tristam R. 2004. "Plazas as Architecture: An Example from the Raffman Site, Northeast Louisiana." *American Antiquity* 69, no. 3:514–32.

Kidder, Alfred Vincent, and Anna Osler Shepard. 1936. *The Pottery of Pecos: The Glaze Paint, Culinary and Other Wares, Vol. 2.* Papers of the Phillips Academy of Southwestern Expedition. New Haven CT: Yale University Press.

Kramer, Barbara. 1996. *Nampeyo and Her Pottery.* Albuquerque: University of New Mexico Press.

Kunin, Seth D. 2001. "Juggling Identities among the Crypto-Jews of the American Southwest." *Religion* 31, no. 1:41–61.

Lamadrid, Enrique R. 1992. "Ig/noble Savages of New Mexico: The Naturalization of 'El Norte' into 'The Great Southwest.'" *Working Papers of the Southwest Hispanic Research Institute of the University of New Mexico,* no. 121:1–24.

———. 2000. "The Indo-Hispano Cultural Legacy of New Mexico." In *Albuquerque Teachers' Institute Seminars.* Albuquerque: University of New Mexico.

———. 2003. *Hermanitos Comanchitos: Indo-Hispano Rituals of Captivity and Redemption.* Albuquerque: University of New Mexico Press.

Lambert, Marjorie F. 1981. "Spanish Influences on the Pottery of San José de los Jémez and Giusewa, Jemez State Monument (LA 679), Jemez Springs, New Mexico." *Archaeological Society of New Mexico Anthropological Papers,* no. 6:215–36.

Lang, Richard W., and Arthur H. Harris. 1984. *The Faunal Remains from Arroyo Hondo Pueblo, New Mexico.* Arroyo Hondo Archaeological Series 5. Santa Fe NM: School of American Research Press.

Lapham, Heather A. 2005. *Hunting for Hides: Deerskins, Status, and Cultural Change in the Protohistoric Appalachians.* Tuscaloosa: University of Alabama Press.

Lawrence, Robert. 1996. *Las Casitas Fence Inspection Report (nmcris activity 60090).* El Rito Ranger District NM: Carson National Forest.

LeFree, Betty. 1975. *Santa Clara Pottery Today.* Albuquerque: University of New Mexico Press.

Lemonnier, Pierre, ed. 1993. *Technical Choices: Transformation in Material Cultures since the Neolithic.* London UK: Routledge.

Leroi-Gourhan, André. 1943. *L'homme et la matière.* 2nd ed. Paris, France: Albin Michel.

——. (1943) 1973. *Evolution et techniques ii—Milieu et techniques.* 2nd ed. Paris, France: Albin Michel.

——. 1981. "Les signes parietaux comme 'marqueurs' ethniques." *Proceedings of the Altamira Symposium, Ministerio de Cultura, Direccion General de Bellas Artes*: 289–94. Madrid.

Levine, Daisy F. 1985. *Archaeological Test Excavations at la16769: Faunal Analysis.* Santa Fe NM: Public Service Company of New Mexico.

——. 1990. Tewa or Hispanic Manufacture? Pottery from Eighteenth- and Nineteenth-Century Spanish Sites near Abiquiú. In *Clues to the Past: Papers in Honor of William M. Sundt*, edited by M. Durán, S. Kirkpatrick. and D. T. Kirkpatrick, vol. 16, 173–84. Archaeological Society of New Mexico, Albuquerque NM.

——. 1996. *Ceramic Analysis and Interpretation for Two Chama Valley Sites.* Santa Fe NM: Laboratory of Anthropology.

Levine, Frances. 1992. "Hispanic Household Structure in Colonial New Mexico." In *Current Research on the Late Prehistory and Early History of New Mexico*, edited by G. E. Bradley J. Vierra, and T. E. Clara Gualtieri, vol. 1, 195–206. Special publication (New Mexico Archaeological Council). New Mexico Archaeological Council, Albuquerque NM.

——. 1999. *Our Prayers Are in This Place: Pecos Pueblo Identity of the Centuries.* Albuquerque: University of New Mexico Press.

——. 2001. "Traditional Use in a Changing Landscape." In *Native Peoples of the Southwest: Negotiating Land, Water, and Ethnicities*, edited by L. Weinstein, 125–42. Westport CT: Bergin and Garvey.

Lightfoot, Dale R. 1993a. "The Cultural Ecology of Puebloan Pebble-Mulch Gardens." *Human Ecology* 21, no. 2:115–43.

——. 1993b. "The Landscape Context of Anasazi Pebble-Mulched Fields in the Galisteo Basin, Northern New Mexico." *Geoarchaeology* 8, no. 5:349–70.

Lightfoot, Dale R., and Frank W. Eddy. 1995. "The Construction and Configuration of Anasazi Pebble-Mulch Gardens in the Northern Rio Grande." *American Antiquity* 60, no. 3:459–70.

Lightfoot, Kent G. 2005. *Indians, Missionaries, and Merchants: The Legacy of Colonial Encounters on the California Frontiers.* Berkeley: University of California Press.

Lightfoot, Kent G., Antoinette Martinez, and Ann M. Schiff. 1998. "Daily Practice and Material Culture in Pluralistic Social Settings: An Archaeological Study of Culture Change and Persistence from Fort Ross, California." *American Antiquity* 63, no. 2:199–222.

Lightfoot, Kent G, Thomas A. Wake, and Ann M. Schiff. 1993. "Native Responses to the Russian Mercantile Colony of Fort Ross, Northern California." *Journal of Field Archaeology* 20, no. 2:159–75.

Lister, Florence C., and Robert H. Lister. 1976. *A Descriptive Dictionary for 500 Years of Spanish-Tradition Ceramics (13th–18th Centuries)*. Special Publications Series 1. Winnipeg MB: Society for Historical Archaeology.

Lycett, Mark T. 2005. "On the Margins of the Peripheries: The Consequences of Differential Incorporation in the Colonial Southwest." In *The Late Postclassic to Spanish-Era Transition in Mesoamerica: Archaeological Perspectives*, edited by R. Alexander and S. Kepecs, 97–115. Albuquerque: University of New Mexico Press.

Lycett, Mark T., Philip O. Leckman, Jun U. Sunseri, and Noah H. Thomas. 2004. *Report of Archaeological Excavations at la 162, Bernalillo County, New Mexico*. Santa Fe NM: Cultural Properties Review Committee, Historic Preservation Division.

Lyman, R. Lee. 1987. "On Zooarchaeological Measures of Socioeconomic Position and Cost-efficient Meat Purchases." *Historical Archaeology* 21, no. 1:58–66.

———. 1994. *Vertebrate Taphonomy*. Cambridge UK: Cambridge University Press.

Madrigal, T. Cregg. 2004. "The Derivation and Application of White-Tailed Deer Utility Indices and Return Rates." *Journal of Taphonomy* 2, no. 4:185–200.

Magnaghi, Russell M. 1994. "The Genízaro Experience in Spanish New Mexico." In *Spain and the Plains: Myths and Realities of Spanish Exploration and Settlement on the Great Plains*, edited by R. H. Vigil, F. W. Kaye, and J. R. Wunder, 114–30. Niwot: University Press of Colorado.

Marshall, Fiona. 1990. "Origins of Specialized Pastoral Production in East Africa." *American Anthropologist* 92, no. 4:873–94.

Martinez, Felipe. 2005. Personal Communication: Livestock Productivity at Zenitram Farm Complex, El Rito NM.

Martinez, Thomas D. 1993. *Abiquiú Baptisms 1754–1870: Database of Archives Held by the Archdiocese of Santa Fe and the State Archive of New Mexico*. Abiquiú NM: Pueblo de Abiquiú Library and Community Center.

Matthews, Kay. 2008. "Rural Villages vs. Forest Guardians." *La Jicarita* 13, no. 1:3.

Maxwell, Timothy. 2000. "Looking for Adaptation: A Comparative and Engineering Analysis of Prehistoric Agricultural Technologies and Techniques in the Southwest." Ph.D. dissertation, Department of Anthropology. Albuquerque: University of New Mexico.

McGuire, Randall H. 1982. "The Study of Ethnicity in Historical Archaeology." *Journal of Anthropological Archaeology* 1:159–78.

McKusick, Charmion R. 1982. "Avifauna from Grasshopper Pueblo." *University of Arizona Anthropological Papers* 40:87–96.

Mera, H. P. 1939. *Style Trends of Pueblo Pottery, 1500–1840*. Albuquerque: University of New Mexico Press.

Metcalfe, Duncan, and Kevin T. Jones. 1988. "A Reconsideration of Animal Body-Part Utility Indices." *American Antiquity* 53, no. 3:486–504.

Mick-O'Hara, Linda. 1992. "Game Depletion and Selection in the Late Prehistoric Southwest." In *Current Research on the Late Prehistory and Early History of New Mexico*, edited by G. E. Bradley J. Vierra, and T. E. Clara Gualtieri, vol. 1, 37–49. Albuquerque: New Mexico Archaeological Council.

Moore, James L. 1992. "Spanish Colonial Stone Tool Use." In *Current Research on the Late Prehistory and Early History of New Mexico*, edited by G. E. Bradley, J. Vierra, and T. E. Clara Gualtieri, vol. 1, 239–43. Albuquerque: New Mexico Archaeological Council.

——. 2005. *Report on Chipped Stone Artifacts from San José de las Huertas*. Santa Fe: Office of Archaeological Studies, Museum of New Mexico.

Munro, Natalie D. 2006. "The Role of the Turkey in the Southwest." In *Environment, Origin, and Population*, vol. 3, *Handbook of North American Indians*, edited by D. H. Ubelaker, 463–70. Washington DC: Smithsonian Institution.

Nicklin, Keith. 1979. "The Location of Pottery Manufacture." *Man* 14, no. 3:436–58.

NMCRIS. 2006. *New Mexico Cultural Resource Inventory System*. Santa Fe NM: Laboratory of Anthropology, Museum of Indian Arts and Culture.

Nuttall, Zelia. 1921. "Ordinances Concerning the Laying out of New Towns." *Hispanic American Historical Review* 4, no. 4:743–53.

O'Connell, J. F., and K. Hawkes. 1988. "Hadza Hunting, Butchering, and Bone Transport and Their Archaeological Implications." *Journal of Anthropological Research* 44:113–61.

O'Hara, Matthew. 2009. *A Flock Divided: Race, Religion, and Politics in Colonial Mexico 1749–1859*. Durham NC: Duke University Press.

Oleson, John Peter. 1984. *Greek and Roman Mechanical Water-Lifting: The History of a Technology*. Toronto ON: University of Toronto Press.

Olinger, Bart. 1988. "Pottery Studies Using X-ray Fluorescence, Part 3: The Historic Pottery of the Northern Tewa." *Pottery Southwest* 15, no. 4:1–6.

Ortiz, Alfonzo. 1969. *The Tewa World: Space, Time, and Becoming in a Pueblo Society*. Chicago IL: University of Chicago Press.

Orton, Clive. 1993. "How Many Pots Make Five? An Historical Review of Pottery Quantification." *Archaeometry* 35, no. 2:169–84.

Orton, Clive, Paul Tyers, and Alan Vince. 1993. *Pottery in Archaeology*. Cambridge UK: Cambridge University Press.

Outram, Alan K. 2001. "A New Approach to Identifying Bone Marrow and Grease Exploitation: Why the 'Indeterminate' Fragments Should Not Be Ignored." *Journal of Archaeological Science* 28, no. 4:401–10.

Pallant, Julie. 2005. *spss Survival Manual*. Berkshire ME: Open University Press.

Parsons, Elsie Worthington Clews. (1929) 1974. "The Social Organization of the Tewa of New Mexico." In *Memoirs of the American Anthropological Association*. Millwood NJ: Kraus Reprint Co.

Pavao-Zuckerman, Barnet. 2011. "Rendering Economies: Native American Labor and Secondary Animal Products in the Eighteenth-Century Pimeria Alta." *American Antiquity* 76, no. 1:3–23.

Pavao-Zuckerman, Barnet, and Vincent M. LaMotta. 2007. "Missionization and Economic Change in the Pimería Alta: The Zooarchaeology of San Agustín de Tucson." *International Journal of Historical Archaeology* 11:241–68.

Perkins, D., and P. Daly. 1968. "A Hunter's Village in Neolithic Turkey." *Scientific American* 219:96–106.

Peterson, Susan. 1977. *The Living Tradition of María Martínez.* Tokyo, Japan: Kodanisha International.

Pierce, Christopher. 2005. "Reverse Engineering the Ceramic Cooking Pot: Cost and Performance Properties of Plain and Textured Vessels." *Journal of Archaeological Method and Theory* 12, no. 2:117–57.

Pikirayi, Innocent. 2007. "Ceramics and Group Identities: Towards a Social Archaeology in Southern African Iron Age Ceramic Studies." *Journal of Social Archaeology* 7, no. 3: 286–301.

Pitts, Martin. 2004. "Regional Identities and the Social Use of Ceramics." *Proceedings of the TRAC 2004: Fourteenth Annual Theoretical Roman Archaeology Conference.* University of Durham UK.

Poling-Kempes, Lesley. 1997. *Valley of Shining Stone: The Story of Abiquiú.* Tucson: University of Arizona Press.

Potter, James M. 1997. "Communal Ritual and Faunal Remains: An Example from the Dolores Anasazi." *Journal of Field Archaeology* 24:353–64.

———. 2000. "Pots, Parties, and Politics: Communal Feasting in the American Southwest." *American Antiquity* 65, no. 3:471–92.

———. 2002. "Hunting and Social Differentiation in the Late Prehispanic American Southwest." In *Behaviour behind Bones: The Zooarchaeology of Ritual, Religion, Status and Identity*, edited by S. J. O'Day, W. Van Neer, and A. Ervynck, 285–92. Oxford UK: Oxbow.

Preucel, Robert, ed. 2002. *Archaeologies of the Pueblo Revolt: Identity, Meaning, and Renewal in the Pueblo World.* Albuquerque: University of New Mexico Press.

Prummel, Wietske, and Hans-Jörg Frisch. 1986. "A Guide for the Distinction of Species, Sex, and Body Side in Bones of Sheep and Goat." *Journal of Archaeological Science* 13:567–77.

Quintana, Frances Leon, and David H. Snow. 1980. "Historical Archaeology of the Rito Colorado Valley, New Mexico." *Journal of the West* 19, no. 3:40–50.

Rabasa, José. 2000. *Writing Violence on the Northern Frontier: The Historiography of Sixteenth-Century New Mexico and Florida and the Legacy of Conquest.* Durham NC: Duke University Press.

Radding, Cynthia. 1997. *Wandering Peoples: Colonialism, Ethnic Spaces, and Ecological Frontiers in Northwestern Mexico, 1700–1850.* Durham NC: Duke University Press.

Rael-Gàlvez, Estèvan. 2002. "Identifying Captivity and Capturing Identity: Narratives of American Indian Slavery, Colorado and New Mexico, 1776–1934." Ph.D. dissertation, Department of American Cultures, University of Michigan, Ann Arbor.

Ramenofsky, Ann Felice. 1987. *Vectors of Death: The Archaeology of European Contact*. Albuquerque: University of New Mexico Press.

Ray, Isha, and Jeffrey Williams. 2002. "Locational Asymmetry and the Potential for Cooperation on a Canal." *Journal of Development Economics* 67:129–55.

Rebolledo, Tey Diana, and Maria Teresa Márquez, eds. 2000. *Women's Tales from the New Mexico wpa: La diabla a pie*. Houston TX: Arte Público Press.

Reitz, Elizabeth J. 1991. "Animal Use and Culture Change in Spanish Florida." In *Animal Use and Culture Change*, edited by P. Crabtree and J. Ryan, 62–77, MASCA Research Papers in Science and Archaeology. Philadelphia: University of Pennsylvania Museum, Applied Science Center for Archaeology.

Reitz, Elizabeth J., and Stephen L. Cumbaa. 1983. "Diet and Foodways of Eighteenth-Century Spanish St. Augustine." In *Spanish St. Augustine: The Archaeology of a Colonial Creole Community*, edited by Kathleen Deagan, 151–86. New York ny: Academic Press.

Reynoso Ramos, Citlalli. 2008. "Table of Wheat/Table of Corn: Consumer Choice, Foodways, and Social Prestige in Early Colonial Pueblo and Cholula." *Proceedings of the Annual Meeting for the Society for American Archaeology*. Vancouver BC.

Rice, Prudence M. 1987. *Pottery Analysis: A Sourcebook*. Chicago IL: University of Chicago Press.

———. 1991. "Specialization, Standardization, and Diversity: A Retrospective." In *The Ceramic Legacy of Anna O. Shepard*, edited by R. L. Bishop and F. W. Lange, 257–79. Niwot: University of Colorado Press.

Rivera, Jose A. 1998. *Acequia Culture: Water, Land and Community in the Southwest*. Albuquerque: University of New Mexico Press.

Rixson, D. 1989. "Butchery Evidence on Animal Bones." *Circaea* 6, no. 1:49–62.

Roberts, S. J., C. I. Smith, A. Millard, and M. J. Collins. 2002. "The Taphonomy of Cooked Bone: Characterizing Boiling and Its Physico–Chemical Effects." *Archaeometry* 44, no. 3:485–94.

Robin, Cynthia, and Nan A Rothschild. 2002. "Archaeological Ethnographies: Social Dynamics of Outdoor Space." *Journal of Social Archaeology* 2, no. 2:159–72.

Rodinson, Maxime, A. J. Arberry, and Charles Perry. 2001. *Medieval Arab Cookery*. Devon UK: Prospect.

Rodriguez, Sylvia. 1996. *The Matachines Dance: Ritual Symbolism and Interethnic Relations in the Upper Rio Grande Valley*. Albuquerque: University of New Mexico Press.

———. 2002. "Procession and Sacred Landscape in New Mexico." *New Mexico Historical Review* 77, no. 1: 1–26.

――――. 2006. *Acequia: Water-Sharing, Sanctity, and Place.* Santa Fe NM: School for Advanced Research.

Rodríguez-Alegría, Enrique. 2002. "Food, Eating, and Objects of Power: Class Stratification and Ceramic Production and Consumption in Colonial Mexico." Ph.D. dissertation, Department of Anthropology, University of Chicago, Chicago IL.

――――. 2005. "Eating Like an Indian: Negotiating Social Relations in the Spanish Colonies." *Current Anthropology* 46, no. 4:551–73.

Rodríguez-Alegría, Enrique, Hector Neff, and Michael D. Glascock. 2003. "Indigenous Ware or Spanish Import? The Case of Indigena Ware and Approaches to Power in Colonial Mexico." *Latin American Antiquity* 14, no. 1:67–81.

Rothschild, Nan A. 2003. *Colonial Encounters in a Native American Landscape: The Spanish and Dutch in North America.* Washington DC: Smithsonian Books.

――――. 2006. "Colonialism, Material Culture, and Identity in the Rio Grande and Hudson River Valleys." *International Journal of Historical Archaeology* 10, no. 1:72–107.

Rye, Owen. 1981. *Pottery Technology: Principles and Reconstruction.* Washington DC: Taraxacum.

Sahlins, Marshall. 1985. *Islands of History.* Chicago IL: University of Chicago Press.

Sanchez, Joseph P. 1992. Pueblo Indian Warfare in the Spanish Colonial Period, A.D. 1540–1680. In *Current Research on the Late Prehistory and Early History of New Mexico,* edited by G. E. Bradley J. Vierra and T. E. Clara Gualtieri, vol. 1, 93–99. Special publication (New Mexico Archaeological Council). Albuquerque: New Mexico Archaeological Council.

Sando, Joe S. 1979. "The Pueblo Revolt." In *Handbook of Native American Indians,* edited by W. C. Sturtevant, 194–97, vol. 9. Washington DC: Smithsonian Institution.

Schiffer, Michael B. 1972. "Archaeological Context and Systemic Context." *American Antiquity* 37, no. 2:156–65.

Schortman, Edward M., and Patricia A. Urban. 1998. "Culture Contact Structure and Process." In *Studies in Culture Contact: Interaction, Culture, Change, and Archaeology,* edited by J. G. Cusick, 102–25. Carbondale: Southern Illinois University Press.

Schulz, Peter D., and Sherri M. Gust. 1983. "Faunal Remains and Social Status in 19th Century Sacramento." *Historical Archaeology* 17, no. 1:44–53.

Schutt, Jeanne A. 1979. "LA 13291." In *Archaeological Investigations in Cochiti Reservoir, New Mexico,* edited by J. V. Biella, 174–97. U.S. Department of the Interior Contract No. CX702960151 (UNM proposal No. 101–127B) for U.S. Army Corps of Engineers. Vol. 3: *1976–1977 Field Seasons,* F. J. Broilo, principal investigator, general editor. Office of Contract Archaeology, Department of Anthropology, University of New Mexico, Albuquerque.

Seetah, Krish. 2006. "The Importance of Cut Placement and Implement Signatures to Butchery Interpretation." *Proceedings of the 10th Conference of the International Council for Archaeozoology.* Mexico City, Mexico.

Shennan, Stephen. 1997. *Quantifying Archaeology.* Edinburgh UK: Edinburgh University Press.

Shepard, Anna Osler. 1956. *Ceramics for the Archaeologist.* Washington DC: Carnegie Institution of Washington.

Sherman, Diana C. 2004. "Unraveling Subsistence and Dietary Patterns: A Study of Faunal Remains from Tecolote Pueblo, Northeastern New Mexico." Master's thesis, Department of Anthropology. Las Vegas: New Mexico Highlands University.

Shipman, Pat, George M. Foster, and M. J. Schoeninger. 1984. "Burnt Bones and Teeth: An Experimental Study of Color, Morphology, Crystal Structure and Shrinkage." *Journal of Archaeological Science* 11, no. 4:307–25.

Simmons, Marc. 1969. "Settlement Patterns and Village Plans in Colonial New Mexico." *Journal of the West* 8, no. 1:7–21.

———. 1983. "New Mexico's Colonial Agriculture." *Palacio* 89, no. 1:3–10.

———. 2001. *Spanish Pathways: Readings in the History of Hispanic New Mexico.* Albuquerque: University of New Mexico Press.

Skibo, James M., and Michael B. Schiffer. 2008. *People and Things: A Behavioral Approach to Material Culture.* New York NY: Springer.

Smith-Lintner, Cheryl Ann. 2007. "Becoming Californio: Archaeology of Communities, Animals, and Identity in Colonial California." Ph.D. dissertation, Department of Anthropology, University of California, Berkeley.

Snow, David H. 1979. "Rural Hispanic Community Organization in Northern New Mexico." *Colorado College Studies* 15:45–52.

———. 1981. "Protohistoric Rio Grande Pueblo Economics: A Review of Trends." In *The Protohistoric Period in the North American Southwest, AD 1450–1700,* edited by D. R. Wilcox, 354–77. Anthropological Research Papers. vol. 24. Tucson: Arizona State University.

———. 1982. "The Rio Grande Glaze, Matte-Paint, and Plainware Tradition." In *Southwestern Ceramics: A Comparative Review,* edited by D. A. Breternitz and A. H. Schroeder, 235–78. Arizona Archaeologist no. 15. Arizona Archaeological Society, Phoenix.

———. 1983. "Note on Encomienda Economics in Seventeenth-Century New Mexico." In *Hispanic Arts and Ethnohistory in the Southwest,* 347–57. Santa Fe NM: Ancient City Press.

———. 1984. "Spanish American Pottery Manufacture in New Mexico: A Critical Review." *Ethnohistory* 31, no. 2:93–113.

———. 1992. "A Review of Spanish Colonial Archaeology in Northern New Mexico." In *Current Research on the Late Prehistory and Early History of*

*New Mexico*, edited by G. E. Bradley, J. Vierra, and T. E. Clara Gualtieri, vol. 1, 185–93. Albuquerque: New Mexico Archaeological Council.

——. 1996. *New Mexico's First Colonists: The 1597–1600 Enlistments for New Mexico under Juan de Oñate, Adelante & Gobernador.* Albuquerque: Hispanic Genealogical Research Center of New Mexico.

Snow, David H., and Joanne V. Bowen. 1995. "No Scum, No Vermin: Seventeenth Century Faunal Remains from Santa Fe's Downtown Historic District." Report Prepared by Cross-Cultural Research Systems for Archaeological Review Committee, under Professional Services Agreement to the Office or Archaeological Services, Santa Fe NM.

South, Stanley. 1978. "Research Strategies for Archaeological Pattern Recognition on Historic Sites." *World Archaeology* 10:36–50.

Speller, Camilla F., Brian M. Kemp, Scott D. Wyatt, Cara Monroe, William D. Lipe, Ursula M. Arndt, and Dongya Y. Yang. 2010. "Ancient Mitochondrial DNA Analysis Reveals Complexity of Indigenous North American Turkey Domestication." *Proceedings of the National Academy of Sciences* 107, no. 7:2807–12.

Speth, John D. 1963. "La Casita Notes." In unpublished notes, property of Martha Dick. Ranchitos NM.

Speth, J. D., & Spielmann, K. A. 1982. "Energy Source, Protein Metabolism, and Hunter-Gatherer Subsistence Strategies." *Journal of Anthropological Archaeology*, 2, 1-31.

Spicer, Edward H. 1962. *Cycles of Conquest: The Impact of Spain, Mexico, and the United States on the Indians of the Southwest 1533–1960.* Tucson: University of Arizona Press.

Spielmann, Katherine A. 1991. "Coercion or Cooperation? Plains-Pueblo Interaction in the Protohistoric Period." In *Farmers, Hunters, and Colonists: Interaction between the Southwest and the Southern Plains*, edited by Spielmann, 36–50. Tucson: University of Arizona Press.

——. 2002. Feasting, Craft Specialization, and the Ritual Mode of Production in Small-Scale Societies. *American Anthropologist* 104, no. 1:195–207.

Stahl, Ann Brower. 2001. *Making History in Banda: Anthropological Visions of Africa's Past.* Cambridge UK: Cambridge University Press.

——. 2002. "Colonial Entanglements and the Practices of Taste: An Alternative to Logo-centric Approaches." *American Anthropologist* 104, no. 3:827–45.

——. 2009. "Material Histories of Global Entanglements: Re-centering Africa and Provincializing Europe." *Proceedings of the Emerging Wolds Lecture Series.* University of California, Santa Cruz.

Stark, Miriam T. 1998. "Technical Choices and Social Boundaries in Material Culture Patterning: An Introduction." In *The Archaeology of Social Boundaries*, edited by M. T. Stark, 1–11. Smithsonian Series in Archaeological Inquiry. Washington DC: Smithsonian Press.

Stone, Tammy. 2003. "Social Identity and Ethnic Interaction in the Western Pueblos of the American Southwest." *Journal of Archaeological Method and Theory* 10, no. 1:31–67.

Sunseri, Charlotte K. 2015. "Taphonomic and Metric Evidence for Marrow and Grease Production." *Journal of California and Great Basin Anthropology* 35, no. 2:275–90.

Sunseri, Jun Ueno. 2015. "A Horse Travel Approach to Landscape Archaeology." *Historical Archaeology* 49, no. 2:72–92.

Swadesh, Frances Leon. 1974. *Los Primeros Pobladores; Hispanic Americans of the Ute Frontier.* Notre Dame IN: University of Notre Dame Press.

———. 1979. "Structure of Hispanic-Indian Relations in New Mexico." *Colorado College Studies* 15:53–61.

Szuter, Christine R. 1991. "A Faunal Analysis of Home Butchering and Meat Consumption at the Hubbel Trading Post Ganado, Arizona." In *Animal Use and Culture Change*, edited by P. J. Crabtree and K. Ryan, 79–89. MASCA Research Papers in Science and Archaeology. Supplement to vol. 8. Philadelphia: University of Pennsylvania.

Thomas, Alfred Barnaby. 1931. "Governor Mendinueta's Proposals for the Defense of New Mexico, 1772–1778." *New Mexico Historical Review* 6, no. 1:21–39.

Thomas, Noah H. 2008. "Seventeenth Century Metallurgy on the Spanish Colonial Frontier: Transformations of Technology, Value, and Identity." Ph.D. dissertation, Department of Anthropology, University of Arizona, Tucson.

Tixier, Jacques. 1974. *Glossary for the Description of Stone Tools with Special Reference to the Epipalaeolithic of the Maghreb.* Translated by M. H. Newcomer. *Lithic Technology* Special Publication no. 1.

Tjarks, Alicia V. 1978. "Demographic, Ethnic and Occupational Structure of New Mexico, 1790." *Americas* 3, no. 1:45–88.

Toulouse, Joseph H. 1949. *The Mission of San Gregorio de Abó.* Monographs of the School of American Research. Albuquerque: University of New Mexico Press.

Trigg, Heather B. 2004. "Food Choice and Social Identity in Early Colonial New Mexico." *Journal of the Southwest* 46, no. 2:223–40.

Tsing, Anna Lowenhaupt. 2005. *Friction: An Ethnography of Global Connection.* Princeton NJ: Princeton University Press.

Turner, Frederick Jackson. 1894. *The Significance of the Frontier in American History.* Madison: State Historical Society of Wisconsin.

Twinam, Ann. 1999. *Public Lives, Private Secrets: Gender, Honor, Sexuality and Illegitimacy in Colonial Spanish America.* Stanford CA: Stanford University Press.

Upton, Dell. 1996. "Ethnicity, Authenticity, and Invented Traditions." *Historical Archaeology* 30:1–7.

Usner, Don J. 1995. *Sabino's Map: Life in Chimayó's Old Plaza*. Santa Fe: Museum of New Mexico Press.

Valdez, Facundo. 1979. "Vergüenza." *Colorado College Studies* 15:99–106.

Van Ness, John R. 1991. *Hispanos in Northern New Mexico: The Development of Corporate Community and Multicommunity*. AMS Studies in Immigrant Communities and Ethnic Minorities in the United States and Canada 76. New York NY: AMS Press.

Voss, Barbara L. 2002. "The Archaeology of El Presidio de San Francisco: Culture Contact, Gender, and Ethnicity in a Spanish-Colonial Military Community." Ph.D. dissertation, Department of Anthropology, University of California, Berkeley.

——. 2005. "From Casta to Californio: Social Identity and the Archaeology of Culture Contact." *American Anthropologist* 107, no. 3:461–74.

——. 2008. *The Archaeology of Ethnogenesis: Race and Sexuality in Colonial San Francisco*. Berkeley: University of California Press.

Wagner, Mark J. 1998. "Some Think It Impossible to Civilize Them at All: Cultural Change and Continuity among the Early Nineteenth-Century Potawatomi." In *Studies in Culture Contact: Interaction, Culture, Change, and Archaeology*, edited by J. G. Cusick, 430–56. Carbondale: Southern Illinois University Press.

Waguespack, Nicole M. 2002. "Caribou Sharing and Storage: Refitting the Palangana Site." *Journal of Anthropological Archaeology* 21:396–417.

Waines, David. 2003. "'Luxury Foods' in Medieval Islamic Societies." *World Archaeology* 34, no. 3:571–80.

Warren, A. Helene. 1979. "Historic Pottery of the Cochiti Reservoir Area." In *Archaeological Investigations in Cochiti Reservoir, New Mexico*, edited by J. V. Biella and R. C. Chapman. vol. 4. Albuquerque NM: Office of Contract Archaeology.

Weber, David J. 1991. "Introduction: Bolton and the Idea." In *The Idea of Spanish Borderlands*, edited by D. J. Weber. New York NY: Garland.

——. 1992. *The Spanish Frontier in North America*. Yale Western Americana Series. New Haven CT: Yale University Press.

——. 2005. *Bárbaros: Spaniards and Their Savages in the Age of Enlightenment*. New Haven CT: Yale University Press.

Weigle, Marta. 2003. *The Lore of New Mexico*. Publications of the American Folklore Society. Albuquerque: University of New Mexico Press.

Wheelwright, Jeff. 2008. "The Secret of San Luis Valley." *Smithsonian* 39, no. 7:48–56.

Whitaker, John O. 1996. *National Audubon Society Field Guide to North American Mammals*. New York NY: Random House.

White, Richard. 1991. *The Middle Ground: Indians, Empires and Republics in the Great Lakes Region, 1650–1815*. Cambridge UK: Cambridge University Press.

White, Timothy D. 1992. *Prehistoric Cannibalism at Mancos 5mtumr-2346.* Princeton NJ: Princeton University Press.

Wilk, R. R., and R. McC. Netting. 1984. "Households: Changing Form and Function." In *Households: Comparative and Historical Studies of the Domestic Group,* edited by R. M. Netting, R. Wilk, and E. Arnould, 1–28. Berkeley: University of California Press.

Wilson, S. E. 2004. "The Fauna of San Lazaro: A Pueblo Located in the Galisteo Basin of New Mexico." Master's thesis, Department of Anthropology, Northern Arizona University, Flagstaff.

Wolf, Eric R. 1982. *Europe and the People without History.* Berkeley: University of California Press.

Yellen, John E. 1991. "Small Mammals: !Kung San Utilization and the Production of Faunal Assemblages." *Journal of Anthropological Archaeology* 10, no. 1:1–26.

# Index

Note: Page numbers in *italics* indicate figures, tables, and illustrations.

To order or obtain more information on these or other University of
Nebraska Press titles, visit nebraskapress.unl.edu.

CPSIA information can be obtained
at www.ICGtesting.com
Printed in the USA
LVOW07*1629050118

561969LV00003B/9/P

9 780803 296398